A LITERARY ADVENTURE!

"Nothing less than a road map to cut through the hazards, detours, bottlenecks and speed traps of life in the next millennium. His approach to spirituality is refreshing and insightful. Sharp's book is FILLED WITH WISDOM, HONESTY AND LOVE."
—Glenda Gnade,
Author, *Return to Paradise in New Heights of Glory*

"This inspiring book guides the reader through the challenges and ordeals that come from following the path to our fullest potential. Sharp writes about the enhancement of our inner self, how we can influence our thoughts, reshape our character, and then experience the blissful spiritual alchemy that inevitably follows."
—Mathias B. Freese,
Psychologist, Author, *I*

"SUPERB! READING THIS BOOK HAS BEEN A JOY. Sharp's words resound like the notes of a symphony—exquisite, precise, purposeful and beautifully blended together. The way he is able to convey his ideas and insights is dazzling. On reaching the end, one of my first thoughts was: 'I've got to give this book to my children.'"
—Robert Listou, Corporate Executive,
U.S. Air Force Pilot, Ret.

"Sharp's book provides us with a framework to help deal with—and even challenge—our basic assumptions of life. The process he has come up with is as unique as it is playful and the result gives us the way to savor the wonder of our daily lives. It's an illuminating, revelatory book—the kind of book I would like to write."
—Robert Vance,
Clergyman, Business Consultant

"Sharp gives us a way to dynamically interact with the universe in our own Kosmic story. He enhances our understanding of the Mysterious Force, what he poetically calls 'the wild wind that blows through and creates our lives.' He encourages us to live our lives at the edge of our experience with questions—not with answers. He inspires us to spiritual enchantment. And finally, he provides us with the key to writing a new world mythology with a radical set of fresh ideas and inventive imagery. A TRULY REMARKABLE BOOK."
—Dr. Sara Little, Ed.D.,
Psychologist

"A TREASURE TROVE OF HEAVENLY PERCEPTIONS. This ingenious book has the ring of authority and depth of understanding that most recent works on spirituality are sadly lacking."
—John Pellicano,
Historian, Author, *Conquer or Die*

The Adventure of Being Human

A Guide to Living a Fuller Life

*Living Where No Humans
Have Lived Before*

by Basil Sharp

Integrated Life Architects
Washington, D.C. 20003

The Adventure of Being Human: A Guide to Living a Fuller Life
by Basil Sharp

All rights reserved. No part of this book may be reproduced, disseminated or utilized in any form or by any means, electronic or mechanical, including photocopying, recording, or in any information storage and retrieval system, or the Internet/World Wide Web without written permission from the author or publisher, except for the inclusion of brief quotations in a review.

For additional copies of this book, please send $14.95 plus $3.00 shipping & handling for *each* copy to:
Integrated Life Architects
1354 K St. S. E.
Washington, D.C. 20003
(202) 546-6549
or credit card orders via the Internet
@ http://www.wel.net/integratedlife

Book design, production, and cover art by:
The Floating Gallery
331 West 57th St. #465
New York, NY 10019
(212) 399-1961; FloatinGal@aol.com

Copyright © 2000 by Basil Sharp
PRINTED IN THE UNITED STATES OF AMERICA

Sharp, Basil
    The Adventure of Being Human
    1. Author 2. Title 3. Religion 4. Self-Improvement

    Library of Congress Catalog Card Number 98-90936
    ISBN 0-9668726-0-6 Softcover

*This book is dedicated to
my Family,
Marie, Heidi, Jane and Otto,
the dream team for exploring
and savoring life in the New Kosmos.*

"By deliberately changing the internal image of reality, people can change the world. Perhaps the only limits to the human mind are those we believe in."
—Wilis Harman, former president of the
Institute for Noetic Science
from his book, *Global Mind Change*

Contents

Acknowledgements 11

Foreword 13

Chapter One
AT FIRST 17

Chapter Two
THE UNIVERSE 32

Chapter Three
THE PLANET 59

Chapter Four
THE INDIVIDUAL HUMAN 94

Chapter Five
THE HUMAN COMMUNITY 154

Chapter Six
THE ULTIMATE 190

Chapter Seven
DANCING 232

Addresses 273

Bibliography 275

About the Author 277

Acknowledgements

So many people have contributed to this book through comments, suggestions, sharing of ideas, encouragement and especially reflecting about life. Then there are all those people who contributed to my experiences of life that are the basis of my reflections. These are far too many to name. Nevertheless, I must acknowledge my deep sense of honor, gratitude and joy for their participation in my life.

There are, though, five contributors to whom I want to express particular thanks.

The first contributor was the team who worked to produce and facilitate the Kosmic Life Story Workshop—the genesis of the book. I am deeply grateful to them for their contributions, both as individuals and as a team.

For the second, imagine a picture of a person doing cartwheels while another kneels on two knees with head bowed, arms extended, palms up. Such a picture expresses my profound feelings of joy and gratitude for Pat Nischan and the visual representations that she created for each of the six basic images.

The third contribution was made by several dear friends who read and commented on the manuscript. I am humbly thankful to them for their time, attention and thoughtfulness.

The fourth particular "thank you" goes to Tree for all its insights, advice and patience. I find that talking with a tree (referred to in the book by the representative name Tree) provides a different and refreshing perspective on life. It is a means to stop, step back, and permit deeper insights to emerge. It is a way to allow new perspectives to contribute to one's life and to take new relationships to aspects of life. So, "thanks Tree!"

Finally, for editing, a special word of thanks both to Eric, who did not spare the "red pen" or the helpful comments and to my wife, Marie, for her patient attention to the details of words on paper.

Now, on to the adventure—just watch out for the tornado.

Foreword

There are some people who are always tinkering around with things to find out what makes them "tick," like car motors, computers, plants, animals, brains, hearts. It seems that I have always been tinkering around trying to find out how life, human life in particular, "ticks." What is going on with this thing called life? How do we humans fit in? And, the bottom line, how do we get the most out of our time here in this planet?

While my studies, research and explorations resulted in exciting and helpful understandings along with rich experiences, there was always a sense of something missing. Then there were always a few "parts" lying around that did not fit anywhere or did not seem to fit well. In one of my explorations, someone pointed out that wisdom about life was the result of people reflecting deeply upon their own experiences of life more than research into other people's reflections. I decided that I should take time, reflect more on my experiences and explorations, and try to "put all the parts together."

The chance came while developing a workshop to provide people with an opportunity to reflect on their life and on a new story of life for our times. In order to provide a coherent foundation for the workshop I wrote a "white paper" pulling together my own reflections on life. In the process I made some surprising discoveries. 1) I enjoyed writing. 2) The world in which I was living was very different from the world in which previous generations of humans had lived—which was one reason that their reflections/wisdom did not fully speak to me. To include all the new parts, a larger understanding of life would be required. 3) To pull together my reflections on life into some systematic and larger understanding of life would take more than a short "white paper."

So I began writing. Page flowed after page. As the volume grew, I thought, why not make it into a book? And so I have. Because I was writing "around the edges" of a busy schedule, it has taken a few years. During that time, as a result of my writing, my experiences and reflections have matured. I would likely write some of the earlier chapters slightly different now.

But this is the very nature of the book. Our reflection on life, like life itself, is always a "work in progress." It is a never-ending story that is constantly being expanded and refined in the living and exploring of life and in the telling of it. As such, this book represents notes of an explorer. The book invites you not to debate but to explore life, to reflect upon your own experiences and to contribute your "findings" in developing a new common Story or understanding of life.

I had fun writing the book. I hope you have fun reading it.

The Adventure of Being Human

A Guide to Living a Fuller Life

*Living Where No Humans
Have Lived Before*

Chapter One

AT FIRST—

<u>SHOWING UP</u>
The alarm!
　　Flailing arms and groggy mind search for the clock.
What the! . . . I'm on vacation, and . . .
　　　VACATION!!!
　　　　　Today's the day we take off on our trip of a lifetime!
Time's a-wastin', let's move!
　　The adrenaline is pumping;
　　the adventure has begun.
　　　　　　Exciting scenery.
　　　　　　Discovering new places.
　　　　　　Great food.
　　　　　　Interesting people.
　　　　　　Challenging, thrilling activities.
　　　　　　Doing fun things.
　　　　　　A different pace.
　　　　　　　　And savoring every moment.
Adventure—
　　the different,
　　　　the exploring,
　　　　　　the unexpected,

> the change of pace.

Adventure—
> an outing, an evening,
>> a trip, a new job,
>>> a new place to live, a new friend,
>>>> a new style, a new school,
>>>>> a new skill, a new assignment.

Living is an adventure.
The adventure of being human
> begins with being born.
>> No one asks us or invites us.
> We just show up
> in Planet Earth.

Living through each day is an adventure.
> It begins in a very mundane manner,
>> an intrusion—
>>> an alarm clock,
>>>> the brightness of the sun,
>>>>> the sound of "time to get up!"—
>> and there we are,
>>> smack dab in the middle of an adventure.
>> What will I discover?
>> What will I see?
>> Who will I meet?
>> What challenges will I face?
>> How will I get through it?

You're right. It usually begins less dramatically.
> Where did I put my glasses?
> What am I going to wear?
> What day is it, anyway?

The day may bring
> changed situations, new places,
> **different people,**
> new issues,
> different activities.

But more likely,
> we will notice new things on the same old street;
> see familiar places in a new light;
> discover a new dimension in long time associates;
> or face new demands from the same old situations.

Be it the way you feel upon waking or

the day's weather, or
deciding what to wear—
we participate in the adventure of living,
    day in and day out.
Be it the stack of dirty dishes in the kitchen,
    the needs of the kids,
    the requests of a parent—
we participate in the adventure of living,
    day in and day out.
Be it the unfinished assignment,
    the obnoxious kid, or the smile of a friend—
    Be it the "in box" stack, the notes on the "to-do list,"
    or "Can you help me with this?"—
    Be it the notice of sales, the bills in the mail,
    the note from the teacher,
    or "Honey, I'll be late getting home"—
we participate in the adventure of living,
    day in and day out.
Be it "What do you think about . . .?"
    "Why?"
    "What are we going to do about . . .?"—
    be it ordinary,
    be it momentous,
    we participate in the adventure of living,
    day in and day out.
No matter our circumstance when we wake up . . .
    no matter what life gives us during the day . . .
    we assess each situation and
    we decide how we will function.
    What an adventure!
And now
there is an added dimension,
    which makes the adventure even more challenging and
    exciting.

**We wake up in a universe
in which no other humans have ever lived.**

We are like Dorothy who was deposited in the Land of Oz by a tornado. After looking around she says to her dog, "Toto, I don't think we're in Kansas!" People today awake in a very different universe from the universe in which people of previous generations awoke. We are no longer in "Kansas."

But someone is bound to say, "the universe has been the same for millions of years! The mountains have stood, the rains have fallen, the Earth has circled the sun and the moon has circled the Earth for millions of years. What do you mean 'we live in a new universe?'"

This statement in itself reveals how universes change. There was a time when people lived in a universe in which the Earth was flat and fixed, and the sun and moon were manipulated across the sky by gods. It was a radical shift for people to learn to live in a universe in which the Earth was round and no longer the center of the universe. And shall we mention the shift from the spirit-controlled universe of the hunter-gatherer and the farmer to the mechanical universe of the industrial age?

Then we could mention that the universes of the ancient Chinese scholar and the Iroquois warrior were very different. In the same vein, the universe in which we live is altogether different from any of the previous universes.

[As you may have noticed, the word universe *shifted in meaning from objects in space to an understanding of life as a whole. Because the more common use of* universe *refers to the totality of physical things, including celestial bodies and space, this book will use* universe *to refer to the **sum of all physical existence and their governing principles as a single operating system.***

To talk about the total design and functionality of existence as a whole, I will use the word Kosmos. *Ken Wilber defines* Kosmos *as the "**patterned nature and process of all domains of existence**"[1] . This was the original meaning of the word* cosmos. *But since* cosmos *now is commonly used to speak of outer space and heavenly bodies, I will use the original Greek spelling of* Kosmos *to refer to the totality of existence. The word* Kosmos *will hold the oneness of existence and the integral relationship of all its aspects—external and internal, objective and subjective, individual and corporate.]*

So, like Dorothy in the Land of Oz, our daily adventure of living involves learning to function in a new and strange world—with one marked difference. Dorothy's adventure was focused toward getting back to Kansas. For us, "Kansas" no longer exists. Our adventure of exploring the new universe is not that of a visiting tourist; but rather it

---

1. Wilber, K. *Sex, Ecology, Spirituality*, p.38

is the serious adventure of people making their home in a new world and establishing a whole new way of living—for themselves and for future generations.

"But this *new Kosmos* is just a new way of seeing the Kosmos," the voice of protest says, "It is just a new understanding of the Kosmos. It's just a new assumption about the Kosmos."

True! And this is exactly the point.

The way people collectively *see* the Kosmos—their understanding, their reference points and images, their common assumptions of the Kosmos—IS their Kosmos. In fact, these assumptions are so pervasive they become reality for us. They go largely unnoticed and unchallenged until something drops into the mix and changes everything—sometimes dramatically, sometimes so gradually that changes go unrecognized for years.

So to say that we live in a new Kosmos is to say that we live with a new understanding and new images of our existence. Furthermore, this realization is itself one aspect of the new Kosmos of which we are a part. We know that the Kosmos is only a human interpretation of our particular observations and experiences. As such, we can and do change our understanding of the Kosmos. Also we know that there is more to be discovered about our Kosmos.

More about this later.

Now back to the adventure of waking up each day in this new Kosmos. We wake up to, and participate in, an adventure of exploring a new world. This is not an option. It is the nature of being alive today. Exploring the new world and developing a new way of living are not things we "ought to do," nor are they things that would be "good to do." It is what we do when we do anything. Some people do it more self-consciously than others do. Some people enjoy it more than others do. But each of us do it just by living.

Why write about it?

Why read about it?

Because living is a series of experiences. Living is reflecting on our experiences. Living is dialoguing with our experiences. Human living is more than just physically getting through a day. Human living has to do with savoring our experiences.

I want to experience being *ALIVE*!

Being *ALIVE* has more to do with expanding my self-consciousness of my experiences than it does with changing the nature or content of my experiences. Whether I plant flowers or watch TV or bake cookies is not, in the first instance, important relative to experiencing life. The excitement and vibrancy of life has to do with expanding my self-consciousness of a particular experience—both of the participation in the event and the reflection on the experience. True, some experiences are more pleasant than others; but if I removed the unpleasant and mundane from my life, I would reduce my life significantly. If I include them as significant parts of my life, I increase both the volume and the richness of my life. As we will explore later, we may have limited control over the nature and content of our life's experiences, but we seem to have extensive control over how we experience our experiences. In this way we have extensive control over being ALIVE or not!

Thus, this writing is an expansion of my self-consciousness of life experiences—a savoring of life. I would like to think that your reading would be an expansion of your self-consciousness of life experiences—a savoring of life

This book is about being aware of the new reality in which we live—the new universe, the new planet, the new human individual, the new human community and the new Ultimate. This book is about expanding our self-consciousness of being alive as part of this new Kosmos. This book is about savoring our experiences of living the lives that we have. This book is for the pioneer and explorer in each of us.

Those who want to continue with the adventure, you may go directly to the next chapter. Those who want to explore more of the rationale of this book are invited to continue with the following section of this chapter.

DECISIONS AND PICTURES

As we go about our adventure of living as a human being, we implement decisions—big and small, consciously and unconsciously—day in and day out. Every action is the implementation of some decision. Non-action is an implementation of a decision. Decisions begin early in the morning with deciding to get up (or some other relationship to one's place of sleep) and decisions continue throughout the day . . .

how to relate to that face in the bathroom mirror . . .
    what to wear . . .
        if, how, and what for breakfast . . .
            the way you respond to people all day long . . .
what you buy or don't . . .
    what you read or don't . . .
        what you listen to . . .
            how well you do your work . . .
                what work you do . . .
                      to go to meetings or not to go . . .
to speak up or be silent . . .
    how you spend your evenings or weekend . . .
        how you deal with a crisis . . .
        etc., etc., etc. . . .

These myriad decisions and actions merge together, like raindrops into rivulets, to form individual life patterns. These patterns merge together, like rivulets into streams and then into rivers, to form group and social patterns.

As long as our decisions and actions help us and society to function reasonably well, things continue without much change. In fact, we don't even think much about our decisions. But when our decisions and actions do not produce acceptable results, or when different results are desired, we begin to analyze the situation and seek corrective alternatives. When things don't go well for us or when things become unpleasant, we reflect and seek to understand what is happening. Why did I lose my job? Why did my life-partner leave? Why are the kids doing poorly in school? Why am I not popular? Why did the crops fail? Why do I have this disease? (This is why people who suffer, people facing loss, the poor and people on the "low end of life's scales" seem to be the most religious. Their situations lead them to ask very basic questions and seek very basic answers about life.)

Now, "fellow decision-makers," when we step back and take a look at our previous decisions and actions, we notice something interesting. Every decision and action, no matter how insignificant or important, is based on a variety of mental pictures or assumptions about life.

"Spinach! Yuck!"
"I'm too old to try to learn new office procedures."
"I will get a better paying job if I go to college."
"I would not be caught dead wearing those!"
"Why would you want to live in the city?"

When we are in a situation that involves a new and different set of operating assumptions or images, we become very aware of our assumptions:

- You are used to the family getting up at 6:00 a.m. and having a sit-down breakfast at 7:00. Then you visit a friend where everyone gets up at different times and fixes their own breakfast whenever they feel like it. At such times, you become very aware of a different set of operating assumptions about family life.
- In your former office, no one assumes responsibility for a task until formally assigned by a supervisor. In your new job, everyone does what needs to be done without being asked—a very different picture of how an office functions.
- You get married and find that your partner has a very different set of assumptions as to who does what in the household.
- When visiting another country or cultural setting, we become irritatingly aware of very different assumptions about the way things operate. Our first reaction is that the other people's assumptions are wrong! If we are lucky, we stop and think about our own assumptions rather than grow irritated.

We all have preconceived notions—assumptions or images—about the way life should function. Behind these preconceived notions, are the basic or fundamental assumptions about life itself. These primal assumptions and images relate to the whole *System of Life* and how *The System* functions. They are assumptions

—about the universe
(where we come from; what is going on here; where we are going.)
—about the planetary environment
(what is natural; how humanity fits in.)
—about humans and our role in life
(are we in control or are we pawns? are we good or evil?)
—about community and our life together
(how we live together; how values and meaning are determined.)
—about Ultimate Reality
(who or what is "running the show," if anyone or anything?)

All of our basic life assumptions and mental pictures are woven together to form the Story of Life—of life in the Kosmos. This Story supports and guides the functioning of individuals, families, groups and whole societies. From birth to death, from getting up in the morning to going to bed in the evening, these basic assumptions provide the means for experiencing and relating to life. They provide the deep basis for our decisions and actions. This Story gives meaning to events and provides the means for evaluating alternatives. Above all, this Story is the "flavor" of life, which we savor.

"OK, Sharp, so our decisions and actions are based on deep assumptions and basic mental pictures of life! What's the big deal?"

"For starters, if things are not working out the way you would like them to, one of the reasons may be that your basic assumptions are inadequate. Perhaps you did not adequately interpret the situation.

"More importantly, if you are doing more and enjoying life less, if the experiences of life are leaving a 'bad taste in your mouth', you just might want to update your Story of Life."

Today, in all countries, in all societies, people are experiencing the fact that life does not seem to be functioning adequately for them—as individuals or as groups. Families, individuals, local communities, educational institutions, businesses, nations, cultures, religious groups, ethnic groups—you name it—do not seem to be functioning as well as people would like. Individuals increasingly experience emptiness and meaninglessness, are feeling "out of it", are spending more money and enjoying life less. Human decency, civility, and values are disappearing. People feel ineffective. We experience deep unfulfilled yearnings. One reason may be that the basic assumptions of life (the Stories of Life) are no longer functional—the basic mental pictures about life may no longer be accurate.

If this reasoning is at all true, then the decisions/actions based on these assumptions will not produce the desired results. If we are no longer in "Kansas," decisions and actions that worked well in "Kansas" will not produce the same results in this "new place." Assumptions that were adequate for "Kansas" may not be adequate for this "New Land of Oz."

In fact, this is the situation in which we find ourselves. We wake up and get out of bed in a new Kosmos, different from any previous Kosmos. Thus, it is very likely that the basic assumptions and Stories about life which helped people function in any previous Kosmos will be of little help in our new Kosmos. Just like assumptions about life that work in rural areas may not help us function in the city, just like assumptions about life that work in America may not work in China, so basic assumptions about life that worked in any previous Kosmos may not work in the Kosmos in which we live today.

Therefore, part of the adventure of living involves developing new mental pictures of life which will enable us to function in our new Kosmos. Not only do we get to experience the adventure of exploring this new Kosmos, we also get to share in the adventure of developing a new Story of Life, which will help us function more effectively.

[*Use of Ancient Stories/Myths:*

Many people today are searching among previous Stories or Myths of Life to discover models for living in the present Kosmos. The promoted value and authenticity of these models and practices are somehow related to their "ancient and honored" source. As much as I rejoice in their concern for more adequate models for living, their effort has a fatal flaw. These previous Stories/Myths/Assumptions were developed to help people to function in the Kosmos of their day—which these Stories did very successfully. For this these Stories/Myths deserve all the credit and honor we can give them. But these previous Kosmoses no longer exist. So assumptions about life in any such previous Kosmos are no longer useful for life in the new Kosmos in which we find ourselves. Just as previous societies struggled to develop these basic assumptions/mental pictures for living in their Kosmos, so we struggle to develop new basic assumptions/mental pictures for living in our new Kosmos. We can certainly learn from the past, but it will not be helpful to adopt those past assumptions, images, and models for living in the present.

And those who seek to re-interpret previous myths/life stories, in order to make them meaningful in the present, often read current assumptions/images BACK INTO the previous myths/stories. This, to me, is an injustice to our ancestors and the myths/stories by which they lived, and which helped us grow into the present Kosmos.

Now, if these previous myths/stories suggest what seem to be helpful insights about life today, by all means, make use of such insights. I would only encourage us to be aware as to whose insights they are—yours or some present day author's. In addition, you and/or the author have rejected the other parts of such previous myths/stories as not relevant for living today. The criteria for evaluating, selecting, wording and usage of such "ancient insights" is a person's understanding (story) about life today. One could drop all references to the ancient myth and the insights would still be just as applicable and would be evaluated the same as any other insights—does it help in living today.]

Furthermore, this New Story of Life will be a common global story. As we realize more and more that there is only one System, one Kosmos, and that we all live and function as part of this one System/Kosmos, we realize the usefulness of having shared views of life that help us to communicate and work together for our mutual benefit. As we face the challenges of living in this new Kosmos, we sense that a common global Story of Life is fundamental—

- fundamental for meaningful dialogue;
- fundamental for developing solutions;
- fundamental for building new social structures;
- fundamental for exploring and sharing life's experiences;
- fundamental for experiencing and savoring being alive.

A common global Story of Life is fundamental to moving beyond the equally destructive tendencies of desiring "sameness" and of stressing "our uniqueness." All of us, most of the time, find it difficult to deal with real differences. We desire to live in a "mono-cultural" situation where "our unique diversity" is the norm. (This is basically the same motivation behind the establishment of suburbs, the struggles in Northern Ireland, ethnic cleansing by the Serbs, hippie communities and the "good life.") It will take a common global Story of Life to honor, promote and appropriate our real differences and diversity—and thus not to seek a Lake Wobegon society "where everyone is above average." It will take a common global Story of Life for people to be able to say "men are men, women are women; youth are youth, elderly are elderly; black are black, white are white, red are red; Jews are Jews, Arabs are Arabs; rich are rich, and poor are poor; the fast runners are fast and the slow are slow . . . viva la difference! What difference does it make?! Let's get on with the adventure of being human!"—all in the same breath.

The new Story of Life will not be delivered "from on high" in "tablets of stone." Nor will it be channeled "from the depths" in best seller books. The new story, the new set of mental pictures, the new basic assumptions, will come from the experiences and reflections of people living their normal daily lives. Our daily experiences of life provide the basis for rethinking of our basic assumptions about life. In fact, we already have begun the process of rethinking our basic pictures of life and of creating the New Story. We need only to increase our reflection on and dialogue about our life experiences so as to articulate our new mental pictures of life and the story they tell. As we reflect and have dialogue with two or three or more people, the images will emerge, will be confirmed and passed on—not unlike the way previous stories of life emerged while two or three or more people gathered around fires and talked about their experiences. As the new basic assumptions are absorbed, enhanced and/or modified by others, the Story will grow. As we test the Story in the decisions and actions of our daily lives, the Kosmic Story of Life will evolve.

In beginning to explore our *new world*—the New Kosmos—I have found it helpful to use five basic pillars to focus reflections and to articulate observations. These five pillars are the five basic arenas of functional Myths (Stories) which have operated on planet Earth. I have titled these arenas:

> THE UNIVERSE
> THE PLANET
> THE INDIVIDUAL HUMAN
> THE CORPORATE HUMAN
>   and
> THE ULTIMATE

Each arena will be presented and explored separately in the following chapters. If the ideas in this book do not adequately articulate the way you experience life, by all means, write your own section, chapter or even a book. In fact, the response to this book I most desire is for two, or three or more people to get together and write their reflections about the adventure of living. Above all, it is critical that we share and discuss our experiences, observations, comments, questions or suggestions about living fully in the Kosmos of our era. Such sharing and discussion is the way to confirm, reject or validate any aspect of the Kosmic Story of Life. I invite you to send observations, comments, questions, etc. to me and to share them with others. I plan to compile the responses and distribute them to the contributors and others. (Various addresses for communicating with me are listed at the end of the book.) In such ways, the story will grow to reflect the vast and varied experiences of human existence.

A word about how you might use this book in reflecting on the happening which you are and all of life is: Life is as playful as it is serious. It does not lend itself to being "wrapped up" or "nailed down"—similar to the content of this book. I would, therefore, recommend a bit of playfulness in reading it.

The structure of each chapter is the same. First, the pillar is presented as a story-poem. This is followed by some suggested exercises to help the reader experience the subject pillar directly and to reflect more deeply on it. The third section of each chapter is the presentation of my reflections on the pillar from my experiences of life—an effort at a more rational discussion of the subject. Following this, is an introduction of some implications for living our lives. Each chapter will conclude with a holding image—both verbal and artistic—for the pillar.

There are at least three ways to approach the materiel presented in this book. (You will likely think of others.)
1) Read straight through from beginning to end.
2) Read all the poetry first, then the prose, or vice-versa.
3) Stop periodically to explore your experiences and reflect on them. You may find meditative or visualization exercises helpful for doing these exploratory trips—use your own or use/adapt the ones presented in each chapter.

Basically, this book is an opportunity for you to reflect on your own experiences of the essential components of life.

All parts of the book—poetry, exercises, reflection, implication, images—are starters to bring more self-consciousness to a common, global Kosmic Story of Life. You are invited and encouraged to join the adventure and exploration. Verify, refine, re-define, and discover the new at each step along the way. Record your observations and reflections. Even though we have increased our powers of observation, recording, and communication through time, life is, as it has always been, an experiment. Sharing your responses and reflections enhances the experiment. We are all newcomers to this Kosmos, so any observations about how to look at it, how best to enjoy it, what works or what does not work, will be of help to others learning to participate.

Now, on with the exploration and adventure of being alive as part of the new Kosmos!

As *we travel*, perhaps these lyrics will make good company.

NEW WORLD NOW[2]
We are in a New World now,
We never can go back.
Our eyes have seen a thousand years,
Our mind has bridged the gap;
And here we stand, we hear the Cry,
Creation surging on,
Our hearts beat wildly and we sigh,
No thing to lean upon.

We are in a New World now,
The light still blinds our eyes.
We weep and soar and shout aloud,
We dance between two pyres;
Like clowns who merge with time and space,
We run and jump and fall,
We beckon to the endless race,
We play the fool for all.

We are in a New World now,
No longer is it hidden.
We struggle to create the edge,
Our local passion given;
We were born to build the Earth,
Our lives consumed with praise,
Gazing straight with open eyes,
The phoenix does arise.

RIDE THE WHIRLWIND[3]
(Tune: El Condor Pasa)
We came upon a world we did not know
Filled with pain, yet not in vain
Born of innocence.
The awesome scope of power is in our hands
To create, or finally devastate
The choice is ours.
Forever ours.

2,3. Words from the "Singing of the Institute of Cultural Affairs", Chicago, IL.

Refrain:
>We hear the thunder, see the sun
>That will shine on everyone.
>The whirlwind carries us along
>It will not stop
>'Til we are done
>New World begun.

To ride the whirlwind 'round the planet Earth
Releasing hope to celebrate
The great new birth.
The winds of time are blowing fiercely now
Calling forth new resolve
To care for all
A common Earth . . . *Refrain*

Chapter Two

THE UNIVERSE

A. SWIRLING ENERGY—A STORY-POEM
Energy swirls
  —expanding, dividing, taking many shapes and forms
     —shifting, changing, dividing, uniting,
        —spinning, exploding, colliding,
           —dancing, joining, growing,
              —through space and time,
                 creating space and time . . .
Ah! The wonder of the forms and expressions
     —massive galaxies of flaming stars, ringed planets, comets,
        —atoms, electrons, protons,
           —snowflakes, beetles, horses, bacteria, flowers,
              —clouds, oceans, ears, eyes, mountains,
                 —cars, shoes, brains, cities,
                    —a kiss, a curse, a wink, a scream,
                       —a song, a painting, a meal . . .

From whence? how?
Why this particular form? that balance? this tension?
Why that path? this leap?

Physical forces and "laws"—yes.
Chemical reactions—yes.
Biological processes—yes.
Mental processes—yes.
Cause and effect—yes.
Randomness and probability—yes.
Some mixture of all of these—surely;
    but why any particular mixture?
All of the above,
    plus another force,
        an unknown force,
            that moves in, and through, all forces and all events.
A mysterious factor
is present in everything
        in every event.
Every happening seems to be a physio-mystery event.
    From the total universe
        to mighty galaxies
            to minute particles,
energy swirls in a myriad of combinations.

One such focused swirl of energy is Planet Earth,
    a dance of energy forms
        —dances within dances—
            twirling, clashing, pulling, leaping, dividing, joining!
Earth dances are erotic dances,
    giving birth to life,
        to an extravagant variety
            of expressions, forms and systems of living organisms.
The journey has been one
    of an ever increasing diversity and complexity
        of life forms
            —dances—
            functioning within, and as, one energy system—
            A LIVING ORGANISM!
                functioning within, and as, one dance—
        A COMMUNAL DANCE!
Ah,
    the clouds, the mountains, the streams,
    the flowers, the fungi, the fish,
    the insects, the birds, the monkeys . . .
        Each dance is composed of many smaller dances.

All participating in the one communal dance known as
Planet Earth.

And one of those life forms
    knows that it dances!
  It thinks and decides how it will step and move.
    It looks at its feet.
    It hesitates and stumbles.
The rhythm has changed,
  or has been disrupted.
A new rhythm will emerge
  as before,
  when a new dancer
    and a new dance pattern was introduced
      to the Planet Earth community dance.
The self-conscious units of the Human Dance are creative artists,
    creating new patterns of energy,
      even new forms of life.
  Self-consciously sensitive to the dance as never before,
    they create new responses.
They appreciate and enjoy
    the swirling expressions and the variety of dances—
They rejoice,
  cry,
  laugh,
  shout, sing,
    write, argue,
    teach,
    build, destroy,
      hurt and heal.
They are clumsy artists at this point,
    but creators nonetheless.
And with this,
  new components are added
    to the physical, chemical, and biological lists.
The human mind
  and human passion
    come now to be operative factors
    in the life of Planet Earth.
Energy now has the ability of
  self-direction,
  self-creating,

self-development and
   self-destruction.
Energy is mindful of itself!

As these humans focus and function
   as communities of mindful energy,
      their power
      is enhanced.
A planet-wide nervous system is emerging.
The planet is
   becoming sensitive to itself and
      carrying out its own mental activity.

And in the midst of this continuum of energy is
      a Mysterious Force,
   the Unknown Unknowable Factor,
A Wild Wind,
   which is the source,
   the enlivenment,
   the sustainer,
   the destroyer and
   re-designer of the swirling patterns.

I,
   like you,
   am a continuation of the original cosmic energy happening.
   I am an exploding, swirl of energy!
   You are an exploding, swirl of energy!
The energy that launched the universe and
      spins the stars and galaxies,
   now takes form in you and me.
   That energy empowers you and me.
      It launches us from bed each day
         to spin our own particular universes
         —clashing, dancing, interacting with other energy swirls.
      We,
   like all elements,
are subject to cause and effect.
   The gravity that holds our clothes on a hanger
   has held galaxies together from the beginning.
      Heat expands elements and burns them away
         —be it gases on Jupiter or the skin on my finger.

When no rains come, the crops die.
    You step on the gas and the car moves faster.
    We,
        like all swirling energy patterns before,
are subject to random fate.
    Orbits intersect;
    a few seeds happen to fall on good soil;
        one of a million sperm
        with one in a billion possible DNA combinations
        fertilizes one particular egg.
            A car goes out of control at 4:35
            and hits six other cars
                that just happen to be coming along,
                    also at 4:35.
And yet
    there is more than mechanistic cause and effect;
    there is more than the wild fortunes of fate.
There is pure mysterious spontaneity and synergy.
    People's lives are far more,
        than the sum of their parts.
    Strange coincidences happen.
        The Earth just "happened"
    to be in the right orbit to sustain life.
    There is more design and purpose to life
        than can be explained by natural causes.
            Matter, forms, patterns leap into being
                out of nothing and
                      disappear again.
                    Life appears on Planet Earth out of non-life.
        Photosynthesis "happened" and we have oxygen and food.
Nervous systems function.
    Mozart writes symphonies.
        My passion and energy swirls high and crashes low.
        Things "work out";
            things fail to "work out."
            I swirl on.
Why are things the way they are?
    A mysterious force operates like a dream fulfilling itself.

The universe is filled with surprises,
    awe and wonder,
        of energy spinning and patterning itself.

Our lives are filled with surprises,
  awe and wonder,
    as energy swirls and patterns itself.
You are a star of exploding brilliance
  —we circle and pass by each other,
    pulling, tugging, impacting, repulsing each others orbit.

The new revelation
  in all of this
    is
      seeing
        the universe as a living, ongoing, creative process.
From swirling energy forms
  to swirling energy forms,
life creates life.
  Each "child" reflects the "parent"
    yet is a unique self—
life moves wonderfully and uniquely from point to point.

So what's new?

As an ongoing process,
the universe
  is not a fixed-in-place system
  nor a pre-set design
    (that we know of).
The universe
  is not some grand, pre-determined plan,
    nor is it heading toward some projected defined goal
      (that we know of).
It is creating itself as it goes.
Thus we can
  never be "off course,"
    or "out of harmony,"
      or "out of step."
Similarly, there is no "grand design"
  to find and
    attune to.
There is no "path"
  to find and
    to flow with effortlessly.
There is no cosmic purpose

with which to be in harmony.
There is no cosmic plan
    to obey, follow, or implement.
Now there may be some cosmic principles
    and processes
        with which to be in harmony—
            like constantly creating—
but no plans, blueprints, or designs.

Furthermore,
    the universe is not "out there."
We are "out there"
    —expressions of, and participants in,
        the ongoing creative process.
Since we are part
    of the ongoing, creative process,
        since our very "seeing" is part of the process,
there is nothing that is objective to us.
    What we know
        is only what we perceive and
            interpret
        with our particular and unique means of perception.
Evaluations are subjective,
    valid only
    to the group or to the person
        at a particular time and place
            making the evaluation.
Ideas of
    "improvements to life,"
    "goals for life" and
    "solutions for life's problems"
        are relative to the people who have such ideas.
What we have is
    complexity within complexity,
    tensions within tensions,
    variables within variables
        —processes, relationships, creativity.
There is no firm, secure place
        to "rest" and take a "break" from creating life.

Cosmic energy is constantly

The Adventure of Being Human

     exploding,
          dying, and
               giving birth to new forms.
                    Even so our lives.
A star exploded and our solar system was formed.
          Our sun will explode some day.
The tomato's energy explodes
    in my stomach,
        releasing energy through my muscles and
        into writing a letter
            which, in turn,
        releases energy in the reader
              —energy swirls on
                  from form to form.
Earth spins in tension
    between the pull of the sun
        and the push of the original exploding force.
Water is formed from the
    attraction of hydrogen and oxygen.
Plants are attracted to light,
    driven to grow, but
        limited by available water and nourishment.
Darkness repulses light,
    light repulses darkness—
        both are necessary for life.
Positive and negative charges attract
    and repulse—holding life together
        as well as creating new life.
So it is with our lives—
    attracted to people, things and situations as well as
        being repulsed by the same.
We are "driven"
    by care,
    by fear and
    by longings.
We are limited
    by time, resources, energy, people, knowledge, skill . . .
We are pushed and pulled
    this way and that
        by all manner of "forces."
From galaxies
    to Earth systems,

　　　　　to groups of people,
　　　　　　　to atoms . . .
　　　tension, stress and struggle
　　　　　between swirling energies
　　　　　　　seems to be the standard mode of operation.
　　　Such tensions
　　　　　and stress
are the source
　　　of creativity,
　　　of the new,
　　　of life itself.
　　　　　In this way stars are created.
　　　　　In this way the Planet Earth is created,
　　　　　　　along with mountains, planets, new species,
　　　　　　　babies, novels, highways, neighbors, ideas. . . .
We seek to escape such tensions.
　　　　　We seek to reduce
　　the stress of the push and pull of exploding energy swirls.
　　　　　We constantly reject
　　getting sucked into the energy systems of others.
　　　　　We feel uncomfortable,
　　pulled between the present and some future destination.
　　　　　We do not like to deal
　　with conflicting demands
　　　　　on our lives, time, energy and resources.
Tension
　　　　　—being pushed and pulled—
　　is the natural pattern of the universe.
As we embrace it,
as we participate in it,
we participate in
　　　the ongoing expanding creative process of the universe.
This tension,
　　　　　this push and pull of the universe
Is
　　　　　nonetheless
held within a mysterious unity,
　　　　　a oneness.
The Mysterious Force
　　　contains all within
　　　　　a wholeness,
　　　　　　　a unity.

WE,
    AS UNITS OF ENERGY,
CANNOT HELP BUT
    BE PART OF THE UNIVERSE EVENT.
If you feel your life is an uncontrollable swirl of energy
    —pushed and pulled here and there,
        torn by tensions,
    swirling out into seemingly meaningless darkness—
then you are authentically
        experiencing yourself as Universe energy.
If you experience yourself as exploding passion
    —spinning out wondrous patterns,
    erotically creating new forms and expressions of energy—
then you are authentically
        experiencing yourself as Universe energy.
But, as self-conscious participants,
    a willing embrace of the tension
        seems to be more satisfying and productive.
The excitement of life is thus enhanced
    by going into the
        "void of the beyond" with eyes open—
          "beyond" what we can handle
            into the "not yet"—
And find . . .?
        I'll just let you discover it for yourself.
Dare we
    live our part in such a universe—
        an exploding, swirling, ongoing, creative energy event!
Dare we
    participate self-consciously
    in the ongoing cosmic energy happening!
Dare we
    be the creative energy swirls that we are!

B. CONSCIOUSNESS EXERCISES

1. General Introduction

You may read about another person. People may tell you about that person. But it is only when you have personal conversations with that person and share experiences that you begin to know each other. When you interact and reflect upon things with someone, you develop adequate images of and meaningful relationships with that person.

The same is true for the profound dimensions of life. It is one thing to read and talk about the Universe, the Planet Earth, the Human Individual, the Human Community and the Mystery. It is quite another matter to have personal conversations, shared experiences and reflections with these basic aspects of the Kosmos. We develop new operating images and mental models from personal experiences and reflections, not from abstract discussions.

Furthermore, the scientist in each of us wants empirical evidence. That is, we want evidence that has been or can be corroborated by others as true, as real, as valid. The basic scientific process to obtain valid knowledge involves three steps:

1) An Injunction: "if you want to know if 'abc' is true, then do 'xyz'";
2) Direct Apprehension: do the injunction (do 'xyz') and directly experience or apprehend the data;
3) Communal Confirmation: (validation or rejection)—checking the data/evidence with others who have also adequately completed the injunctive and apprehension steps.[4]

It is important to remember that this approach to valid knowledge is applicable to all arenas of knowledge, not just to the physical arena.

The critical step is the communal confirmation—either validation or rejection. But only those who have done the injunction and collected data are able authentically to engage in the confirmation. Only those who have learned to use a microscope and who have looked through the microscope at the sample can legitimately participate in the discussion of the nature of the microorganism under investigation. It is those who have reflected deeply and/or meditated on these pillars that can authentically participate in the confirmation of the New Kosmos.

---

4. Wilber, K. *The Marriage of Sense and Soul*, pg. 155-6 and fully discussed throughout the book.

The Adventure of Being Human

Section B of each chapter provides a series of exercises designed to assist us in personally experiencing the Kosmic dimension presented in the chapter and reflecting on that experience. Through these exercises we can collect, enhance and evaluate direct experience/data about these pillars for use in confirmation with others.

Though we experience the Universe, Planet, Human Individual, Human Community and The Mystery each moment of each day, these exercises provide us with an opportunity to be self-conscious of our experiences, to reflect on them and to relate to each pillar at a deeper and more profound level. These exercises are opportunities to "know what we know" and to integrate the knowing at a deeper, more authentic level.

Such exercises are normally classified as meditation or contemplation. The general preparation for meditation involves relaxing our bodies, minds and emotions. When we are uptight physically, absorbed in thought about something else or in an anxious mood, it is difficult to enter into a meaningful relationship with another. It is therefore recommended that each exercise session begin with a few moments of relaxation.

If you already practice some form(s) of relaxation that are helpful to you, I suggest you use those forms for your preparation.

If you do not have a method of relaxing, I recommend the following:

Sit on the front edge of a solid chair; feet apart and firmly flat on the floor; knees at right angles; back and neck straight; hands resting on your knees or in your lap. (You may also sit on a cushion on the floor with legs crossed in front, weight on knees, with back and neck straight. Or you may lie on your back on the floor.)

Breathe through your nose deeply enough to swell your stomach like a balloon. Push the air out slowly through your mouth by contracting your stomach muscles. Do this several times, concentrating on breathing in and out, until your breathing slows down and you are aware and in control of your breathing.

Now, at the end of the "in breath," hold it a moment or two, then release and breathe out slowly. At the end of the "out breath" continue letting the air flow out. Empty your mind with the out flow of air (go blank) and wait until your body automatically begins to inhale. Repeat the sequence.

After a few such breaths, focus your attention on the top of your head. Then move your attention slowly down your body—focusing on each part (from outside to inside) of your body. Let each part relax or "melt." Continue down your body to your toes.

Be aware of two or three more slow breaths. Now proceed with the chosen exercise(s). If at any time during an exercise your mind wanders or strays or loses focus, return to being aware of your breath going in and going out. Then return to the exercise at the place where you had been at the time of the loss of focus.

When you have finished the exercise or come to a stopping point in the exercise, move your attention to your breathing and then slowly return your attention to your surroundings.

I have found visualization and reflective meditations most helpful for me personally. Thus, most of the suggested exercises in Section B of each chapter, are of these types. But if you have meditative/contemplative practices of your own which you are comfortable with, feel free to make use of them.

In each chapter, the Section B exercises may be used at any point during that chapter. It is suggested that you do one exercise before reading the Section C, then do one exercise after reading the Section C and do another exercise at the end of the chapter. The exercise instructions are not meant to be followed word for word. You may interpret things for yourself and modify as you see fit. Trust your own interior to provide a meaningful experience.

2. Exercises For Relating to the Universe

• The Big Bang:

In a relaxed state, with eyes closed, picture your mother and the world as it was at her birth; then move back to her mother (your grandmother) and the world at her birth; move back to her mother (your great-grandmother) and the world at her birth. Continue back through your mothers to the human situation 2,000 years ago, 10,000 years ago, 100,000 years ago. Now begin following your ancestry back through their pre-human development, back to the earliest animals on Earth. Follow them back through reptiles; follow the reptiles back to the sea and to fish; follow fish back to the organisms from which they arose; follow back through the one-cell life forms to the emergence of life. From this point follow back through water, through rocks and their cooling to the molten hot planet. Follow back through the swirling dust and gases that were coming together to form the Planet Earth. Continue on back to the explosion of the star that produced these gases and dust to that star's own formation from gases and dust and its swirl in the galaxy. Continue back to the formation of the whole Milky Way Galaxy. Continue on to time before the galaxy, to rushing, expanding energy and on back to the first pin-point of matter and to the great explosion that sent that matter expanding—creating time and space as it expanded. Pause there. Now go to the moment before the "Big Bang" that launched the Universe.

Return to the explosion; follow the explosion and expansion of energy back through the previous path to your birth and to the present moment. If you so desire, you can follow the evolution of the Universe into the future to the point where our star, the sun explodes and the Planet Earth along with it—sending swirling gas, dust, and "stuff" into space to gather and form yet another "heavenly body." Then retrace your steps to the present. Slowly move a foot or hand and gently become aware of your surroundings. Reflect on your experience and note any responses, emotions, or insights. You may want to keep a journal and record your reflections.

- **Expand Yourself:**

In your meditative state, imagine yourself standing in the place where you are. Imagine yourself growing tall, so tall that you can see the surrounding community from above. Imagine that you grow even taller, and are able to see the whole city or county, then the whole state/province, then the whole nation, then the whole continent. You grow large enough to step off the Earth to see the whole of it. You grow larger still and you place the whole Earth in your stomach. You continue to grow so that the sun and all the planets of our solar system circle in your stomach. You continue to expand to include our whole galaxy in your stomach. You continue to expand to include more and more galaxies in your stomach until the whole cosmos is moving within your mid-section. Look tenderly upon all of existence as it moves within you—as part of you. Stay there for a few moments and savor the situation. Then begin the return journey as you gradually reduce in size back to your present size. Open your eyes slowly and sit in the relaxed state a few moments more.

- **Edge of the Universe:**

In your relaxed meditative state with eyes closed, travel to the edge of the Universe and explore the other side of the Universe.

- **Talk to a Tree:**

   [Note: In this book, trees, water, rocks, sandwiches and various other objects can play the role of a teacher or guru—a source of information and wisdom. They are far more accessible and often more wise than human gurus. To the realist in all of us I would say, "You are correct in thinking that this is likely a form of talking to yourself. But it provides us with a variety of new perspectives and permits unrecognized wisdom to emerge to consciousness. Try it before you dismiss it. And, like any of these exercises, if it does not work for you, don't use it."]

Begin by sitting near a tree, preferably right in front of one. If there is no tree immediately available, while in your meditative state, imagine one right in front of you. Relax and ask the tree to tell you about the Universe. Ask the tree where the universe comes from? Where is it heading? Why is it here? Ask it any questions you might have. Then listen. The tree will communicate with you. You can carry on as an involved conversation with the tree as you wish. Most trees can easily keep up their end of the conversation, but you do need to be quiet and listen attentively for the tree to speak.

- **Other Sources of Wisdom/Insight:**

You can do the above exercise with a rock, a pool of water in a stream, a wise being, or a deep well of water. Usually, these items will have to be visualized in your mind's eye. With the pool of water, it may be muddy or cloudy when you first imagine it, so wait quietly while it clears and then look into the deeps. With the well, you will go down into it and follow the underlying stream to a place of deep wisdom. The wise person, in your mind's eye, can be a real historic person or can be an imaginary one. In each case, talk with them about the Universe—ask whatever you wish to know.

C. REFLECTIONS ON OUR UNIVERSE

1. The First Pillar

The first part of any major Kosmic Myth addresses the questions "Where did everything come from?" "Where is everything going?" "Why are things the way they are?" "Why do things operate the way they do?" And these questions usually continue with a secondary part, either explicit or implicit, which adds "including me?"

Classical Myths or Stories of Life were created to explain observable existence, the basic "stuff" of life. They began with the physical aspects of life. People looked around at all the things that surrounded them—the sun, moon, stars, sky, Earth, rocks, sand, mountains, bodies of water, animals, plants. As makers of things, people assumed that all these things were made by someone, somehow. So, the first part of their stories sought to explain how all this stuff came to be and how it functioned. The first part of these stories/myths laid out the basic framework and operating principles of observable existence. This was their Universe.

Every story of life begins with a basic image of how life began, a basic assumption about how and why the observable phenomena of life are as they are and function as they do. Every understanding of life has a basic framework within which life operates. The UNIVERSE chapter addresses this pillar of the Kosmic Story of Life.

2. The Previous Universes

Throughout history, there have been various creation stories about how the universe came to be and how it functions. In most of these stories the universe was fixed and set in place like a stage on which life takes place. How much of an active role the "creator" played in the ongoing operations of the universe varied from culture to culture. Some gods intervened only on special occasions, for good or for ill. Other gods took a more active role in the day to day management and operation of the universe (the heavenly bodies, Earth and human affairs).

In some stories/myths, there was a perfect, ideal design for the universe and its operations. But its material expression was somehow imperfect because of faulty material or the fact that creation was still moving towards the completion of the ideal design.

Other stories or myths described the universe as a giant machine, created by a god, which was set in motion and left to run by its own principles.

The basic assumption about the universe, described in all of these stories, was that it was a fixed operating system. And if the universe was not operating satisfactorily, there were three basic reasons to explain why. One was that the gods were interfering. Another assumption was that something or someone had "messed up" the original operating design, or was not following the operating instructions properly. The third basic explanation of undesired happenings attributed the source of such happenings to "fate."

The assumptions about the role of humans, the products par excellence of creation, varied from story to story and within stories. According to some assumptions, humans were to play their assigned part, to fit in, and to cooperate with the design of the universe. Humans were to get "in tune with" the universe and adjust to its design. According to others, humans were to "use" and "manipulate" the universe—like it was our private garden or play ground. In some stories, humans were to accept their "fate." Still others just considered the universe as a "staging" area for humans to exist in before moving on to something better.

Though each of these stories and myths had various expressions, the basic understandings and assumptions about the universe inherent in them are still operative for many people today.

3. The New Universe

For over three hundred years now, the scientific community has been contemplating the universe and its many aspects with the focus and dedication of a religious monk contemplating a flame. Recently, a new understanding of the universe began quietly and gradually to come into being.

As a result, people are becoming aware that the universe in which we live today is unlike any universe in which humans have lived previously. That is to say, it is dawning upon us that we show up in a universe that is totally different from the universe(s) in which humans have previously lived.

Someone might be inclined to say that the universe has been the same at all times, only our perception of it has changed. This is true. At any given time (era), the universe is the universe as perceived by the people of that time. For example, people who perceived that they lived on a flat Earth were in a different universe—with a different set of operating principles—from those who perceived that they lived on a round Earth. Similarly, those who perceived that disease is caused by the affliction of some god or spirit lived in a different universe—with

The Adventure of Being Human 49

different health practices—from those who perceived that disease is caused by bacteria and viruses. So, as people's understanding and perception of the universe changes, grows and expands, the universe in which they live changes.

With human senses extended by means of scientific technology, the understanding of the universe has extended into the vast reaches of time and space, into the most minute details of organisms and matter. As a result, you and I show up in a vastly larger and more complex universe than any previous universe.

We live in a universe that is perceived to be a massive force of energy which has been expanding, from a single point of undifferentiated energy, for about 14 billion years—give or take a few billion. And it is still expanding. For the first time ever, we can see (with scientific instruments and calculations) the beginning of the universe and the edge of the universe. This single, expanding, swirling force of energy takes many increasingly varied and complex forms from atoms to galaxies, from raindrops to soaring eagles. And these forms are not fixed and stable—they expand, collide, explode, collapse, and transform themselves into yet other forms and patterns of energy. (Death and resurrection to a new form were fundamental dynamics of the universe from the very beginning.)

One of these energy forms is the Planet Earth, which is a product of, and a participant in, the universe's energy. This particular expression of the universe's energy, existing for over four and a half billion years, is an ongoing, evolving process that includes an extravagant array of diverse forms and patterns of energy—all interrelated and interacting as a single energy system. And each of these forms and patterns themselves has a long history of evolution with its own intricate array of forms, patterns and sub-systems of energy. The Earth energy system began with the geo-sphere (land, solid structural forms), added the hydro-sphere (water forms), the atmo-sphere (air forms), and finally the bio-sphere (life forms). With these basic forms in place, Earth went wild.

One of the Earth's energy forms of particular interest for us is the human species, with its many forms and interrelationships. The human species is also a product of, and a participant in, the universe's energy. And like all other expressions of energy, humans evolved and developed over time. The human bio-system is the most recent bio-system to arrive on the scene and, with a relative short period of development to date, is considered to be in its early phases of development. The human bio-system, like other energy systems, is itself a single energy system composed of a variety of forms, patterns and interacting energy swirls.

Self-consciousness makes the individual and collective life of humans more complex and rich. Within the human bio-system, the universe has developed a fifth basic planetary form—the mind-sphere (self-conscious mental forms). As a functional process, this mental activity now joins the processes of physics, chemistry and biology as a basic operating "law" in the Earth energy system.

Much of the universe, its operation and development, can be understood in terms of the intricate workings of the laws of physics, chemistry and biology and in terms of the principles of *cause and effect, randomness/probability, and chaos*. Years of scientific "meditation" about the universe has raised these laws and principles—along with their methods and tools—to a high degree of precision and sophistication.

This rigorous application of the rational, objective, scientific approach has also uncovered many facts that cannot be contained or understood within our rational framework. There are many happenings during the evolution of the universe—many beginnings, leaps and gaps—which cannot be explained or grasped by our objective scientific processes. These seem to point to the presence of an unidentifiable force or factor—a numinous aspect—which is still beyond the realm of comprehension by human minds.

Science can do a fairly good job of describing *what has happened* in the universe and *how it happened*. But Science cannot describe *why it happened* or *why it happened as it did*. Clearly, there is an unknown factor, an unknown force operating at all levels and at all points in the universe. We have objective evidence of occurrences. But we do not always know or understand what produced them. Often, what we desire to know is unknowable—at least at the present level of development of our minds. We are dealing with pure mystery—the unknowable unknown. The mysterious factor is not a riddle that we have not yet figured out. The mysterious factor is something that we currently do not have the capacity to comprehend.

Because there seems to be a mysterious aspect to all events, it might be said that every event in the universe is a "physio-mystery" event. That is, every event or happening involves physical energy in some form and a mysterious factor. In every event there is more than "meets the eye." There is present another aspect or dimension to existence that we cannot grasp with our minds or with physical forms. The word *mystery* may not be the best word, but we do not have good language at the current time for dealing with the non-object, non-physical, non-rational dimensions of life.

The new universe in which we live is a single, expanding,

interacting, constantly creating, multiform, physio-mystery energy happening. We humans, along with the planet, stars, rivers, trees, cars, frogs, lettuce, pencils, guns, snow storms, mushrooms, viruses, ... you name it, are part of an ongoing energy event. Someone has called this process *cosmo-genesis*—the universe is in a constant state of ongoing creation.

Creation arises from tension. An initial explosion set particles both moving outwards and spinning—exerting force on one another. The counter balancing of forces (tension) holds patterned energy forms together. This counter balance between attracting and repulsing forces is the operating mode of the universe.

If this counter balancing tension was perfectly balanced though, everything would be stable and constant—nothing would ever change. But there is, built into the scheme of things (there's that mysterious factor again!), just enough unevenness to permit tensions (attraction or repulsion) to over-load or under-load which results in inter-action between masses of energy. A slight imbalance or unevenness of tensions allows for variation, growth, destruction, change and creation. Tensions from a variety of sources can build up over time and violently erupt—an exploding star, a lightning bolt, a hurricane, a societal eruption, personal anger—rearranging the conditions of life, rearranging surrounding energy forms and patterns and releasing new energy to take new forms. Tensions can weaken and breakdown—decaying fish, falling rain, boredom, a burning log—releasing energy that can form into new patterns. Opposite energy patterns attract each other and new forms emerge—all processes of reproduction. Similar energy patterns repulse each other—the basis of electric motors. Human creativity is the product of forces of attraction and repulsion.

The universe we live in is a multi-form, ongoing, creative energy event. Humans are swirling energy patterns, a product of, and a participant in, a vast continuum of swirling energy patterns within swirling energy patterns where new forms and patterns of swirling energy are constantly being created. So it has been for billions of years, and so it will most likely continue for billions of years to come.

(This is not meant to be a precise or exhaustive description of our new universe. It is meant to help us get a "feel" for this new understanding of the universe and to begin to create images/metaphors/basic assumptions, which permit us to savor more authentically and fully the universe in which we participate.)

D. IMPLICATIONS OF LIVING IN A NEW UNIVERSE

When I first moved to Taiwan, it was like moving to a different world. I had to change the way I interpreted situations, the way I responded to people and situations, and some of the ways I functioned. People would say "yes" even when they intended "no"—being polite, not to offend in person. Pedestrians walked, without looking, across the street because larger moving objects on the road were responsible for not hitting smaller moving objects. A polite refusal really meant "Yes, I want it." I had to learn to be circumspect in admiring another person's possession because, if I admired it too openly, they would try to give it to me. Traffic did not move in a straight stop-and-go line. Rather, traffic kept moving by weaving in and out and around anything that would threaten to impede forward progress. Bargaining was the accepted mode of determining the price of goods and services. And "How much did you pay for that?" as a main topic of conversation was not being nosy; rather it was the way people kept abreast of the going price of things.

Section D of each chapter sets forth some implications and possible changes for us, now that we find ourselves in a different world—a new Kosmos. If you find yourself disagreeing with something presented in these sections, I would ask that you to write down the assumptions upon which your evaluation is based. Analyze your assumptions. If your assumptions "hold true," then we have the starting point for a dialogue. Let me hear from you.

For the new universe pillar of the new Kosmos, here are a few possible new orientations for our lives.

1. We Live in an Expanding Universe—Always Changing

Nothing about our universe is fixed, static, or in final form. Thus there is no "golden age" to which we can return, even if it were possible to go back in time. There is no good, pure and perfect original creation which has been lost, and which we should seek to re-establish. Thus there is no need to blame human society for having lost paradise. Nor is there cause for laying a guilt trip on humans for messing up an imagined good and perfect creation.

Furthermore, since the universe is not a fixed operating system, it is not helpful to attempt to make some adjustments so that it will function "the way it was designed to function." Since it is not a fixed system, it is irrelevant to try and learn its "operating instructions" in order to make the world function better.

2. An Open-Ended Creative Process Rather Than a "Production"

In all our observations of the workings of the universe, there has been no sign of any pre-determined or projected design of the universe—perfect, ideal, encoded, or otherwise. At least there is none to which we have access. Thus, there is no system, or design, or standard that should be implemented or to which we should be conforming. There is no grand design to harmonize with. There is no universally correct or ideal standard by which events are judged. That is not to say that there are no standards or criteria by which we make judgments. It is just that we need to remember that any standards or criteria are social (human) creations—products of the ongoing creative tensions of the universe. There is no escape from responsibility. There is no way to claim, "I am just following the plan."

The universe is a happening. Each day we stand naked on the raw edge of the universe and participate in the creation of the next expression of the universe. (We also create the next expression of the planet Earth and our own personal journey—but more about that later.) The challenge is to bring as much self-consciousness to this creative process as possible, and to savor it.

3. Humans Are An Expression of the Energy of the Universe

In one sense, we humans are just a "hunk of meat." In another sense, we are the new leading edge of the universe's development. As we will see later, the self-reflective human mind is part of a daring universal experiment. But for sure, humans are not the primary focus or the "last word" in the operation of the universe. We are just one of many participants in the ongoing drama which is the universe.

In fact, the universe does not seem to attach much importance to human concerns or values. It will drown, freeze, burn, crush, starve, destroy, and otherwise play havoc with humans, just as it does with stars, trees, tomato plants, cows or any other energy pattern. It will also feed, warm, water, heal, protect, enrich and otherwise promote human life, as it does with a planet, a flower, a bug, a loon or any other energy pattern. The basic pattern of development in the universe goes from simple to more complex wholes. This would seem to favor the human mind as the leading edge of evolution. But the process of evolution seems to meander rather than to proceed in a linear fashion. Evolution produces more surprise results than predictable results. We humans should not count on any preferential treatment.

4. Universe is Not an Objective Reality

For us, the universe is not an objective reality, as it was for people of previous ages. We know that whatever a person observes is affected to some degree by the person who is doing the observation. Thus every observation contains something of the observer. Not only do we know that all ancient ideas (Stories) about the universe are human creations, we also know that our current perceptions (Stories) of the universe are human creations. It is true that there is some external, commonly observed and measured data available to us. But its interpretation is very subjective. Do you know where you are? Do you even know which way is up? (Earth is up from the moon.)

How often have you heard or said the phrase "that's just the way it is?" This phrase usually means, "that's a fact of life, and there is no use trying to deny it." But there is no "way it is." There is only "the way somebody perceives it." True, there are many commonly agreed upon perceptions. But they are just that, the perceptions of a given person or group of people, at a given point in time.

Since there is no true objectivity, each of us has to take responsibility for our observations. Also, it might help to be slow to judge the observations of others and to be quicker to see value in the observations of others. Somehow, this is not easy for any of us.

5. Tensions Are Normal

Tensions are part of the normal operating mode of the universe. This flies in the face of our concerns and efforts to reduce tensions, to escape from tensions, to resolve tensions, to blame tensions for undesired results and to otherwise demonize tensions. Tensions help the universe hold together. Tensions are a source of creativity. The most basic tension is the tension between life and death. We will deal with tensions in more detail in Chapter 4—THE INDIVIDUAL HUMAN. Suffice to note here that the challenge is to embrace and work with as much tension as one possibly can. Use tensions to increase your creativity. When they get too much to bear, use something to help deal with them—only use it self-consciously so that you use it and it does not use you. If we do not learn to embrace "the life that is death and the death that is life," we can be paralyzed by the tensions. To put it more positively, the message of the universe is that tensions are our friends, the source of creativity. Welcome them—don't run from them.

6. We Live in an Era of Surprise, Wonder and Enchantment

The more data we gather, the more mystery, wonder and awe are conjured up. An unknown factor, a mysterious force, seems to surround and infuse each aspect of the universe. Who can contain it? Who would want to contain it? From the smallest particle of energy-matter to the wrinkled edge of space, the universe is comprised of swirling energy forms. Exploding stars, sun-spots, solar winds, storms, lightning, rivers, a bird in flight, a newborn baby—all are swirling energy rippling through space and time. Each morning I go forth, a swirl of energy, setting off other swirls with each word, each action, each interaction with other swirls of energy. The water molecules that flow in my blood stream crashed on beaches millions of years ago. The basic energy pattern of the tree in my yard struggled into being millions of years ago. The minerals in my car were created during the explosion of the star that gave birth to our solar system.

Ours is a universe of surprise, wonder and enchantment. Each morning we wake up in the midst of a great drama that has been billions of years in the making. The Mysterious Force that sparked the first minds, the Mystery that spaced the notes of the nightingale, the Force that set the hundred billion galaxies spinning across the sky, now awakens you and me, and sets us forth to participate in the ongoing creation of the drama that is our universe and our Kosmos. The more self consciously and intentionally we participate, the more satisfying and exciting it is for us.

We do not know what mystery awaits us in the very next moment. We do not know, cannot know, how our decisions or actions will turn out. How the drama will proceed, we cannot tell. We can be sure, though, that we will continue to be astonished and enchanted.

E. AN IMAGE

Stories of Life are composed of vivid images or metaphors that communicate rich understandings about the way life functions. Such images represent basic assumptions about life—what life is, how it operates, and how humans can best participate in it.

Image is here used as a *basic operating picture*—something that effects the way we operate. Image refers to how we understand (see) ourselves, others, things and happenings. Such an image determines how we relate and respond to life. More importantly, these foundational assumptions or operating images affect (positively and negatively) the way a person experiences life. For instance, if you have a preconceived notion that something is *fun*, you will participate differently than if you see it as *serious*. Have you ever noticed how your body reacts when you encounter something that you image as scary or evil? And like a picture, they express more than any amount of words.

The primary function of *images* in a Story of Life is to express compactly and directly fundamental assumptions about the Kosmos. Such primal images help a person experience life more fully and savor life more subtly, more intensely—to expand one's range of sensitivity and appreciation of life.

For each pillar (chapter) of this Kosmic Story of Life, a fundamental operating image is presented. They function as a basic holding image for our understanding of and relation to each pillar. Each of these images has come from my personal experience and reflections. Each one is not my first image for that chapter, nor will it likely be my last. You are invited to test each image relative to your own experiences and reflection. If the provided image does not *work* for you, if it does not seem to enhance the vitality and excitement of life, then by all means, please experiment with various other images until one does *work* for you.

As we encourage the poet, the artist, the dancer, the singer, and the storyteller aspect of our lives to express our experiences of life in metaphors and images, the new "Story of Life" will emerge. It is this new *story* of life which will enable us to sing together, to dance together, to laugh together, to talk together, to work together—together with each other as humans and human communities, together with all systems of the planet, together with all aspects of the universe—as the grand Kosmic drama.

The image for the UNIVERSE is that of *SWIRLING ENERGY*. Swirling like a galaxy, like an atom, like water in a stream, like a child with outstretched arms trying to get dizzy. Swirling . . .

. . . powerful forces pushing outward;

The Adventure of Being Human

   . . . powerful forces pulling inward;
   . . . powerful forces, intense swirls;
   . . . powerful forces held in place with just enough imbalance to permit movement and change.

Swirling energy forms interact with each other to create yet new energy forms. Then when the tension breaks or collapses, energy swirls into new and different energy forms. Creation is a constant, ongoing process.

You are invited to contemplate this image of SWIRLING ENERGY. Create your own image for the Universe. Create several. Play with them; test them; use them; share them. I am starting a repository to gather such fundamental operating images (metaphors, "pictures," assumptions) of life.

58 Basil Sharp

"Swirling Energy"
By Pat Nischan

Chapter Three

THE PLANET

A. THE COMMUNAL DANCE—A STORY-POEM

1. The New Reality

A star blazed brightly . . .
    and exploded!
God! What a dust bowl.
    sweeping through space!
There, as dust has a habit,
    it collected into giant dust balls.
One burst into flame;
    the sun was born!
        Nine smaller hot dust balls circled round the sun.
Ball number three cooled with a hard crust and
    produced a strange substance—
        water
        —dissolving and carrying chemicals.

Somewhere,
    somehow,

(the mysterious factor again!)
in that water
    appeared a living cell—a process
        of transformation began.
Single cell and multi-cell organisms began to appear—
    functions within functions,
        organism within organism.
Over time,
    the Earth gave birth
        to an extravagant diversity of living systems,
            forms and expressions
                —a variety of shapes, colors, textures, and odors.

All of this took place within a developing,
    complex support system.
A geological system provided physical structure
    —bones and flesh.
Then, water and air circulating systems—flowing and breathing—
    supplied chemicals for growth
        and helped to regulate temperature to sustain that growth.
Next, the living biological systems
    made it possible to transform sunlight,
        chemicals and other organisms
            into usable energy.
And lastly,
    a mental system
        began developing
            for the appreciation and enhancement of the Planet.

Balanced mutual support—
    yet enough instability
        pulling, pushing, joining, separating,
    to create improvements and new expressions.
The journey of Planet Earth has been one of increasing diversity and complexity of life forms—
    organisms within organisms,
    living systems within living systems—
        each living off of the other,
        each supporting the other
        each pushing and limiting the other.
    All functioning within,
        and as,
    one energy system, the planet Earth.

The Adventure of Being Human

    Roots, branches, leaves, flowers, fruits and seeds;
    Muscles, lungs, eyes, stomachs, bones and skin;
       Plants, insects, animals, hills and streams.
   Seasons and storms; night and day;
     Action upon reaction;
       adjustments and readjustments.
From bare rock and empty seas
   to forests, jungles, plains and teaming seas.
From a single cell groping for a molecule of building material
to the fine coordination of eye, claw, tongue,
   stomach enzymes, blood cells, and muscles.
The Earth,
   a giant living organism
   developing as a complex unit of life.
      Some have given it a name—
       Gaia.
With the development of a nervous system,
   organisms took on self manipulation and responsiveness—
fish swam, birds soared,
   monkeys swung, toads hopped, tigers pounced.
    They hunted and hid;
    they attacked and defended;
    they screamed and they purred;
    they raised young and they formed groups;
    they played and they felt fear;
    they basked in the sun and froze in the snow.

The journey took another mysterious leap.
   Self-conscious thought
      was developed by Earth
      in one of its organisms –
        the human.
With this ability,
   the universe and the planet became aware of itself
        and could
      for the first time
        appreciate itself
      as well as fear itself.
With this ability,
   the Earth began to learn about itself;
     began to research and analyze itself.
   It learned to evaluate and respond;
    to regulate, improve, screw-up, hurt, and enjoy itself.

With self-conscious reflection,
  the Earth took some measure of self-conscious control of
    its own development and destiny—
      with all the accompanying potential for a royal mess
        as well as for glorious achievements.
Earth had reached a new level of maturity.

It might be said,
  with this ability,
  the Earth,
    as an organism,
  is developing
    its own nervous system,
    its own mental process,
    its own mind.
The human community functions as the mind of the Earth,
  composed of innumerable nodes of mental activity.
          Like the individual human mind,
  the Earth's mind is at times brilliant,
    at times sluggish and stupid,
    sometimes insightful and sometimes unseeing.
          Like the individual human brain,
  the Earth's mind is influenced by a variety of factors,
    as yet, not fully understood.

Some few humans, at times,
  have experienced themselves as one with all creation,
    beyond the individual self.
Beyond the rational and in the realm of Spirit,
  some even, at times,
          have experienced the oneness of existence—
    as the ONE,
      the ALL.
Beyond Mind,
  will the Earth develop Spirit?

2. The Wonder

Ah, the wonder of it!
  The pure, unadulterated wonder of it!
You and I are part of the Gaia's mental process.

The Adventure of Being Human

Our efforts to investigate,
   discover and learn about life on Planet Earth
      is Gaia investigating and discovering itself.
When you and I explore, experiment, evaluate,
   the Earth is exploring, experimenting and evaluating itself.
When we humans invent, create, order, solve, envision,
   Gaia is inventing, creating, solving, envisioning.
When humans make mistakes, become perplexed,
      learn from them and make corrections,—
   Gaia is making mistakes, feeling perplexed,
      learning from them and making corrections.

When our bodies do not function correctly,
   our nervous system registers pain.
When things do not function well for the planet,
   the human system registers pain and suffering
   and responds to relieve that pain and suffering.
What may be years of response time to us,
   may be almost immediate response
         in terms of Earth's geological time.
So our pain at the plight of victims of natural disasters,
   our anger over the hatred and
      killings from religious and ethic conflict,
   our frustration with pollution,
         is the Earth being sensitive to its pain.
As you and I remember, think and
   store up our learning in books and other media,
   Gaia is remembering, thinking and storing up knowledge.
As we sing and cry, weep and laugh,
   the Earth sings, cries, weeps and laughs.
Through us
   Gaia raises questions and wonders out-loud.

And what might the Earth's mental capacity be
   in another 1,000 years? 10,000 years?
We are a young species,
      a very young species,
      a newly formed organism in Earth time.

This reflective quality has enabled humans
   to develop tools and technologies,
      which enhance the speed and power to build up, break down

and re-organize the structures and systems of the Earth.
The Earth is taking a risk with humans.
Within the past few decades,
    humans have developed the ability
        to destroy life on the planet—either partially or totally.
But, as with all young things,
    the human is just beginning
        to experience its power and
            learn how to use it.
Thus, the dance of Planet Earth bio-systems,
    dances within dances,
        an Earth Community Dance,
which seemed to be functioning harmoniously
(though never as smoothly as we are want to imagine)
        is now going through an awkward phase
        as the human bio-system
            creates its steps
            and learns to dance in the Community Dance.
The human bio-system is learning to respond
    to the intricate dance of the other bio-systems
        and to the passion of Earth itself.
I wonder,
    how long did it take the trees
to learn their place in the dance?
        What plants and animals did
        trees tromp upon and destroy?
And how the trees did pollute!
        They saturated the air with their toxic waste
            called "oxygen."
Earth does find ways of taking care of itself!
With the human journey,
    Planet Earth is learning and struggling to be itself.
With the human journey,
    Gaia is not only learning to improve its dance;
        it is learning to enjoy its dance.

The Earth produced the human community.
        (Yes, humans are a product of Earth's evolution
            just like mountains, snails, roses,
                algae, blue birds and cows.)
    In producing us humans,
Planet Earth is developing a brain,

a mind,
a psyche,
a personality,
that can fully appreciate itself and
improve itself.

The Earth is becoming enchanted with itself!

With the development
of the human mind and capabilities,
even the ability to destroy itself,
Earth has entered a new geological age of its development
—the Ecozoic Age—
the age
when the Earth takes self-conscious responsibility for itself;
the age
when the human bio-system learns to dance creatively
with all the other bio-systems.

3. Implications

I no longer live ON the Earth.
 I participate IN the planet's life.
 I am a living part of
  a whole being,
  a living organism.
To get in tune or harmony with nature is pointless.
 I am nature!
 We are nature!
  Nature is learning a new tune.
 To be sure, Earth has hit a few sour notes recently,
  but that's nothing new for Earth.
Humans do not live ON Earth.
 We are a bio-system of Planet Earth
 We are PARTICIPANTS in the Great Communal Dance,
  of bio-systems,
   that is Planet Earth.

Cities are as natural as beaver dams, bird nests, and anthills.
There is no leaving the city to get back to nature.

We are all participants in the life of the planet.
Each day we are learning how to participate.

It is not easy.
No one before us has tried to function as a living planet.
    There are no rules,
    no instructions,
    no guidelines on how to participate.
There is no script,
    no program,
    no system for us to learn and to follow.
As the *Mind* of Planet Earth,
    what will it mean for us to have the well-being
    of Planet Earth as our primary point of reference
    for observing, evaluating and deciding?
Normally,
    we measure things by our own subjective standards.
    "What's in it for me?"
    "What's in it for us?"
Now we will be saying
    "What's in it for Planet Earth—
    Not just for me and my community,
    Not just for humans,
    Not just for trees,
    But for Earth as a living body?"
We feel a need for
    new education,
    new economics,
    new politics,
    better health care, . . .
To be effective
    the whole planet will be the basis of our response.
We are,
    and will continue,
        creating
Earth-based education,
Earth-based politics,
Earth-based economics,
Earth-based health care,
Earth-based language,
Earth-based sociology,
Earth-based theology,
Earth-based architecture,
    and on and on.
We are,

and will continue,
> learning to function as a living planet.

No illusions
> about the pain and struggle to kick some bad habits.
> > It is no easier for the human bio-system
> > > than for an individual human
> > > > to change lifestyles.

With the Gaia as our reference,
answers become more complex,
> not simpler.
There are many variables
> —most unknown;
> and the impact of each variable upon the others
> > is unknown.
How often has a good solution only created more problems!
> Do you close down an unsafe nuclear plant
> > and cut off half of the electrical supply of a country
> > struggling to recover,
> > > or risk the plant's continued operation?
> At the grocery check out,
> do you choose paper or plastic bags?
> > Paper bags, destruction of trees,
> > consumption of energy,
> > with increased pollution.
> > Plastic bags, use of oil,
> > environmental hazard.
> Do you decrease child mortality
> > and increase the population explosion;
> > or do you change mating practices?

There are no perfect answers.
There are no clear right answers.
> So what does one do?
> How decide?
> How act?

4. The Challenge

We are the Mind of Earth.
    We participate in a living Planet.
        We dance the Great Community Dance.
Dare we be it—intentionally?
        HOW?
Hang loose!
    Be cool!
        With detached sensitivity,
    be open
        to the total picture and
        to the particulars at hand.
Listen to the human community—the collective mind of Gaia.
Use all of the rational power
    and resources you have at your disposal.
        Then let the focus emerge,
        trust the "force,"
        trust your intuition or judgment.
            Decide the necessary deed—
                necessary because you have to act
                one way or the other.
Be passionate!
Put your whole life into your response.
    Be totally engaged.
Commit your whole being to your response—
    Dance!
        Dance!
            Dance!
This is integrity
    —total commitment and engagement.
Let the Earth speak to you,
        let its passion speak through you.
Put your life into your response,
    whatever it may be—
        choosing the grocery bag;
        revamping the education system;
        washing the dishes;
        creating an environmentally friendly dwelling;
        producing a fantastic report on health care;
        repairing a telephone line;
        making a sale;
        changing a diaper;

    attending a meeting;
    making love;
    pulling weeds.
Don't worry too much about accomplishment.
    Your brilliant solution will probably create 15 more problems.
       Besides, you may never see or know the final result.
Trust the Earth with the outcome.
    Trust the Earth to take care of itself.
        It has been doing a fairly decent job
            for over four billion years.

B. CONSCIOUSNESS EXERCISES

The following exercises are provided to help you experience the Planet Earth more directly and personally. These exercises create opportunities for you to visit with and reflect on the Planet Earth—to be more aware of it, to savor it.

- **An Atom**:

In a relaxed state, imagine you are one of the atoms that compose your body. Follow the history of that atom back through time, back to explosion of the star from which the sun and Earth were formed. Try to visualize the various periods of Earth's evolution and development. At the point of the explosion, shift your visualization to another atom. Follow this new atom forward in the formation and development of Planet Earth until the atom arrives in your present body.

- **Bio-Systems:**

Reflect on all of the bio-systems that are part of your day—trees, bacteria, insects, streams, etc. and all the foundational spheres on which they depend—rocks, soil, water, gases. How do you participate in their dances? Where is there pain in the whole Earth-system or dance? Where is there health and joy?

- **Your Hand:**

In a relaxed state, hold your hand in front of you. Make a fist and then open it. Meditate on the evolution and development of your hand. From where did it come? How did it come to be that humans have the capability of hands? How long did it take Earth to develop the human hand? Meditate on what your hands are able to do and express.

- **The Joy of the Earth:**

In a meditative state, try to identify with Planet Earth or take the perspective of the Planet as a living being. Think about the joy of Planet Earth as it evolved and developed over the years to the state that it is today. Recall accomplishments of the past 4.5 billion years, and rejoice. Now, mediate on Planet Earth's hopes and dreams for its future journey and development over the next 100,000 years or as far as your visualization will take you into the future.

- **Planet Earth and the Galaxy:**

In a relaxed state, with eyes closed, imagine that you are Planet Earth. The Galaxy (The Milky Way) speaks to you and asks, "Earth, what is your passion?" You, as Planet Earth, respond to the Galaxy's question. The Galaxy then asks, "Earth, what do you envision or desire for the human race in the next 1,000 or so years?" You again respond to the Galaxy and carry on a conversation about your future as Earth and the future of the human species.

- **Eating a Sandwich or Salad:**
  Some noon, as you are eating a sandwich or a salad, carry on a conversation with the ingredients, as you would with a wise guru. Ask where each came from and how they got into your meal. Talk about their history and evolution. Ask them what they expect to do for you and what you can do to honor their contribution and participation in your life. Talk with them about each of your roles in the life of Planet Earth. Thank them for bringing their particular energy to contribute to your life.

- **Walking as One with the Earth:**
  Meditate while walking. As you walk, concentrate on your breathing. Be aware of the in-breath and the out-breath. Allow your steps to coincide with your breathing—like four slow counts/steps in and four slow counts/steps out. (Or you may go even slower with one step on the in breath and one step on the out breath.) Take soft, deliberate steps. Notice the movement of the foot as it lightly "kisses the Earth" and lifts off again. As you walk, repeat a phrase with 8 syllables, such as "I AM WALK-ING AS ONE WITH EARTH," or "THE EARTH AND I ARE ONE IN LIFE." The main thing is to keep a slow, steady rhythm, so that your being is in tune with your walking, and with everything that surrounds you. You may gaze at the ground just in front of you or slowly look around you—the main thing is to keep your attention on the phrase and the steps.

- **Talk with a Tree, Rock, Pool of Water, or Wise Person:**
  Go sit near a tree, preferably right in front of one. If there is no tree immediately available, while in your meditative state, imagine one right in front of you. Relax and ask the tree to tell you about the Planet Earth. Ask it where it came from? How it got to where it is today? Ask about its current state of being. Ask where is the Planet going from here? Ask it any questions you might have about Planet Earth. Then listen. Your conversion can be as involved as you wish.

  You may carry on a similar conversation with a rock, a pool of water in a stream or a wise person (from history, literature, movies or your imagination). Usually, these will have to be visualized in your mind's eye.

C. REFLECTIONS ON PLANET EARTH

1. The Second Pillar

The second part of any major story of life deals with the everyday physical and biological world around us—the third rock from the sun. The word *planet* seems natural here. But upon reflection, one realizes that the concept of *planet* is a fairly recent one—the result of modern scientific investigation and education. In traditional mythology, this second pillar is known as "nature," "creation," "Earth" or "the world." As such, second pillar deals with basic mental assumptions about the nature of the world around us and of which we are a part. How does it function? And how do humans fit in it?

2. Previous Worlds

People once believed that the world was composed of powerful forces. These forces could destroy and kill as well as create and sustain life. Usually these forces were identified with observed phenomena like lightening, trees, rocks, mountains or animals. Gradually, these forces were personified and thought of as *beings, spirits* or *gods*, or thought to be under the personal control of *spirits* or *gods*. As humans began to manipulate aspects of their surroundings for their own benefit, they sought also to influence these *spirits*, to manipulate their powers in ways beneficial to humans. In seeking to manipulate such forces, humans sought to gain some control over their own destiny.

Since humans made and manipulated things, humans began to explain the existence of things, including themselves, as products of some supreme, powerful, unseen "creator(s)."

Though some stories and myths spoke of the oneness and wholeness of all things, and saw humans as just another aspect of "creation" like everything else, there was little practical understanding of this relationship. It was more of a fusion with nature rather than a oneness. People respected and cooperated with nature, almost unthinkingly, just to function on a daily basis—not because of some mystical understanding of or "spiritual attunement to nature."

[For some peoples, there were spirits and gods living in or expressed as natural objects such as mountains, trees, animals and rivers. These people honored and respected these aspects of nature, not because of the natural items themselves, but to honor, please and gain the favor of the spirits or gods that were thought to be present in nature.]

People's livelihood and successful existence depended upon being aware of and attuned to their surroundings and working with the local environment. But this is no different than any other successful humans. A street person in New York City in the 1990s, needs to be as sensitive and attuned to their environment as any native American was centuries ago. A stockbroker or office secretary, in order to function well and to survive, must be sensitive and attuned to their environments as any farmer of an ancient civilization. Being attuned to plants, animals, streams and forests was not an option or a virtue for people of earlier times. Plants, animals, streams and forests formed their work-a-day world. Furthermore, since these people were powerless before the forces of nature, cooperation was the only way to survive.

Gradually, humans came to view themselves as something distinct from their environment. As human ability to make things and to manipulate the environment increased, humans gained more control over their well-being. Eventually, the distinction between "human-made things" and "natural things" came about. Humans began to see themselves as makers, as controllers, as manipulators—roles previously reserved for the *gods* or *spirits*.

At the same time, humans became more self-reflective. They projected themselves, mentally, into time and space before things were created and into time and space after things ceased to exist. Humans could step back from the physical world and experience time and space in the inner world of the mind. Humans again moved into the realms of the gods and spirits. Humans began to see themselves "above" this world.

Thus, the natural world became something separate from the human world. Nature was first perceived to be a realm that functioned by the dictates and control of spirits, gods, or some force other than human. Later, nature was perceived to function according to the laws of cause and effect, obeying certain physical, chemical and biological laws. Humans on the other hand, had a free will, conscious reflective thought, a soul, a spirit, and the ability to manipulate the world of objects. Not only were humans different from the natural world, they were somewhat superior to it.

The natural world was viewed as something to be used, manipulated and managed for the benefit of humanity. Earth was considered raw material to be used for the enjoyment and benefit of humans. Even more enlightened people thought that the physical world was meant to be harnessed for humans. Whether it was admired, enjoyed, taken care of, overused or trashed, Earth was assumed to be a resource for humans.

Humans came to think of themselves as akin to the gods. Their real home, their real world, was the realm of the gods—above and separate from this created world. With this perspective, the Earth was seen as a temporary home for humans until their return to an eternal home in the realm of the gods.

The scientific and industrial era evidenced a concerted effort to exert human control over the Earth and to manipulate it. In this era, the physical world was viewed as composed of discrete parts. Humans researched, examined, classified and documented these discrete parts of the world in a most remarkable way. It might be said that humans have been meditating on the physical world for 400 years. By gaining an understanding of the discrete parts and how they functioned, humans were able to manipulate the physical world in significant ways and exert powerful control over it. This dissection of the world revealed, among other things, that there were no gods or spirits resident or operative in the world. The physical became supreme. That which could be experienced by the five senses (or the mechanical extensions of them), that which could be measured and manipulated, became the real. All else was either derived from the real or was suspect. Humans were in control. The understanding and manipulation of the physical world were the keys to complete victory by humans. The wonderland of paradise was within our reach.

Then a NEW world came into being.

3. The New Planet

During the extensive and intensive investigation of our world, a new understanding of Planet Earth emerged.

As our investigation of the discrete parts and functions of the human body revealed a complex interrelated, interdependent whole, so our investigation of the discrete parts and systems of the Earth revealed a planet that is a single ecological system composed of complex, interrelated and interdependent life systems (bio-systems). The current basic perception regarding our planet is that it is a living organism. Planet Earth is a self-regulating, growing, evolving organism—an integrated whole.

John Lovelace, Peter Russell and others have developed this perception in what is commonly known as the "Gaia Hypothesis." (You are referred to their writings for details.) A few points about this hypothesis will suffice. To begin, the atmospheric "skin" protects the Earth's surface from harmful radiation and maintains Earth's temperature within acceptable limits for organic life systems. The wind functions as the respiratory system, distributing the supply of oxygen and other gases necessary for plant and animal life. The water systems (clouds, rain, streams, rivers, oceans, etc.) function as the circulation system, supplying necessary liquid and nutrients, and removing and disposing of waste products. Various critical chemicals in land, air and sea are self regulated to maintain the proper levels for life functions. Living organisms support and maintain one another with life processes, protection and nutrients. A balance between supply and demand is maintained within "healthy" parameters. "Wounds" are healed or compensated for. The evolution of Planet Earth, as a whole, follows the same basic developmental steps and processes that any living organism does.

This image of the Earth as a single living organism is dramatically held for us with the view of the Earth from the moon—a blue marble rotating gracefully through space.

No humans before us lived with this perception of Earth.

a. The Planet's Evolution

Planet Earth has grown from simple forms and functions to its current complex forms and functions. In the beginning, over four billion years ago, the Earth was a ball of star dust undergoing a few chemical reactions. It was very explosive and very hot. As it cooled, the Earth developed a hard crust, along with bodies of water and an atmosphere as mediums for dissolving and transporting chemicals and for regulating the temperature of the planet. Layers of crust and rock formations formed the structural "skeleton" of the planet.

Eventually, in the chemical soup of the water, a living cell came into being. The concept of life, the dramatic shift from "no-life" to "life" is difficult to grasp. But once life began, it slowly and gradually expanded. It had the ability to reproduce and to modify itself in reproducing. Simple cells became complex cells, and they, in turn, formed into multi-cell organisms. These new life forms, in turn, developed into ever more complex life forms—functions within functions, organisms within organisms. (In this we see a basic pattern of development—a new unified system that is more than the sum of its components.) The ability to transform sunlight into matter came into being—green plant life expanded across the land masses. As new life forms (bio-systems) interacted with the non-living environment and with each other, the atmosphere, the water and the land were being transformed.

At some point, bio-systems emerged with muscles and a nervous system that could receive and react to complex stimuli from their surroundings. Self-manipulation, responsiveness and rapid mobility came into being. Insects, fish, reptiles, birds and mammals came into being.

These bio-systems followed the basic developmental pattern from simple to complex expressions. As they interacted with each other and with their surroundings (rocks, rivers, plants, etc.), integrated and living ecological systems grew. These ecological systems then participated in even more complex environmental systems, up to and including the Earth as a single, whole ecological system. The mutual give and take among the various systems, from the planetary water system to single cell bacteria to lumbering elephants, is a wonder to behold.

The human species is a very recent bio-system to be produced by the Earth in its development of mammals. The human bio-system is produced by, and is taking its place in, the complex ecological systems of Planet Earth. It is not a separate group of beings that are put here to live ON Earth. We humans are an expression OF Earth.

Humans did not come INTO this world from some other place, they grew OUT OF this world; the same way that an apple comes from a tree or a kitten from a mother cat. We humans are a product of, and a participant in, the happening that is Planet Earth. This is very different from perceiving humans as coming from outside of Earth and living on Earth for a while—as visitors, workers, managers, tourists, or what have you.

Extend your hand. Watch closely as you slowly make a fist. That which was once inert star dust, is now living flesh that moves with intricate precision, control, feeling and passion. Minerals from a cow and from a tomato form bones of your fingers. The oxygen produced by the trees on the hillside is now powering muscles in your arm. Ah, the wonder!

We cannot fully imagine the long, fascinating journey that led to the development of such a hand. Think of all the systems that are necessary to support the existence and functioning of one's hand—air, water, food, blood, bones, skin, nerves and parents. Think of all the help and all the harm that the function of closing the hand can do—carry nutrients to plants and animals, carry destructive chemicals to plants and animals, lift a child to safety, grasp a gun to kill.

In the process of flexing your hand and reflecting on it, you have exercised the latest and most complex of all Earth's evolutionary developments—self-reflective thought.

The possibility of self-reflective thought began with the appearance of a nervous system. The nervous system evolved into even more sophisticated and intricate functions—especially in terms of brains and mental processes. At some point humans developed self-consciousness. Humans are aware of their own thinking processes. Humans are also able to communicate their thoughts to other humans.

Humans not only have an ability to use a conscious reflective feedback loop within themselves, they are able to reflect with other humans. This involves other human minds in a larger, self-consciousness and awareness. Together, the human individual and the human community thinks, learns and remembers.

With the development of reflective thought, humans now have some measure of influence over their situation and destiny. Humans not only have more control over their own responses, they also have more ability to change and shape their environment. Humans can drain swamps and flood valleys. They can turn deserts into green fields and green fields into deserts. Humans can domesticate animals and plants. They can create new species and exterminate already existing ones. Humans can alter the chemical content and pattern of Earth's air and water.

b. A New Level of Maturity

First, the Earth developed its Geo-logical sphere—in simple terms, the Land. The geological sphere is the basic structure which provides support for all other development—the core, the center, and the surface crust of the planet. The surface structure of the Earth, the rocks, mountains, valleys, soil, etc., continually supports and interacts with all later developments.

Second, the Earth developed its Atmo-sphere—the Air. The gases that surround the Earth provide protection from radiation and intrusions from outer space while regulating the temperature of the Earth's surface. The atmosphere provides the gases necessary for the functioning of the living processes of Earth. The winds and air currents distribute and recycle gases and other light particles.

Third, the Earth developed its Hydro-sphere—the Water. Water is a dissolving and distributing medium. It supplies liquid and nutrients to Earth's living organisms. Water removes toxins and wastes, redistributing them or purifying them. Water also helps regulate Earth's temperature.

Fourth, the Earth developed its Bio-sphere—living things, Life. From microscopic single cell amoebas and bacteria, to towering trees and dinosaurs, from simple fungi and algae, to complex hawks and humans, Earth developed an extravagant and wondrous array of life forms—most of which no longer exist today. Not only are there varied and abundant life forms, but these life forms combine to form a variety of complex ecological systems from polar caps to tropical rainforests.

Fifth, and most recent, the Earth developed its Mind-sphere—its mental capacity, its Mind. With the emergence of human self-reflective thought, the Earth has developed a thinking capacity. For an individual human the mind is the body's way of knowing and appreciating itself. In like manner, the mental activity of the human species is the Earth's way of knowing and appreciating itself as Planet Earth. The human mind is the Earth's way of knowing and admiring its mountains, its rivers and its trees—not only the individual grandeur of each, but also the role each plays in the life of Earth.

Planet Earth has entered a new level of maturity. In the self-reflective thought and technological capabilities of humans, Earth has taken some measure of self-conscious control over its own destiny. Not only is the Earth a living organism, it is a self-conscious, self-reflecting, self-directing organism. In the human self-conscious, reflecting capacity, the Earth thinks about itself, appreciates itself, enjoys itself, worries about itself, plans for itself, makes decisions for itself. Through the human race, Earth analyzes and evaluates itself. Through human activity, the Earth seeks to regulate itself and improve itself. Through humans, Earth hurts itself, makes mistakes, learns from its mistakes, makes adjustments, etc. As the human mental ability increases, so the Earth's mental ability and self-conscious control increases. And it is helpful to keep in mind that the Earth's mental development is very, very young.

c. *New Images of Planet Earth*

For the first time ever, a living creature has been able to "step off the Earth" and look at it as a whole. Humans are able to see the whole Earth at once, as a single ecological system—a living organism. And humans are just one part of this body.

But it is not just a simple living organism. In a word, the Earth is a COMMUNITY of life systems—a self-organizing community. Just like a city is composed of smaller communities, so the Earth is composed of smaller communities—bio-systems.

But these bio-systems, these communities, are not static. They interrelate. They support each other. They limit each other. They enhance each other. They destroy each other. It might be said that they DANCE with each other. The Earth is one big dance of bio-systems. They move in intricate patterns and steps. Dances within dances. Patterns within patterns. Some slow, some fast. Some very smooth and harmonious. Others very awkward and discordant. As with all dances, there are balances and counter balances. There are tensions and counter tensions.

The human species is one of the bio-systems in the Earth

Community. The human community is one of the dancers in the giant Earth Dance. We humans are not spectators, we are not visitors, we are not temporary residents just stopping by for a while. Nor are we directors or managers of the dance. We are full-time participants in this complex living system or communal dance that is Planet Earth.

d. Ecozoic Age

The human bio-system, though, is a significant participant. In fact, the human community recently reached a new level of significance. This is the result of two developments.

One is the size of the human population. The ability to have longer and healthier lives has resulted in a dramatic increase in population. As a result, our consumption of resources, our use of space and the amount of waste we produce are putting a strain on Earth's other systems to the point of almost overwhelming them. One person, or even ten, walking across a meadow, picking berries and relieving themselves behind a bush, can be handled by Earth's normal operating systems. But millions of people crossing the same meadow will trample it bare, strip it of food, and leave one big mess behind the bush.

The other development that greatly affects the condition of the Earth is that of technology. We have the ability to level mountains, block rivers, remove forests, make the air toxic, kill bodies of water, make species extinct and extract huge amounts of resources from below the Earth's surface. In fact, we have the ability to destroy the whole Planet, or at least destroy most of the life forms of Earth. On the positive side, we can make the desert bloom, create new and better sources of food, develop new species and plant great forests. We can cure and heal afflictions never thought possible; and we can provide living space, comforts and enjoyments never dreamed of before.

Whether by sheer magnitude of numbers or by the power of technological developments, the human species now has the capacity to alter significantly—both for good and for ill—the major life giving systems of the planet: the air, the water, the soil and the biological organisms.

This awesome capacity of the human species points to the beginning of a new period in the Earth's evolution. For the first time in its existence, the Earth has the possibility of committing suicide. Similarly, the Earth has the possibility of developing itself as a more inclusive, mature, mutually enhancing and self-conscious planet. It has been said by some, that the Cenozoic period, which began some 65 million years ago, has come to an end. During the Cenozoic period wave upon waves of life appeared—flowers, birds, mammals, and human civilizations. This period has been brought to an end by the new human capacities. The Ecozoic[5] period is now beginning. (You may give this new age any name that you wish. What is being emphasized is the magnitude of the change as a major period in Earth's history, not just a change in human history, such as the change from the Agricultural Age to the Industrial Age.) In this emerging period, the self-conscious development of the integral community life of the Earth's bio-systems and ecological systems will be the focus.

In this new age, humans will develop their important role in the larger Earth community. We will be learning how to function effectively as the mental activity of the Planet Earth. We humans are new comers to the Communal Dance that is Planet Earth—and we are in the process of learning how to dance. In fact, our very presence creates a whole new dance. Slowly, and painfully, we humans are learning how to participate more gracefully in the dance.

e. Living Organism

Before we become too depressed and pessimistic by thinking about the down-side possibilities or too unrealistically hopeful about the up-side potentials, let us remember that the Earth is alive. It and its composite bio-systems participate in the Kosmos' basic growth process of birth, living, dying and rebirth. Every death produces the materials for new life. A fallen tree nourishes new plants. A raging flood fertilizes the valley. A failed experiment opens new paths. The larval stage ends and the adult insect comes into being. Parents expend their lives in giving the next generation life. Death opens the way for new life. Life feeds on other life. Every bite of nourishment is the death of something. There is no life without death. The basic principle is "to live is to die—to die is to live."

As a living organism, the Earth will experience periods of birth, growth and success. The Earth will also experience periods of decline, failure, regression and death. Each experience needs to be seen in relation to the development of the whole organism, the Planet Earth. Human activity contributes to and shares in Earth's ongoing cycle of life and death. Though death and destruction are painful, saddening and discouraging, they are a part of the life processes. They do not necessarily signal failure or the end.

---

5. The term "Ecozoic" is a newly invented term as a possible designation of the new emerging period in the life of the planet. This term has been developed and promoted in writings by Thomas Berry. It refers to the awareness and intentional development of the planet as a single integrated "household" or community ("eco" from the Greek word for "household").

D. IMPLICATIONS OF THE NEW PLANET

We are participants in Planet Earth—an Earth that is a living organism of which we humans are an integral part. What does all of this mean to us and how does it affect the way we live our lives?

In the first instance, the answer is "nothing!" We will get up, eat breakfast, hug our loved ones, go about our daily business, deal with our "to-do" lists, sweat, worry, laugh, cuss and discuss various matters, come home, eat supper, wash dishes, watch TV, read, go to bed and sleep in our normal manner. We will go about business as usual, knowing that we are part of the normal, maturing, evolving process of Planet Earth. As a self-organizing, ongoing process, the Earth makes use of any and everything you and I think, do or say for its own development. So we can calmly go about our lives, knowing that in and through us, Earth is doing "its thing" just like it does with flowers, catfish, rivers, ants, foxes, and red birds.

For those who desire to be more aware of Planet Earth and their relationship to it, who decide to be more self conscious about the way in which they participate in the Earth's development, there are many implications of the previous reflections.

1. Earth-Centric Orientation

The first of these implications is that we humans have a new orientation. We function within a very different context than previous humans. For centuries humans have been judging and evaluating situations in terms of their benefit to themselves—how much food, housing, control over illness, supplies, speed and ease of travel, amusement, etc. is provided to humans? Progress was judged as to its benefit to humanity. Humans judged events and their results in terms of benefits to their nation, their clan, their city, their group, their family and their person—"what is in it for me and those I value?" It was necessary to be that way previously in order to advance the Earth to its current level of development.

Until recently, this approach presented no real problems for the Earth. Furthermore, it has only been recently that we have had the means to reveal and validate the harm humans were beginning to do to the Earth and to ourselves.

We know now that our well-being and survival as a species depends upon the well-being of the Planet. We also now know how radically both the large human population and the technology at our disposal can impact the Earth, both destructively and creatively. Therefore, events will now be judged and evaluated in terms of the benefit for the whole Earth. This is not some "do good" idea or some moralistic nicety. This is basic well-being and survival. Humans have no life, no future, separate from the life and future of Planet Earth. Yes, we will continue to be concerned for our personal well-being, our family's well-being, the well-being of our cities and nations; but these concerns will be in reference to the larger community that is Planet Earth. We know that the well-being of ourselves and our communities depend upon the well-being of all the other bio-systems. The simpler life forms—bacteria, fungi, algae, grass, cockroaches—can get along quite well without the more complex life forms. But the more complex life forms cannot exist without the simpler forms. Humans are the most complex and most dependent of all bio-organisms. It is in our self-interest to make sure the whole planet does well.

In the Ecozoic age, we humans will be concerned that our **economics** are based upon Earth's economics. Earth is a very good bookkeeper. When a resource or bio-system is gone, it's gone—no appeals, no extensions! A lot more is included in the Gross Earth Product than in the Gross National Product. It might be wise to set up our human accounting books to match Earth's accounting books.

Education will best serve us when it helps us learn how we can fulfill our role in the larger Earth community. It will not be so much a *teaching* effort as a mutual *learning* effort. Education will be based on the one Great Story of Life.

The **medical** profession has already begun to see that well-being of all the bio-systems of Earth is dynamically interrelated. It is difficult to have well humans on a sick Planet.

Our **political** life may be more meaningful and helpful if it is based on units formed by a combination of geological, biological, economic and sociological considerations rather than units formed by political considerations. We need to remember that the introduction of a new plant or animal to the Earth resulted in changes in the geological and biological patterns of the Earth. We humans are still in the process of finding our place in the scheme of things. Because of our high mobility and adaptability, we may have to learn patterns of participation rather than having a "special niche." Politics, as the art of compromise, can be seen expanding to include all Earth spheres and bio-systems. There may be other rights than human rights to be considered. In fact, *rights* may not even be an operative factor. It may be better to consider who/what will benefit from our actions and decisions. *Mutual Benefit* might be the more fundamental consideration to guide our operations and judgments. Given the mode of constantly shifting patterns of human participation in the "community dance of bio-systems," *mutual benefit* would seem to be a more helpful guideline.

Religious groups are beginning to appreciate that the primary sacred community is the Earth Community as a living whole. Also, the Kosmos is seen as a primary source of divine revelation. I am not suggesting "nature worship," a return to "native religions" or a "spirit" Earth. The Kosmos, in every aspect of its development and its existence is a source of awe and wonder—an expression of the Divine, a means of communication with the Divine. (Chapters 6 and 7 will look more closely at this aspect.)

Cultural values and customs will come to reflect the integral relationship of all aspects of Planet Earth. Limited, incomplete views, values and customs that often divide people will be replaced by integral, global and evolving values.

These examples are not meant to be exhaustive. They seek only to illustrate the new operative mode of the Ecozoic Age. The Earth, as a maturing organism, is the referent and source for all life disciplines. We humans will spend the next hundred or so years reworking all of our social, cultural, educational, economic, and political disciplines and structures.

2. Participation

Humans have no present and no future, except within the great Communal Dance of the larger Earth Community.

Each day, we are learning and practicing how to participate more constructively in this Communal Dance that is Planet Earth. It is not easy. It will not be easy. There are no rules, instructions or guidelines as to how we are to participate. There is no script, no program, no choreographed steps, and no system for us to learn and to follow. We are writing the script, developing the guidelines, designing the system, choreographing our dance, as we live each day. This is, and will be, very disconcerting to those who think that they have "the answer" or think there is "a correct and right way to do things."

There will major changes in our lifestyles—as individuals and as a society. We should have no illusions about the pain and struggle involved in "kicking some bad habits." (Bad in the sense that certain habits and living patterns no longer contribute to the well-being of the planet.) It is not easy to change, especially for human society as a whole.

Will we make mistakes? Fail? Not even try? Sure we will! But the Earth Community can deal with the results of our mistakes. Earth bears the pain, adjusts, compensates, learns and moves on. By the same token, Earth accepts, incorporates and rejoices in the positive results that happen, often in spite of ourselves.

3. Corporateness and Care

A third implication: Corporateness is not a goal or an option—we are corporate.

We have been aware that we are part of a group—our family, our clan, our tribe, our interest groups, our community, our team, our nation. Now we realize that we are one body, one team, one tribe, as humans on the planet. Not only this, we are also a living component of the one Planet Earth.

In previous times, if a person did not like the people on the other side of the cave, they could move to the next valley and start their own clan. In previous times if a person did not like the people in their community, they could move to another community or start their own community. But if a person does not like our community, Planet Earth, they cannot leave and go start their own planet (not yet anyway). Thus, we have to make do as the one community that we are. This corporateness involves not only China, USA, Mexico, Kenya, India, men and women, young and old, dumb and smart, it also involves weeds, rocks, rats, mushrooms, woodpeckers, polar bears, ants, wind, lakes and tadpoles. Oh! The ocean, don't forget the ocean!

As one increases self-consciousness of this corporateness, the size and richness of one's life increases.

Furthermore, it is no longer appropriate to make a distinction between *nature* and *human*. It is no longer valid to pit *human* against *nature*. Humans are natural organisms—a natural bio-system. Humans are a product of nature, just like flowers, elephants and guppies. Human productions are just as natural as beaver dams, bird nests, ant farms and bee's honey. This will not "sit well" with some folk, but cities are a natural eco-system just as any forest or prairie dog town. "Leaving the city to get back to nature" not only represents an incomplete understanding of Planet Earth, it may also be harmful to the Planet. Cabins in the woods and their compromise version as suburban houses erode field, stream, coast and mountain ecosystems along with their beauty and "wildness."

Responsible participants we are. We respond all the time. Each response has many ramifications—whether we like it or not. Team members we are. We cannot live without the assistance of other members of the Planetary Community. Our actions or inability to act affects all members of community Earth. We are part of the Earth Community Dance—no choice about that. There will be times when we seem to have "two left feet," when we are out of step, when we step on some toes. But that is the way we learn to dance. Because we have the ability to think and decide about our responses, we have the power to change and the ability to initiate a course of action. We can create. By the same token, we can destroy. Thus, we are more than simply responsible, we self-consciously participate in the life patterns of Earth.

Please note that humans are participants in, not "caretakers" of, Planet Earth. We are not "children of *Mother Earth*." If the image of *Mother Earth* is to be used, then we should consider ourselves a part of Mother Earth—like her tonsil, her kidney, or her nervous system. And as such, we are not "responsible for Earth." Yes, with our self-reflective capacity, we can step back, observe, reflect and decide things about the Earth. But this is really Earth observing, reflecting and deciding about itself. No, we do not take care of Earth. Earth takes care of itself.

In light of this, it is not too helpful to "beat up" on us "bad" humans for "messing up" Earth. Such judgments upon humans are a continuation of the invalid distinction of *humans* versus *nature*. Such condemnation of humans reflects an anthropocentric, paternalistic view of humans in relation to "mama Earth." These judgments also reflect a continuation of a religious evangelistic approach to life. Previously, people were condemned to "burn in hell" unless they changed their ways and were good. Now we're told that the planet is "going to hell in a hand basket" if we do not become better caretakers of the Earth. Besides being ineffective, such an approach stems from fear, not love.

True, we humans have done and are doing things that are not helpful for the well-being of the planet. But it is not necessarily because we are bad or stupid. We are in the middle of a learning process. A child is not bad for touching a hot stove, or for dropping a glass, or for a loving embrace that squeezes the life out of their guinea pig. It is part of the process of learning about life. Humans are not bad for polluting the air and doing other harmful practices. It is part of the process of learning about our participation in the planet. Now some humans learn by means of their brain while others learn by means of their pain. Also some of us humans learn more slowly than others. This is not bad, just a bit more painful. However we learn, we will learn about participating helpfully in Planet Earth. In addition, we should keep in mind that what was considered "brilliant" and helpful by one generation, is seen to be horribly stupid by another.

We humans are in a learning mode. And if we are somewhat destructive in the process, this is nothing new in the history of Planet Earth. Other bio-systems through the ages have been rather destructive in the process of learning to participate helpfully in the life of the Planet.

The Earth is not a simple system. Our efforts to *manage* Earth, both as "promoters of progress" and as "promoters of ecology," have often created more problems than they have solved. Because of the magnitude and power of human efforts, because destructive and harmful effects seem to spread so rapidly, it would be wise to proceed with caution.

On the other hand, Earth is patient and is a good teacher. Let us be open, use our common sense, and help each other to decide what is the most mutually beneficial way to proceed. Let us be sensitive to the Earth and follow its guidance as to its own health.

4. The Journey of Humans

A fourth implication has to do with our perceptions of the human journey.

One classical story describes a previous time when humans lived in simple innocence and perfect harmony. At some point humans did something to disrupt this paradise. Since then, we have been "going downhill," suffering because of our bad deed. It is also assumed by many that life in the past was better than in the present. "We used to have it good until we messed it up." In this story, humans have done something wrong, which has resulted in the problems, pain, suffering and the so-called *terrible* situation of the world today. The proposed solution is to correct our mistake and return to a harmonious relationship with god or nature. Then the good life will be ours again.

Another classical perception describes life as repeating cycles. There are ups and downs, better times and worse times, growth and decay, but basically nothing ever changes.

According to another classical assumption, humans are evolving. Paradise is in the future. Humans began as primitives and have been improving ever since. And now, we humans are getting close to perfection. With just a little more learning and a few improvements of character, humanity will achieve the ideal, and live in perfect peace and harmony. But how long will this process take? While future humans may get to enjoy this paradise, what about those of us here and now?

But looking at the journey of Planet Earth, life seems to grow. The pattern is to begin small—a single cell, a seed, a sperm and egg—and then grow. This growth is set within limits and constraints. This growth reacts to changing situations. This growth continues with increasing complexity, diversity, sophistication and specialization. This seems to be the pattern for the whole species as well as for individual units of a species.

Thus, a more sound assumption would seem to be that we humans are in the process of maturing. Humans are on their way "up from the Garden of Eden." "The Garden of Eden" symbolized the innocence and simplicity of the pre-consciousness *womb* from which humans were *born*. Since that time, they have been maturing. There are always new challenges to meet, new visions to pursue, new improvements to be made, new situations to respond to, new problems to solve and new areas to explore.

As the human species matures, the new situations challenge and push it to its limits. As we humans mature, we face struggles and situations that we are not fully prepared for. We feel very threatened and unsure of ourselves. Often we fail. We yearn for the good old days when life was simpler. It is a common fantasy to want to go back to an earlier phase of life with the wisdom and skills that we presently have. We tend to romanticize the past and forget the fears, dangers, struggles and pain of ages gone by. But we cannot go back in time, and we cannot repeat the past. We are able only to live in the present and to prepare for tomorrow.

The thing to realize about the process of maturing is that both the capacity for positive action and the capacity for negative action increase equally. With increased power for creativity comes increased power for destruction. With an increased capacity for love comes an increased capacity for hate. With increased sensitivity to experience pleasure comes an equally increased sensitivity to experience pain. A tadpole cannot experience much suffering, neither can it experience much joy. A fish cannot hate you, neither can it love you. A small child can do only a little damage with a hammer. By the same token, a small child can only do minimally constructive things with a hammer. A mature adult can do many constructive things with a hammer. By the same token, a mature adult can do much damage with a hammer. With increased intelligence, creativity, determination, commitment and passion, a person has the capacity to make substantial, constructive contributions to society as well as to make substantial destructive contributions. The same is true for the human species. Maturity brings with it an increased capacity for good as well as evil, for love as well as hate, for joy as well as suffering. We do not have one without the other.

The human species is constantly maturing. Current humans are part of a continuum. People are not getting better or worse. People are not becoming more evil or more righteous. Humans are increasing their capacities—self-consciousness, technological power, understanding how the universe functions, sensitivity, emotions . . . With these increases comes the constant challenge to use them for the mutual benefit of all Earth components. It is not a question of returning to simpler, less complex situations. It is not a question of solving all the problems so that we will not have to struggle. Life is struggle, constant struggle. What is important is how we relate to the challenge and struggle involved in continuing the journey of maturity—the maturity of humans and the maturity of the Planet Earth.

Many of our current imperfections or inabilities as the human race are because of our immaturity as a species. We humans are a very young species. We have much more to learn about being human and how to play our role in the life of the planet. To be sure, we will make mistakes. We will "goof up." We will go down some unhelpful paths. We will cause pain, suffering and make a general mess of things as we learn—especially since we have no set of operating instructions and have to learn mostly by trial and error. But this is not bad. This is not a mistake. This is the way that the Earth develops. It is not helpful or effective to react judgmentally or moralistically to our actions as a human species. Working together to evaluate the current situation and to develop appropriate ways of living would be more effective.

5. Decisions and Actions

This brings us to another implication having to do with decisions and actions as humans:
- Given that we are participants in the living organism Earth, participants in the Great Earth Community Dance of Bio-systems;
- Given that there is no script, no program, no operating instructions—we are the first humans to live in this Ecozoic age and we are writing the script as we go;
- Given that we are responsible participants in the corporate body Earth and are in the process of learning how to participate, to the mutual benefit of all;
- Given that we are a young and maturing species with much to learn;

What do we do tomorrow? How do we decide upon any action? How do we respond and participate appropriately? How can we respond with any kind of authenticity? How can we reduce or minimize the harm and pain that our choices and actions cause?

The Adventure of Being Human

We observe, evaluate, weigh up the alternatives, decide and act. We humans have done this for ages and we will continue to do so. Whether decisions are quick and unconscious, like throwing a ball, or whether they are long and laborious, like deciding which house to buy, we go through these basic steps: Observe, evaluate, weigh, decide and act. (Deciding not to act is an act that has as much consequence as any direct action.)

Nowadays, we are aware of the complexity of life. In fact, we are overwhelmed by the complexity of life. At times we seem paralyzed by the complexity. We can never know all of the factors and variables involved. There are so many ways of looking at the situation. There are so many possibilities of combinations, timing and quantity. We cannot know all of the implications or ramifications of an action. We try to predict—"all things being equal." But "all things" do not stay equal. The rules of tension and counter-tension come into play along with the rules of "chaos." Plus, there are those factors that no one could have foreseen, along with the ever-present "wily human factor." Yes, my friends, we decide and act in pure ambiguity.

Life comes mainly in hues of gray. It is not black and white. Choices are usually between several combinations of good and bad. It is a constant struggle to survive, to grow, to expand, to change, to live, to heal. It is a constant challenge to deal with one situation after another. And usually we are not provided with all of the resources that we need to deal with the situation successfully. We are not smart enough, tall enough, experienced enough, strong enough. We do not have enough power, or enough money, or enough time. Or there is too much time, too much to do, too many people to help, too many choices, too much rain. Or things don't work out. People don't respond. Yes, life is a constant struggle.

Regardless, we are forced to act. Life constantly puts us in situations where we have to respond—ready or not. We observe and get as much information as we can. We evaluate what we have at our disposal. We apply our best judgment. Then we make our decision and act.

Will it be right? Good? Helpful? Harmful? A mistake? How do we determine the value of an action? From whose point of view do we decide? What is right for the winning side is wrong for the losing side. From what point in time do we decide? What is good this year may be seen as a disaster in ten years. Most of our actions are a mixed bag—beneficial in some respects, destructive in others. History will finally decide.

From Planet Earth's perspective, what is success? What is failure? Is a cold day a success or a failure? Is a dandelion in my yard good or bad? Is rain and a flood that sweeps away trees, land, cows, rabbits, houses and humans a success or a failure? Is the rise and fall of a tree a success or a failure? Is the rise and fall of a nation a success or failure?

Earth is a self-organizing organism that encourages and permits things to happen within certain limits. The Earth is very malleable. Earth incorporates all happenings and events, adapts to them, neutralizes them, lets them run their course, builds on them, lives with them, lives without them, suffers with them, rejoices in them or any of a thousand other responses. As "Chaos Theory" points out, Earth, at times, increases the complexity of things to a point that there is a total breakdown of a situation and then it re-organizes life into a new, higher level of order. So, finally, nothing we do can be a failure—unless the entire Earth is destroyed. In the scheme of the Universe, who is to say even that is a failure—we would not be the first planet or star to die! In fact, if a star had not exploded and died (possibly taking a few planets with it), Planet Earth would not exist.

Our decisions and actions, while very serious with far-reaching implications, cannot be taken with final or absolute seriousness. While our participation in life is highly significant, it is not possible to "wrap it up" or "be on top of a situation." It is not possible to completely succeed or fail. The best way to learn to dance is not to worry about doing it right. Rather, look your partner in the eye, feel the music and just dance. And, above all, appreciate the experience!

So how is it to dance the Earth Community Dance? How do we decide and act?

At first, I would stand in awe at the wonder of Planet Earth—from snowflakes to hurricanes, from bacteria to elephants, from birth to death, from grasshoppers to CEOs, from the Grand Canyon to Los Angeles. I would seek to be as sensitive to the Planet as possible. It would be helpful to be sensitive to what the Earth is telling us or asking us. This takes a bit of practice and attention. Soon though, we become "accustomed to her ways." We begin to sense when things are strong and vital, slightly out of rhythm, not quite right or seriously wrong. In the same way, we become able to sense what needs to be done and *sense* if our response is appropriate or not.

Next, I would listen to the human community. This is listening to what groups of people are saying with their movies, songs, actions, art, styles, writings, etc. Observe where people really put their time, money and personal energy. Listen to what the community is saying with its life, not its opinion polls. Trust the human community. Its corporate mind is rather phenomenal in its wisdom and sense after what is most practical and beneficial—though not necessarily the most perfect.

Finally, there is commitment to the Earth. It has to do with making our best choice and then putting our whole being—our wisdom, our energy, our bodies, and our passion—into it. We dance with our whole being. We give ourselves fully to the path we have decided to take. We let Earth take its course.

Deciding and acting goes something like this:

Stand back from the situation so that one may get as broad a view and be as sensitive as possible. Listen to what the situation is "telling you," what the Earth is "asking of you." **Make the necessary decision. Involve yourself totally**—your passion, your energy, your life—when responding to the situation. Then, **turn loose** of the situation. Offer your detachment and your engagement as a gift to the Planet to use as it will.

6. Trust the Earth

One final implication: we can trust the Planet Earth. We can trust the Kosmos and the Planet to continue what they have begun. We can trust the Planet to continue to take care of itself. It has had over 4.5 billion years of experience.

We can decide, act, respond as well, or as poorly, as we will. I am sure the range will continue to span the spectrum from brilliant to stupid to just plain maliciously harmful. Some results will be heart warming while others will be heart ripping. When all is said and done, we can trust the Earth to accept and incorporate everything human into the process of life. We can enter the dance and participate in the dance with confidence. The dance will always accept us and rejoice in our participation. We can trust the Great Community Dance that gave birth to us and continues to teach us. With confidence we continue the adventure of inventing our role in the dance that is Planet Earth.

Life is not a problem to be solved or a goal to be achieved. Life is a dance to be danced—and savored. The Planet is a corporate adventure to be experienced and appreciated. The Earth is a never ending adventure story to be enjoyed.

E. AN IMAGE

For the PLANET pillar of the Kosmic Story of Life, the image of living organism seems very appropriate and useful. The various life systems of the planet function together as a self-organizing, living organism. The Earth is a growing, evolving, maturing organism with humans functioning as its mind.

Good as it is, the image of *living organism* is not as powerful or as dynamic I would like.

The fundamental operating image that I would set forth for the PLANET is that of a *COMMUNAL DANCE*. It is like a neighborhood happening, with every element of the neighborhood participating. The rocks and trees, the clouds and seas, the bugs and slugs, the whales and porcupines, fishes and humans, all living and dancing together as one tribe, as one "hood."

Dancing . . .

All the various life systems and ecosystems, members of the one community Earth, are moving and functioning together as a single dance. The humans are one of the life systems participating in the dance.

We humans are still a bit awkward; still learning our steps. Humans dance in groups and sub-groups, human groups dance with each other and in various ecosystem dances—dances within dances within dances.

The Earth—dances within dances—a single, living community.

Dancers trip, stumble, miss a step, introduce new steps—and the whole dance is affected; but the other dancers incorporate these missteps and new steps into the ongoing dance.

Dancing . . .

    sometimes solemn;
    sometimes stately;
    sometimes wild;
    sometimes fast;
    sometimes slow;
    sometimes passionate;
    sometimes cold.
    sometimes tender and dreamy;
    sometimes frenzied and chaotic;
but dancing—
    always dancing—
        a single community—
            a single, living entity.

Play with this image. Create several of your own. See which one "works" for you.

The Adventure of Being Human

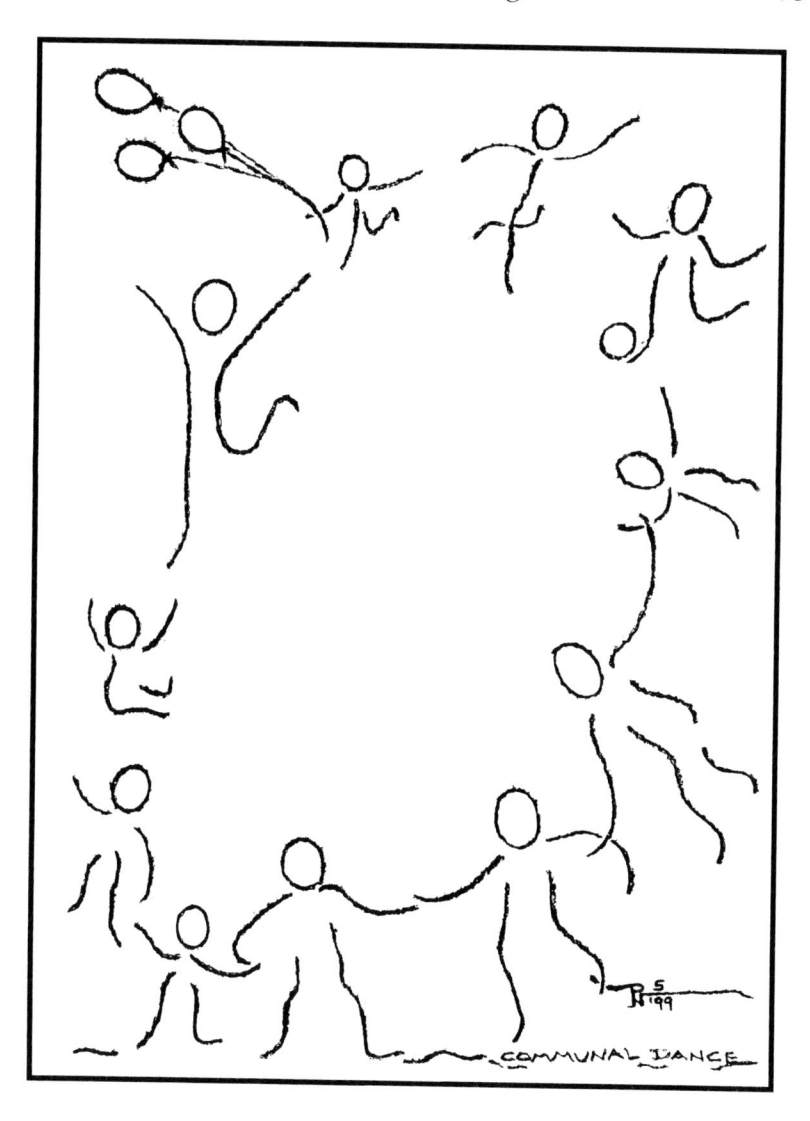

93

"Communal Dance"
By Pat Nischan

Chapter Four

THE INDIVIDUAL HUMAN

A. CREATIVE JOURNEY—A STORY-POEM
WHO AM I?
I gaze at the setting sun. Who am I?
I argue with my friend. Who am I?
I walk in the starry night. Who am I?
I work in the heat of day. Who am I?
Why am I?

A star explodes.
    Energy expanding through space,
      Star dust, atoms, swirling through space,
        Forming a sun,
          Forming Planet Earth.
Earth gives birth to rivers, plants, animals,
    made of star dust.
Earth gives birth to humans,
    to me,
        made of atoms from that exploding star.
Star dust,
I am star dust.

An energy form . . .
   of swirling atoms from an exploded star.
I AM
   <u>Sensitive</u>
The human eye is very sensitive—
   to colors, shapes, shades,
      movement, minute details, grand vistas.
The human ear is very sensitive—
   to tones, rhythm, melody, words, nuances, noise, cries, wind.
The human nose is very sensitive—
   to fragrant perfume, body odor,
      clean air after a downpour, apple pie.
The human skin is very sensitive—
   to a soft finger, a hot cup, a cool breeze, a pin prick.
The human tongue is very sensitive—
   to sweet and sour, hot-dogs and cokes, spinach and ice cream.
Aided by a variety of equipment,
   microscopes,
   telescopes,
   stethoscopes,
   video recorders,
   sensors,
   spectrographs,
   meters of every kind,
humans are ultra-sensitive.

This raw sensory data
   is perceived by,
   is filtered through,
      is processed by,
   a complex web made of
one's body condition,
one's emotional makeup,
one's mental processes,
one's psychological composition,
one's personality makeup,
one's consciousness of consciousness,
one's relation to the Ultimate.

I AM
   <u>Responsive</u>
Like all nervous systems,

a human responds to that which it senses.
We blink, laugh, cry,
    write, build, sing,
        hit, go to meetings, sweep the floor,
        cook a meal, argue, take a quiet walk,
        dream, repair the faucet, get angry,
            go to the bathroom, answer the phone.

At every moment,
    We are sensing and responding.
We are one continuous stream of
    Sensing-Responding-Sensing-Responding-
        Sensing-Responding-Sensing-Responding . . .
And our responses create
    something else
        to which we and others—respond.
So we participate in a continuous complex stream of
    Sensing-Responding-Sensing-Responding-
        Sensing-Responding-Sensing-Responding . . .

I AM
    <u>Aware</u>
We humans are **AWARE**
    of our sensitivities and our responses.
Not only that,
    we are aware that we are aware.
Humans are self-conscious.
A human is a self-
    Awareness
        filtered and
        processed
            through a complex web of our
        physical,
        emotional,
            rational,
            personality,
                psychological and
                      spiritual
                makeup.
    I've got to go to the bathroom,
        but I don't dare climb over six people to the aisle.
    I've got to go to the bathroom

and I don't give a damn if I have to climb over six people.
"That's a beautiful dress and you look good in it."
What did he mean by that comment?
What did I mean by my response?

Each human
    an energy form,
    a focal point of self-consciousness,
        conscious of our self-consciousness.
Our complex stream is now a complex web of
    Sensing-Aware-Responding,
        Sensing-Aware-Responding ...
Not only that,
    we humans
    self-consciously participate
        in this complex web of
    Sensing-Aware-Responding-Sensing-Aware-Responding ...

I AM THAT I AM
<u>My Journey</u>
Each human response is pure creativity.
So many complex variables,
    combinations, nuances, possibilities,
        plus that illusive factor of the *self*—
            more than the sum of all our experiences.
Pure, original creativity,
    each human response is
        an original creation.

Human life is
    a *jam session*,
        a constant *jam session.*
Each player is sensitive to,
    responding to,
        the music being created by the group
            and each person in the group.
Each player is responding
    to what they hear.
There is no score of music to be followed—
    the music is being created as you go—
        by the individuals and by the group as a whole.
I listen with my whole being.

I respond with my whole being,
    with the instrument and skill I have.
        Pure creativity.

Human life is an improvisational dance,
    a constant improvisational dance.

I move in relation
    to the other dancers,
    to the space,
    to the sounds,
    to the objects
        around me.
Out of my own internal being
    I move in response to my interpretation
        of the moves made by other dancers,
    of the space, sound, and objects around me,
    of the dance as a whole.
I move in response
    to all that I am sensitive and aware of.
I dance
    using the body, mind and spirit
    that I have at the moment.
Each move is pure creativity.
    I decide,
    and I create it.
The other dancers respond to my moves;
    now, there is a new situation to respond to.
I shift my focus—
    and perform very different moves and responses.
I may be intensely involved in responding to one or two dancers
    for a while;
        then I may focus on relating
            to the space around me,
        or to a purely interior image
            to the exclusion of other dancers;
    or I may try to combine the two aspects;
    or I may flow with the whole group.

Our lives are pure improvisation and creativity—
Every response is uniquely our own—
    pure creativity

The Adventure of Being Human

      in response to the situation,
           as we are sensitive and aware of it,
      and out of the totality of who we are
           at that point in time.
Who we are
    is the result of all of the music and dancing.
On, and
on, and
on—
    Our lives are an
ongoing journey—
    creating,
    improvising.

My being
      is constantly
           becoming.
I am my becoming.
I am my journey . . .

. . . In a new universe
      swirling energy
         ongoing physio-mystery creation.
. . . Participating in a new planet Earth
      a living organism,
      a community of dancing bio-systems.
. . . With
      No map,
      No sheet music,
      No script,
      No dance steps,
      No answers
to guide me
    in understanding,
    in responding to,
      the many relationships
      and interrelationships,
        the many possibilities
        present in life.
No answers, no maps . . .
I create the answer each moment
    with each response I make.

I create the map
    with each step of my journey.
Are the choices clear?
    Usually not.
    Life is full of fog and ambiguity.
Will I know the results of my choices, of my steps?
    Not fully.
Are there risks?
    Yes.
    But not to my being.
Life's journey is an adventure;
    not a pleasure cruise,
    not a slave march,
    but an adventure.

This is scary!
I wish otherwise.
No other option
    for us humans today.

My life is the answer.
My life is the music.
My life is the dance.

I am my journey.
My life is the map.
    Follow me!
        Make your own map.

So many tensions—
    headache producing tensions—
        positive and negative
        dark and light
        female and male
        have and have-not
        chaos and order
        life and death
        strong and weak
        failure and success
        likes and dislikes
        pleasure and pain . . .
And there are tensions within tensions,

tensions among tensions,
    along with the gray fog of ambiguity.

Want to run,
want to escape,
    want to have just the pleasant half of life
      (whichever that is),
  want to reduce the tension.
Wait!
How was the Universe created?
  Out of tensions.
How was the Earth and all of life created?
  Out of tensions.
How did I come to be?
  Out of tensions.
      Ah, the alluring magic of male and female!
All existence comes from
  tensions.
All existence is maintained by
  tensions.
All creativity is a response to
  tensions.

I stretch my being,
  Enlarge my arms,
    Embrace as much tension
      as I can.
Out of tension I create,
  I improvise,
    I engineer . . .
  my self,
  my family,
  my groups,
  my community,
  my country,
  my society,
  my world,
  my Planet Earth,
  my Universe.
Out of this tension
  I invent
    life.

In the midst of this tension
> I live the **CREATIVE JOURNEY**
>> that is me.

Maturity is
> embracing and using
>> more and more
>>> tension.

Why AM I?

Why am I here?
What I am doing—
> when I am Sensing, Aware, Responding?
> when I am being my journey?
> when I am creating life?

What is so special about a self-conscious hunk of star dust?
Why is Earth developing self-conscious,
> creative beings
>> like me? Like you?

In me, in you,
> Earth is developing its brain to a new level;
> Earth is developing a minding activity.

In me, in you,
> Earth is being self-conscious of itself;
> Earth is learning about itself;
> Earth is being sensitive, responsive, and aware.

In me, in you
> Earth is imaging its future;
> Earth is inventing itself;
> Earth is taking self-conscious control of its journey.

In human creativity and improvisation,
> Earth is entering a new level of creativity
>> a new level of evolution—
> beyond codes,
> beyond maps,
> beyond answers.

We humans are not co-creators.
We humans are Earth's newest means of creativity—
> in us, Earth is *jamming*;
> in us, Earth is *improvising* the dance.

With increasing tensions,
> Earth,

                humans,
        are entering a new level of being.
Earth and I,
        as fellow adventurers,
                are on a never-ending journey!
Journey to where?
        That's not the point.
What is the point?
        Appreciate!
        Savor!

Human life is not a problem to be solved,
        not a game to be won,
        not a goal to be reached.
Human life is to be lived,
        to be appreciated,
        to be savored.

Like good wine and
        fresh baked bread,
Life is to be rolled round on the pallet
                and savored.

Stare at,
Be sensitive to,
Be aware of,
        every crack and line,
        every pebble and stick,
        every flower and thorn,
        every success and failure,
        every cry and laugh,
        every face and word
        every joy and sorrow.
Savor its being.
        Appreciate its contribution to the drama of life.

The galaxies, stars, cosmic space, quarks,
        and the myriad other wonders of the Universe
        are to be experienced, savored and appreciated.
The Planet Earth,
        as a living organism
        is filled with wonders

      under every rock,
      in every house,
      along every pathway,
    to be savored and appreciated.
Each human life is
    a novel to be read,
    a movie to be seen,
    a marvel to behold,
    —to be savored and appreciated.
We are exquisite creations
    to be explored,
    savored and appreciated.
Relationships—
    there are whole galaxies of relationships
    to be tasted, savored and appreciated,
        like a cool drink, a glowing sunset or a good book.

Years of drought, sickness and devastation
    left no food, no work, no hope for the large family.
Into the mountains,
    a father leads two young children—
        to be left.
A child stands beside the house,
    sees,
    knows,
        and **SCREAMS.**
A scream of indescribable pain,
    of utter fear and frustration,
    of total love,
    of bitter protest to the universe.
She was savoring the situation to the depths
    with her very appropriate response.
Now that she owned and savored the situation,
    she re-engineers her life,
        improvises new responses,
            continues her—
                and the Earth's—
                    journey.

Our relations with family members, friends,
    our work situation, the traffic, the TV,
    a rock, a flower, our house,
can be savored and appreciated.

Every situation is a link to the fullness and wonder of life.

Savor the beauty,
Savor the ugliness,
Savor the pleasure,
Savor the pain
    of any situation.
Savor thunderstorms, songs of birds, lines of a building,
    a birth, a death.
Savor your frustration,
        your worries,
                your excitements;
Savor
    the structure of a snowflake or a car,
    the dance of a candle flame, the agony of a house fire,
    the hunger of a child,
    the fear of a parent without work,
    a pay check,
    a letter,
    a criticism and a complement.
Acts
    of pure creativity and inventiveness,
    of pure stupidity and blundering,
    of hatred and destruction,
    of heroism,
    of love,
may be savored,
    and their contribution to the journey of life appreciated.

Everything—
        the dirty dishes,
           a blade of grass—
is a manifestation of,
and a doorway to,
        the richness that is life.

Savor Life!
    What else can you do with it?
In each of us,
Life savors Life.
In each of us,

the Earth is sensitive to,
    is aware of,
        savors and appreciates,
            its life,
            its journey.

We are the Earth's brain,
    the Earth's consciousness,
    the Earth's self-consciousness,
    and even the Earth's budding
        trans-rational/trans-personal dimension.

I AM MYSTERY
Ah,
The wonder of it!
The pure wonder of being a human being!
The pure wonder of being myself,
    of being the adventure that I am!

Who Am I?
    I'll never fully know.
What Am I becoming? What is my journey creating?
    I'll never completely grasp this.
Why Am I here?
    I'll never fully understand.
All my efforts to answer these questions
    ends at the edge of a great darkness,
    at the edge of a great abyss.
This darkness, this abyss
    is not just the Unknown,
    it is the Unknowable Unknown—
        the Great Mystery.

I am surrounded by the Mystery.
The Mystery of the journey that created me from star dust,
    in this place, in this time,
        with these combinations of characteristics.
And my journey's end?
    Pure Mystery.
And in between?
    I am!

plus I know I am.
That is Mystery.
There is so much to discover about me.
There is so much to explore about living.
There is so much I can do,
    can create,
    can think,
    can relate to.

I am a fireball of cosmic energy,
    a result of exploding energy-passion.
I am a fireball,
    an explosion of passion-energy—
        both
            positive passion-energy
            and
            negative passion-energy.
I swirl through life
      day after day.
I attract and am attracted to other fireballs.
      Our orbits and collisions
        produce new thoughts, decisions, actions, objects
          and patterns of energy.
I repulse and am repulsed by still other fireballs,
    causing different patterns of energy.
I sometimes burn bright,
    sometimes mellow.
I sometimes race about,
    sometimes just drift.
Attractions, repulsions, pressures, pushes and pulls,
    limits and constraints,
        my energy patterns reconfigure.
And so I participate in the Universe, the Planet Earth,
        along with other humans
    in one great dance of evolving energy,
    passionate energy interacting with passionate energy
        —creating and being created.

How and why do I participate the way I do?
How and why are the results as they are?
    It is pure Mystery.

At the center of the swirling fireball of self-conscious energy
    is me,
        myself—
            and the Mystery.
At the center
    there is just me and the Mystery.
    And sometimes there is just me.
    At other times, there is just the Mystery.
In reality,
    I am Mystery.
In relating to other humans,
    I am relating to Mystery.

Maybe there is only Mystery
    taking shape in me
        in you
        in a tree
        in a shirt.

Each of us is a fascinating being.
    We are enchanted beings.
I am fascinated with being myself,
    being my journey—
    creating and living the life I am—
    being my Mystery.

BEING MY BEING
Dare I?
    Dare I be myself?
Dare I be the process,
    the journey,
    the becoming,
    the happening
        that I am?
At any moment,
    I am the result of all
        my Sensing, Awareness, Responding, Savoring,
I am a bundle of characteristics—
    conscious and unconscious.
I am a bundle of different selves vying for attention—
    the self I think I am and
        the self I'd like to be,

the selves other people perceive me to be
at any given moment,
the private self and the public self,
the individual self and the community self.
Sometimes I am purely an individual.
Sometimes I sense I am one with the group—I am team.
Sometimes I sense I am one with the Planet—I am Gaia.
Sometimes I sense I am one with the Kosmos—I am Being itself.

I am fascinated and enchanted with myself,
with the journey that I am.
I am also fearful of being myself.
There is a depth, a greatness, and a mystery within me that I dare not touch.
Yet, they fascinate me;
they intrigue me;
they entice me.
They call to me.
Yet I am fearful of responding to their call.
I am fearful of exploring them.
The call haunts me.
Dare I be me?
There is only me,
only my journey.
The challenge is
to expand the awareness,
to deepen the savoring,
to heighten the appreciation,
of participation in
the journey,
the *jam session*,
the dance.
DARE I?

The challenge is to increase the amount of tension we can handle,
to be more creative.
That challenge begins with appropriating
"to die is to live."
From the death of the old,
the new is created.
The Kosmos is constantly re-formatting energy.
The old patterns of life,

of self,
>have to die
in order for the new self,
>the new patterns of life
>to be formed.
As our current self dies,
>as we die to expectations
>>that things will be any different than they are,
>we live as a larger self
>>that includes the old and the new.
As we die, we move into ever newer and larger selves—
>to the one Kosmic Self.
Our sensitivity,
>our awareness,
>>our savoring,
>>>our responding,
>>increases.
>The *jam session* gets bigger and wilder.
>The dance gets more complex and richer.
>The tension mounts.
>The creativity expands.
>The savoring becomes richer.
>The wonder, excitement, and fascination mounts higher.
As we die, the journey expands unbelievably.

The alternative is to
>sit in the corner, suck our thumb,
>>and bitch about life not being the way we'd like it to be,
>>or yearn for some other life, to be some other self
>>(slimmer, younger, healthier, richer, happier . . .).

But this would mean that we'd miss out on the party of life.
>Hey man! No way am I missing this party!
So, with excitement in my voice
>and butterflies in my stomach,
I set off again
>as my creative journey.
I set off to create myself as a surprise to the Kosmos—
>to dance the Great Dance!

B. CONSCIOUSNESS EXERCISES

The following exercises are provided as a means of experiencing (being aware of, savoring) the Human Individual more directly and personally. They provide opportunities to visit with and reflect on the Human Individual journey.

- **Positive Moments:**

    In a relaxed/meditative state, recall a moment in your life when you felt vibrant or joyous. Visualize that moment. What is the setting? Who is involved? Savor it. What are its physical aspects? Biological? Mental? Emotional? Social? "Spiritual?" What makes it so wonderful? What does it have to do with being human? In terms of the total design of things (of the Kosmos), what is happening in that situation?

- **Negative Moments:**

    In a relaxed/meditative state, recall a moment in your life when you experienced intense pain, deep "darkness," intense hatred, fear or anxiety, sickening evil. Visualize that moment. What is the setting? Who is involved? Savor it. What are its physical aspects? Biological? Mental? Emotional? Social? "Spiritual?" What makes the moment so repulsive? What does it have to do with being human? In terms of the total design of things (of the Kosmos), what is happening in that situation?

- **Keep a Journal:**

    Over a period of several days, record in a personal journal or special notebook moments of vibrancy, joy or being "up" and moments of pain, despair or being "down." With each entry, note any reflections about these experiences—what was going on in terms of being a human?

- **Review Your Day:**

    In a relaxed or meditative state, review your day. Recall your actions and sensations, your awarenesses and reflections, your decisions, your responses. Reflect on one or two of them—what life dynamics were involved?

- **The Self:**

    When you say "myself," who is the "self" to whom you refer? In a meditative state, consider who is the self that experiences life, who is the self that is aware. Realize that the self is more than your body, your feelings, your mind, your past, your roles and your relationships. Who is the self that is aware of all of these?

- **Movement:**

    Listen to some favorite music. Relax, be still. Feel your body responding to the music. Let your body move, spontaneously—follow the music and follow your body's lead in moving to the music.

- **Your Death:**

Lie on the floor and create your relaxed/meditative state. Imagine having died and having been placed in your casket. You are now lying in the casket for your wake, and then for your funeral. Who is there? What are they saying? What is the funeral like? Go in the hearse to the cemetery. You are then lowered into the grave and dirt is filled in over you. What is it like being dead? After a few moments, retrace your journey back to the present. Slowly come "alive" to your present situation. What was it like being dead? What is it like being alive again?

- **Talk with a Tree, Rock, Pool of Water, Well or Wise Person.**

This is the same last two exercises as in Chapter 2. Only this time you ask about the Human Individual: Where did I came from? How did I get to where I am today? Where am I going? Why I am here? What is it to live fully and how do I live a full, satisfying life? Ask what human life is about or any other questions you may have about being a Human Individual. Carry on a lively conversation—talk back, argue, debate, explore wild ideas and above all, LISTEN!

C. REFLECTIONS ON THE INDIVIDUAL HUMAN

1. The Third Pillar

What does it mean to be a human? What is an authentic human life?

More particularly, Who am I? What am I to do in Earth? How be I? What is the significance of my life? **How do I participate in the fullness of life?**

A third component of any major cosmic mythology addresses the question of the individual human being. What is it to be an individual human? What is the role of an individual human in the Kosmos and on Earth? How does a person best relate to other people and to his or her environment? Or more to the point, How does a person live well?

Related questions are: Why do we suffer? Why is there evil? Is there a final triumph over destruction and imperfection and an eternal *good life*? And if so, what is it like and how does a person participate in it?

Every major mythology presents basic mental images of the nature and role of the individual human.

2. Previous Humans

Within the previous context of a basically static Universe and Planet, human life was understood as a function of a plan and was to operate according to the plan and/or a set of standards. Such plans and standards for human living were established and enforced by some supreme being(s) or a supreme power. Often they were the same supreme being(s) who had created the heavens and Earth.

Some people lived better than others and everyone could imagine a better life than the one they had. Why did a person not live as well as was possible? How could a person live better?

(It should be noted that for many societies and the Kosmic stories by which they lived, the individual was not the basic unit of society, nor was the individual's well-being of primary concern. Rather, the primary concern was a larger social unit such as the family, the clan or the tribe. The individual's well-being was integrated with and derived from the larger social unit's well-being. Therefore, in the following paragraphs, the words person *and* people *refer both to the larger social unit and to the individuals who participate in it.)*

One reason for a person's poor life, other than the caprice of some supreme force, was that people were not living according to the plans and/or standards that had been established by the supreme forces. Improvement in people's lives was achieved through conformity to the *rules of life* as set forth in the plans and/or standards. One aspect of such *rules of life* involved pleasing the gods—or at least not offending them—who controlled or guided human affairs. If the gods were unhappy or offended, the *rules* set forth the means of placating the gods and/or increasing their happiness. And when the gods were happy, humans had a happier life.

Dark or evil forces (enemy gods) were also seen as responsible for human misery. Usually, the power and influence of the dark forces was seen as a result of human (personal and/or group) failure to follow the *rules of life*. Otherwise, it was believed that the dark force or enemy gods simply overwhelmed the protective gods.

Personal weakness could be understood as the means used by the supreme beings/forces to deny the good life. In some circumstances, an unsatisfactory, painful life was seen as the result of testing or training by friendly gods. Such a life was meant to test a person's allegiance to their god and adherence to the *rules of life* in spite of adverse results. Some saw it as a character building exercise.

In these previous mythologies, the humans were often seen as a *wayward children* or *imperfect subjects* who were striving, more or less successfully, to improve themselves and their lot in life. Such improvement depended upon how well people followed the plan, fit the pattern, or measured up to the standards. Real and substantial improvement depended upon the favorable intervention of a supreme being or a supreme force. (It can be noted that some stories took the stance that the only way to *win* in life was not to play the *game* or to rise above the *game*. But the goal of life was still to *win* as defined by the *game* and its rules.) Though people might experience improvement, the perfect yearned-for-life was in the future—usually after life on Earth. Accommodations and status in that future life depended upon how well a person conformed to the plan and standards while in this life, as well as upon the extent of the favorable intervention of the supreme being(s) or force(s).

To live well—both now and hereafter in some other world—a person need to learn the *standard rules* for human life as set forth by the supreme being(s) and to live accordingly. These *standard rules* set forth the purpose and goals of life as well as the means to live it. The rules were set forth in stories, myths, religious teachings and practices, and other social traditions. Here, the ideal person was described. Success and failure was interpreted in terms of compliance or non-compliance to the *standard rules*. The particular description of the purpose and content of the good human life, or what is meant to succeed as a human, was supplied by each particular human grouping.

More to the point sociologically, each human grouping (be it by territory, clan, tribe, race, and/or culture) had developed certain patterns and norms for human behavior that enabled its society to function. These patterns and norms were enforced by elevating them to the status of laws or will of divine powers. Each society/culture defined its own *good life* and *bad life*. Conformists enjoyed the former and non-conformists the latter. Exceptions could be attributed to the *personal privilege* of the gods.

Since life operated within set rules or standards, humans usually saw themselves as either *winning* or *losing, either right* or *wrong, either as good* or *bad*. The hero was one who, with help from the gods, followed the rules, triumphed over the negative forces, and won (or at least demonstrated) for themselves and for other people the opportunity for a better life.

For some, in more recent history, impersonal *laws of nature* have replaced the rules and standards set by supreme beings. Here, the concern was to discover the laws by which the universe and planet operated in general and the laws by which human beings functioned in particular. Thus, a better life could be achieved by closer conformity to these *laws* or *rules* of nature. Nonetheless, there were some objective standards or rules that humans were to discover and to which they were to conform as the means to participate in the fullness of life—the *good life*.

The fact that a human, individually or as some group, was seen as one who could improve and better their life, as one who could disobey/obey rules, as one would could be *good* or *bad*, meant that a human was special. A human obviously was not just another physical object, not a part of the stage of life. (At least this was true for the people of one's own *Human Group*. There was always some doubt as to whether people of another *Human Group* were considered truly human.) Also, a human obviously was not a god or a supreme being. But a human was seen to have characteristics of both an Earthly object and a heavenly being. A human, therefore, was seen as a special kind of being—somewhere between an unintelligent Earth creature and a divine being. A human was seen as a mixture of flesh and spirit, of body and soul. And since it was understood that spirits and souls lasted longer than flesh, a human was understood to be a living spirit that had some kind of existence after the body died.

It was this living spirit that was to seek and obey the

standards/rules of human life. It was this living spirit which was either *good* or *bad* or *improving*, as evaluated by the rules. The quality of one's life, both *spirit* and *flesh*, both in *this world* and in *another world*, depended upon how well this living spirit related to the standards/rules as well as to the "powers that be." (It should be remembered that the supreme "powers that be" could always find a way to override the *rules* or to grant exceptions.)

To summarize, humans were previously seen as flesh-spirit beings who were seeking to improve their life situation, in this world and in another world to come, by conforming to some set of standard rules which were set and enforced by some superior beings.

3. The New Human

a. No Script; and We Write It

Today, human beings show up in a new Universe and a new Planet Earth which provide a new context for living. The Universe and the Planet are dynamic, expanding, evolving, interrelated energy and biological systems. Nothing is permanent. There are no preconceived designs or plans, of which we are aware. There is no established goal or destination, of which we are aware. There is no pre-set *game plan* other than perhaps our solar system winding down, going super nova and becoming starter material for another solar system. There are limits, constraints, attractions, and repulsions of energy/life forms. There is growth and decay, birth and death, a constant reconfiguring of energy/life patterns. There is movement between order, chaos, new order, chaos (and even chaos is seen as part of a higher order). In the midst of all of this, there is an openness for creativity and the new.

In this new Universe and new Planet, humans are no longer subjects or children of supreme beings. Human beings are no longer actors, sojourners, worker-bees, or pawns in the play on the stage of Planet Earth. Humans are no longer those who fight with, cooperate with, use, control, go native in, or escape from, the Planet. Humans are products of and integral participants in this ongoing, expanding, reconfiguring, creative energy/life event of Planet Earth and the Universe.

Today's exposure to the great variety of human cultures, each of which has its own set of definitive standards or divine *rules of the game* for human living suggests that these standard/rules were designed by humans. The fact that these standards or rules have themselves been changed over time further indicates that they are the work of humans. Not only were they designed by humans, but they were designed to function within a particular understanding of the universe and planet and to function in a particular life environment. Now those Universes, those Planets and those life environments no longer exist. The *computer* on which these previous *programs of human living* were to run has been upgraded or reconfigured. Therefore these old *programs* do not function very well, if at all.

We live in an era in which the universe, the planet and the human all participate in the process of becoming, of evolving, of creating, and of being created. We are the first to live in an era where there are no standard pre-set designs, plans, or rules. There is no *script* given to us to follow. There are no standard answers to the questions of "How do I live?" and "Why do I live?" Today, we must improvise. Even those who belong to sub-groups within society which claim to live by a divine *script*, pick and choose the parts of the script that they follow as the real standards and rules. They too are improvising.

In the past, there were some people who departed from the divinely prescribed *script and music* and improvised their lives. There were individuals who ventured to create their own answers to life's questions. These individuals were the exception and were often rejected by society for doing so.

Today, such departure or venture is not an option. Today, there are no standard rules or script from which to depart. We have to create the standard rules or script. *Have to* not in the sense of a moral imperative with dire consequences if we do not, but *have to* in the sense that there is no other choice. Today, everyone improvises human living. That is just the way life operates for us.

The human today is unlike any that has ever lived. The human today is a participant in creating what is and what comes to be—including the *rules of the game*.

(When you find yourself not agreeing with what is set forth here, I would invite you to articulate the assumptions underlying your position and test them against common experience. And/or you might discuss the matter with a tree.)

b. A Complex Happening

That was a look from the top down, a deductive journey, a theoretical perspective. Now, let's start with our human experience and look from the bottom up, an inductive journey. Let's see what clues there are for what it is to be an authentic human, for how we participate in life fully, and for how we fit into the scheme of things.

A human is an Earth organism. Like a tree, an ant, a cow or a puppy dog, a human being is a living organism that has been produced by the maturing process of Planet Earth. Each one of us is a highly developed and extremely complex organism, but an organism nonetheless.

A human is a very <u>sensitive</u> organism. Besides the five physical senses of sight, touch, hearing, taste and smell, the human also has emotional, mental, psychological, spiritual, personal and trans-rational sensitivities. (At this point, *trans-rational* is a "place holder" for the inexplicable, trans-physical, trans-mental dimension of the human that includes a mixed bag of such aspects as intuition, "sixth sense," soul, "higher self," pure consciousness, trans-personal, direct comprehension, etc. There is no clear understanding of, or precise term for this aspect of a human being. We will look at it in more detail later in the book.) Today, these sensitivities are greatly extended and enhanced by technology. For example, microscopes, telescopes, and other instruments allow humans to *see* wide spectrums of light and other waves, to *see* into the atom, to the edge of time/space and to the beginning of the universe, and to *see* into the smallest cracks and structures of the planet. With microphones we can hear a wide range of sounds from any situation. Information available to the mind comes as a blizzard of snow, piling high all about us. And the list goes on. Technology not only enhances the extent of our sensitivities, but also increases the speed, volume and detailed analysis of our sensory data. Along the same lines, education, psychology and self-help programs have heightened our mental, emotional, interpersonal and trans-rational sensitivities.

In addition, this sensory data is perceived by, filtered through, and processed by a complex web, overlay, interrelationship and interaction of our physical, emotional, rational, psychological, personality and spirit makeup. And each of these aspects of our makeup is highly unique and complex within itself. So much for objective data, observation and experience! The point to be highlighted here is that every instance of sensory data involves a large, complex, interrelated set of variables.

And then, as any sensitive organism and nervous system, humans <u>respond</u> to that which they sense. Humans blink, cry, laugh, run, sweep the floor, watch TV, hit, hug, dance, argue, turn the page, buy a cup of coffee, write a book, go to sleep, climb a tree, wash the dog, turn right, quit our job, change diapers, answer a question, put on suntan lotion, throw a rock, pull weeds . . .

Every moment we are sensing and responding.

Each response is an expression that involves a complex web, overlay, interrelationship, and interaction of our highly unique and complex physical, emotional, rational, psychological, personality and

The Adventure of Being Human

spirit aspects. So much for the straightforward, objective answer! Again, the point to be highlighted here is that every instance of response involves a large, complex, interrelated set of variables—only a small portion of which may be fully perceived by another person observing the response.

Each response creates an occasion to which the person, other humans and Plant Earth respond. Thus, each human participates in a continuous complex stream of *sensing and responding, sensing and responding.* . . .

And for the human organism there is another dimension to this. We are aware, to a very high degree, of our sensitivities and of our responses. Not only that, we are aware that we are aware. We are self-conscious. We are also aware that self-consciousness is a unique personal happening. And shall we say it again—this awareness is filtered and processed through a complex web, overlay, interrelationship, and interaction of our highly unique and complex physical, emotional, rational, psychological, personality and spirit aspects. So much for objective, impartial analysis! And once again, the point to be highlighted here is that every awareness involves a large, complex, interrelated set of variables.

(Now add awareness to the complex steam of sensing and responding. Each human is a participant in an even more complex, interrelated stream of sensing, aware, responding, sensing, aware, responding . . .)

To get a feel for this, imagine this scenario. At a baseball game, score tied, runner racing for home plate, the throw coming in, your camera focused on home plate ready for a great action picture, and the person in front of you stands up. That person had just experienced a half-cup of cold beer in their lap, which had been knocked there by the person to their right getting up to go to the restroom. How many resulting scenarios can you play out, including some of what is going on inside the three heads involved, plus any others who become involved? Or try imaging various scenarios resulting from an "insensitive remark" in the midst of a tense political situation, or in a family that does not relate well.

We are not finished yet. There is one more dimension (are you still with me? even into this fourth dimension?) involved in being a human. As a focal point of self-consciousness, each human actively participates, more or less self-consciously, in a unique, complex web and stream of *sensing, aware, responding, aware, sensing, aware, responding, aware,* . . . As an active focal point of self-consciousness, <u>a human can decide</u> how it participates in this stream of *sensing, aware, responding, aware, sensing, aware, responding, aware* . . . A human being decides, more or less consciously, (1) how to relate to the point of awareness; (2) to what awareness or combinations of awareness to respond, and (3) in what manner to respond. (True, there are instances when instincts, reflexes or unconscious conditioning may function, but these are few and are becoming fewer.)

Now add *deciding* to the complex stream of *sensing, aware, and responding*. Each human is a participant in an even more complex, interrelated stream of *sensing, aware, deciding, responding, sensing, aware, deciding, responding* . . .

(You are perfectly correct. This is not a straight linear process. It is four-dimensionally interactive.)

Each decision is—may I say it again?—filtered and processed through a complex web, overlay, interrelationship and interaction of our highly unique and complex physical, emotional, rational, psychological, personality and spirit aspects. The role each aspect plays in the processes is part of the deciding that takes place.

Who is this *self* that participates in this ongoing, complex stream of sensing, aware, deciding, and responding? Who is this *self* that senses, is aware, decides and responds? Who is this *self* that is conscious of itself? The *self* knows itself as "I." At this point, let the *self* speak:

"I am an interrelated network of a physical body, of emotional patterns, of a psychological profile (conscious and unconscious), of mental patterns, of a personality organization, and of a spirit dimension. Each of these aspects is a highly complex, interrelated dynamic with its own history, development, and current state as a result of the history of all the sensing, awareness, deciding, responses of my life. These interrelated networks—those within each aspect and those between each aspect—exist in an unstable tension. Though this makes for high volatility, it also makes for change, growth, and creativity. Yet, I am more than the sum of my physical, emotional, psychological, mental, personality, and spiritual components. I am a bundle of selves. There is the self that I see myself to be. There is the self that I would like to be. Then there is the self that others see me to be. There is the private self. There is the public self. There is the individual self. There is the community self. And all these selves vary from moment to moment. Who is the I that knows me and all my selves? Alas, who is the primal subject?"

Such is the *self* which participates self-consciously in the ongoing, complex happening that is its life.

The point is that each moment of a human's life is the result of and is involved in a highly complex and interrelated set of variables—both in terms of dynamics and of content. Each moment in the life of a human is a highly complex, creative *happening*. There are so many complex variables, combinations, nuances, possibilities, plus that elusive factor of the self, that it can be said that each of our responses is pure, original creativity.

Living as a human is pure, original, ongoing creativity—like playing in a continual *jam session*. In a *jam session*, each player responds to the music being created by the group and by each person in the group. Each player is responding out of his or her own depths and responds at the moment. Each player is responding with the skill, talent and ability they have at the moment. There is no score of music to be followed. Players listen with their whole being and respond with their whole being. Pure creativity.

Living as a human is pure, original, ongoing creativity—like improvisation dancing. In improvisation dancing there are no choreographed dance steps or movements. Out of your own internal being and vision, you move—move in relation to the other dancers, to the space, to the objects around you and to the music. You are also responding according to your sensitivity, awareness, and interpretation of your internal vision. You also respond according to the other dancer's moves and to the dance as a whole. You move in response to all of which you are sensitive and aware—both of all the givenness of the situation and of all your interior. Your moves are done with the self you are at the moment. As one improvisation dance instructor said, "Each moment, your space is empty. There are ten thousand possible moves. But your space can be filled by only one move—and it will be filled with some move. You decide which move." Each move is pure creativity. The other dancers respond to your moves and thus there is a new situation to which to respond. You shift your focus or your image and thereby create very different moves and responses. You may be intensely involved in responding to one or two other dancers for a while; then you may focus on relating to the space in which you are dancing or to a purely interior image; then you may focus on a particular part of your body or on a particular object or you may just generally flow with the situation. Each dancer's participation and movements create a constantly changing situation to which you respond and within which you create your movements. Pure, ongoing creativity.

Each of our lives is such a *jam session*, is such an improvisation dance—constant, ongoing creativity. Every response (word, thought, action) is pure creativity in response to the situation as we are sensitive and aware of it and as we decide how to relate to it. Every response is unique—arising out of the totality of who we are at that point in time. Who we are and where we are is the result of all the *music* and *dance* that we have created previously. Having responded, we are a new totality out of which we will make our next response.

Not only is the internal dynamic of the human equation one of high complexity and massive variables, but the external situation in which we participate is also one of mind-boggling complexity and innumerable variables. We are aware of so many physical objects, interrelationships, values and implications. There are many social, political, economic, educational, cultural, legal, etc. interrelationships, values and implications. We are sensitive to the existence, personalities, moods and preferences of other individuals and groups. Each of us can add to the list. Furthermore, each of these dimensions impacts, and is impacted by, the others.

Now overlaying these dimensions and relationships is a variety of templates, models, screens, schools of thought, points of view, approaches, value sets, unresolved issues, and explosive ramifications. In addition, all of these dimensions and relationships are open to growth, change and the serendipity of life.

Complexity upon complexity. Variables upon variables. Life swirls like a dervish.

Let's add a little more fun to the situation. Today, more than ever before, we are sensitive to tensions. Tensions between positive and negative forces, between male and female, between haves and have-nots, between strong and weak, between majority and minority, between now and later, between like and dislike, between "I like both and can have only one," between "I dislike both and have to pick one," between values, and you can continue the list. Polar tensions pull us this way and that. The tension of a variety of attractions pulls us. The tension of a multitude of repulsions pushes us. We seem to live constantly on the edge between having order and being overwhelmed by chaos, between life and death, succeeding and failing. We try to escape the tension, or at least reduce the pull of one side or the push of the other.

But we now see that tensions are the basis for creativity, life, and vitality. So the universe has functioned from the beginning. It is out of such polarities that all things have been created—atoms to galaxies, flowers to cats, families to cities. It is by such polarities that all things hold together. Tensions are the source of creativity. They call for and produce a response. Tension has just reached a new level of complexity and intensity in self-conscious humans and with it, a new level of creativity.

c. *No Answer. I Am It*

Complexity upon complexity. Variables upon variables. Tensions within tensions. In the midst of all of this, a human is sensitive, aware, deciding, and responding.

Is there any guidance as to the correct response or at least the best means of response? What is the most helpful set of values or rules for deciding and responding?

In past eras there were myths, stories, social and/or religious laws, standards, patterns and such that set forth the *game plan* of the Kosmos and the *rules* for human participation. They provided the *script* or *directions* to follow in how a human was to look at things, how to interpret experiences, how to decide, and how to respond. They provided the pattern of what it meant to be a human. The challenge was to fit the pattern, to follow the rules, and thus to be a *good human.*

With the massive increase in both the awareness and volume of the variables in the equation of the human happening, these previous guidances or standards have been overwhelmed and "blown away." They cannot handle the magnitude of variables—either in dynamics or in content. The increased complexity breaks down the underlying assumptions upon which these standards were based as well as overwhelms the limited pattern of interpretations and options. The previous standards for human living are no longer effective in providing guidance for human living in our era.

[Part of the increased complexity comes from the exposure to the many different sets of values, standards, or rules of the game from various parts of the globe. This variety undercuts the claim and authority of any one of these sets as the definitive and true way of functioning as a human. In fact, each set becomes another element in the increased complexity and variables for current humans.]

We are the first era in which the majority of people are aware, consciously or unconsciously, that there are no common standards, *rules of the game or scripts* for being and living an authentic human life. **We are the first era—and this is the newness—in which everyone has to improvise their lives.** For us, this is the only option. Efforts to return to the good old days of standard religious, community and family values, or to follow nature as a standard or to seek encoded instructions, all confirm the reality of our era as they seek to deny it. These efforts, while not too realistic, are just one of many ways that a person improvises their response to their situation.

But still we ask, "Is there any help, any guidance, any instructions, as to the correct response? Is there at least a correct means to see, interpret, decide, and respond as an authentic human? Is there any hint as to what *notes* we are to play now or what *dance steps* we are to take next? Are some better than others? What is it to be a true human and how do we become one? How do we become a great human, or at least a good, decent one?"

The word comes back to us, "There is no answer. There is no answer, and you create it. There is no solution, and you improvise it. There is no script, and you write it."

Each response that you make IS your answer. Life honors your answer by incorporating it into its ongoing dance. Each thought, each action is your contribution to the drama of life. Life honors them by including them in its story. Each sensitivity, awareness, decision and response you make is your contribution of the next note in your song of life; and life honors your music by including it in the ongoing music of the universe. Moment by moment, day in and day out, each of us is creating the answer to our life, to human society's life, to the planet's life, and to the life of the Kosmos. Each moment, each day, we improvise our participation in this ongoing dance, this ongoing jam session of being a human.

[For your information! Ken Wilber, in Sex, Ecology and Spirituality *and in* The Eye of Spirit, *deals superbly with the issues of validity, truth, truthfulness, appropriateness (justice, values) and functional fit. Using a combination of the basic three-step validity method, a spectrum of evolution and four quadrants of evolution, he provides a means for evaluating products, statements and conclusions of people. I mention this excellent and solid approach for validity of truth and rightness not as a way to discover or provide answers—it doesn't. I mention it as a way of saying that we are not in "free fall" relative to values and answers. I mention it as an example of a very useful tool in assisting us in evaluating our answers, solutions and scripts. Wilber's approach does not relieve us of the reality and necessity of improvising our responses. It is just a tool to help us. And it is good to know that there are tools available.]*

We decide our response. Out of the myriad of stimuli of a given situation, we choose those things, or those combinations of things, to which we will respond. Of all the people on the sidewalk I notice the man with the black hat, the lady with the wild gray hair, the child with the untied shoe. Of all the items on the news, I am excited by a report on education. Above all the noise, I hear a song. In all the comments in the conversation, I noticed the one about health. And then we decide how we will respond, in what manner and with what intensity that we will respond. We choose the standards, values, screens, guidelines, etc. that we apply to the situation. As Virginia Satir writes in her Declaration of Self-Esteem:[6]

"I am me. In all the world, there is no one else exactly like me; everything that comes out of me is authentically mine because I alone chose it. I own everything about me: my body, my feelings, my mouth, my voice, all my actions, whether they be to others or to myself. I own my fantasies, my dreams, my hopes, and my fears. I own all my triumphs and successes, all my failures and mistakes."

As humans, we cannot necessarily choose what is given to us by any situation. We cannot control how others will act or respond to us. We cannot determine how groups or society will act. Life gives and life takes away. Life builds up and life tears down. But we can choose our relationship and response to every situation.

There is no answer, no solution. You are it. You improvise it.

The challenge to being human today is to bring as much self-conscious intentionality as possible to the process of being sensitive, aware, deciding and responding. As a self-conscious energy/life form, the challenge is to be aware of one's self and the situation to which one is responding, and to be intentional in one's response. You may decide that you do not have the strength to stay in a situation and decide to take a break. But it is your decision; you are in control. You are taking the break. You are not a victim and being forced to *take a break*. You decide that this is the appropriate response as the necessary response. As Virginia Satir continues:

"I can become intimately acquainted with me—by so doing I can love me and be friendly with me in all my parts. I know there are aspects about myself that puzzle me, and other aspects that I do not know, but as long as I am friendly and loving to myself, I can courageously and hopefully look for solutions to the puzzles and for ways to find out more about me. However I look and sound, whatever I do and say, and whatever I think and feel at a given moment in time is authentically

---

6. Satir, V. *Self Esteem*, 1975.

me. If later some parts of how I looked, sounded, thought and felt turn out to be unfitting, I can discard that which is unfitting, keep the rest, and invent something new for that which I discarded. I can see, hear, feel, think, say, and do. I have the tools to survive, to be close to others, to be productive, and to make sense and order of the world of people and things outside of me. I own me, and therefore I can engineer me, create me, improvise me. I am me and I am wonder-full."

As the cosmos is composed of swirling masses of energy—galaxies, solar systems, stars, planets—so a human might be conceived of as a swirling focal point of cosmic energy, a living, self-conscious *fireball*. This complex pattern of energy swirls through life attracting, repulsing, and colliding with other energy patterns, resulting in reconfigurations and new patterns of energy. Subject to a myriad of stimuli filtered through multiple screens and provided with multiple options of response, this complex, self-conscious energy pattern is constantly interacting with other energy patterns. Each response sends waves of energy swirling outward to impact other forms and patterns of energy, causing reconfigurations and reactions. A hearty "good morning" sends energy swirling through the office, impacting and reconfiguring energy patterns. An angry outburst sends different energy swirling through the family.

Each response also sends waves of energy swirling inward to impact the host energy form, causing reconfigurations and reactions within the host energy pattern. The hearty "good morning" and the angry outburst each have their own, special impact and reconfiguring effect on the person who uttered them. All these reactions send even more waves of energy radiating out into the larger systems. (For example, follow the expanding waves of impact from the act of a student shooting a gun in a school.) Each human participates in highly intricate, complex, and constantly interacting energy systems of increasing size from family, to community, to society, to ecosystems, to planet, to solar system and beyond. The universe, the planet, and human selves participate in one great dance of evolving energy patterns—constantly creating and being created.

d. A Journey

As Ms. Satir noted above, "However I look and sound, whatever I do and say, and whatever I think and feel at a given moment in time is authentically me." Our *authentic self* is the self we are at any given moment. It is the only self there is. It is meaningless to talk about the self that I "could be," "should be," or to say "this is not really me." The self we are at any given moment is the only self in existence. To be truly me is to be who I am at any given moment.

But it is also true that a human is an ongoing happening. Each moment presents a new situation in which we are sensitive, aware, deciding, and relating/responding. A human is constantly evolving, is constantly becoming a new individual.

"Ongoing! Ongoing how long? Becoming! Becoming what? On a journey! A journey to where?"

Traditional Kosmic Stories and mythologies provided a design for human life that included an end state that a human was to achieve, an ideal existence that a person was to realize. Having reached that point, a person could stop, relax and enjoy life. These various ideal human end states are still operative for many people today. Other people, who reject the validity of traditional Kosmic designs and plans, operate with their own image of an ideal human and an ideal human existence, if no more than the dream of a *the perfect weekend spent with ideal friends and family.*

But when we stop and think about it, we realize that few people, if any, attain anything close to any envisioned ideal human life. We also begin to realize that daily human life is more than something to bear with until we become that ideal human and live that ideal life. Surely being a human is more than putting up with the weekdays to get to that perfect, dreamed-for weekend. With such views of an ideal human life, it is being to dawn on us that most of one's life is spent in something less than ideal human living. In fact, very little, if any, of one's life is spent as an ideal human in an ideal human state.

So, if a cosmic or ideal destination is non-existent, meaningless or both, then why move from where we are now? Why strive? Why journey? Why not just stop trying to improve and enjoy what we have?

In the first instance, I'd say that this sounds like a good idea. To the degree that one can do it, I would encourage you to do so.

In the second instance, I'd say that we journey because we are sensitive and aware of stimuli and it is in our nature to respond. We are impacted by energy, by forces, by sensitivities and awareness—to all of which we respond. We journey because we are pushed and pulled through life. We are driven by cares—cares for providing for our life, care for others. We driven by fears—fears of the known and fears of the unknown. We are driven to grow and to expand. We are pulled by desires—desires to escape from unbearable, undesirable circumstances, desires to change, to improve, to overcome situations that confront us. We are pulled by fascination—fascination of the unknown, of the possible, of the impossible, of that which is just beyond that which we know and can see and is waiting to be discovered. We are pushed and pulled by the energy of the exploding star that formed our solar system—energy that is constantly swirling and moving within us and around us.

And there is that strange force within us—passion. There is within us a deep force that drives us to act, to work, to strive, to accomplish in spite of the odds, in spite of opposition, in spite of the cost (even the cost of our very lives), in spite of pain and in spite of rewards or lack of them. It may be all-consuming, like painting, dancing, teaching or some cause. It may be specific, like reaching the top of a mountain, completing a building, or cooking a fine meal. It may be general like doing each task well, caring for one's children, or creating a pleasant environment. Passion may be one of those primary dimensions of human life to be included in the basic equation along with body, mind and the rest. Or it may even be a primary force, to be included along with chemical, biological and physical forces.

Why journey?

Being a human is being a journey. A human life is a journey. Not a *Hero's Journey*, but an *Every-person's Journey*. Not a journey to find a solution—life is not a problem to be solved. Not a journey to reach a destination Rather its a journey as a way of life. The human journey is not to achieve some perfect, full, ideal human life—not to arrive at some goal where we then stop, relax, and enjoy the ideal life. No. Our journey is about journeying, per se. Journeying, in and of itself, is being the real, full, ideal human. Will I arrive? I am already there. I am on my journey. Will I become fully human? Fully me? I am fully me, now. I am on my journey. There is only the journey.

There is only the becoming. To be the human that I am is to be my becoming, to be my journey. A human individual is a never ending journey. We are our becoming—nothing more, nothing less. To be human is to be our becoming, to be our journey, as we improvise it. As a fireball of self-conscious energy, we create ourselves as a continual surprise to ourselves, to other humans, and to the Kosmos.

e. Savor It

So why are we humans here on Earth? Why am I here? Why did Earth evolve humans in general and me in particular? And what is it to live a full, satisfying life—to have a *good life*—here and now?

In the first instance, there are no answers; each of us creates the answers. We improvise the answers as we live.

For what it is worth, I would share one answer of mine. Our purpose on Earth as humans is to appreciate and savor. To live well, as a human, is to appreciate and savor life—all of existence.

There is something more than just knowing that my life is an improvisation. There is something more than just doing and being a journey. I can relate to my improvisation. I can relate to my journey. As a human, I can appreciate. I can savor. I can enjoy!

We humans are sensitive to so much. We are conscious of so many things—sunsets, cool breezes, a cut on our finger, the smell of burnt beans, the smile of a friend, anger at a mistake, words on a page, solving a problem, a pleasant personality, being in the dumps, a neat room, a stuffy nose, the report on our desk, the hole in our sock, a kiss, a flower, a new dress. We are aware of such a vast array of things. And the more we inspect any one the more it expands into a vast world of its own.

To appreciate all of which we are aware is to affirm their reality, to say "yes" to their existence. To appreciate something is to recognize its existence, just as it is for what it is. To appreciate something is to accept all that it is as it is: and maybe even to say "thank you" for its existence. Once something is, it is—like it or not. The only basic choices available seem to be to deny it, to complain about it, or to affirm it. And it does not take a "rocket scientist" to figure out that *denying* and *complaining* waste physical, emotional, rational, psychological, spirit and other personal energies. (You are right! It is easier said than done. But then, our *complaining* is just another item that has come into existence, of which we are aware and to which we respond.)

Not only can we appreciate the existence of something, we can also savor it. Life is like fine wine. It is not for gulping down. It is for rolling around on the tongue and slowly letting it flow down our throats, savoring it to the fullest. We sense people, things, places, events—savor them to the fullest. We are aware of people, things, places, events—let them flow over us and savor them, like water flowing over us in a nice cool shower on a hot day. We decide and respond—savor our responses, bask in their wonder and glory like a beautiful sunset. We create—savor our creations. We dance—savor our improvisations. We swirl—savor the energy flows and patterns. We journey—savor each moment.

The meaning and purpose of our life is not to achieve something. Life is not about achieving. Life is to be lived! Life is to be appreciated—the failures as well as the successes, the attempts as well as the achievements. Every moment of our lives—not just the few moments of victory that we are lucky enough to attain—is experienced as significant, wonder-full and satisfying. Our whole life is *flavorful*.

f. Earth's Journey

A human is an Earth organism. Humans, individually and collectively, are living organisms that have been produced by Planet Earth's evolutionary and creative process. The human, individually and corporately, is a creature of Earth's creativity.

[Let's pull off and stop a moment to observe a particular Earth phenomenon. Earth energy bio-systems are composed of individual expressions. Neither the whole system nor any individual expression thereof can exist without the other. Individual humans exist only as part of the human bio-system. The human bio-system exists in and through individual humans. Each individual human exists only as an expression of a race, a culture, a society, or any number of groupings. In turn these groupings exist only as a composite of individual humans. The corporate human journey and individual human journeys impact each other. One is a variable in the other's journey and each is mutually dependent. In this section, in referring to humans, both the corporate and the individual natures of being human are included.]

Earth, as a living system, is stimulated and senses the stimuli. Earth, as a living system, responds. With the development of the human, Earth has developed a new capacity, a new dimension. It is now aware of its stimuli; it is aware of what it senses.

Furthermore, with the development of the human, Earth is developing the capacity to decide self-consciously how it will respond. In and through humans, individually and corporately, Earth senses, is aware, decides and responds—with all the interrelated complexity and variables noted previously in regard to humans.

Thus, in and through humans, the Earth is creating, is improvising, is *jamming* its ongoing song and dance. With the increasing and maturing human capacity to be sensitive, to be aware, and to respond, the Planet Earth is engineering not only human selves but itself as well. In humans, individually and collectively, the Earth is aware of itself as the self, as the being it is.

In my journey, in your journey, Earth is journeying. My journey is an expression of Earth's journey, and at the same time, my journey participates in the creation of Earth's journey. In our becoming as individual humans, Earth is becoming. And Earth's becoming is our becoming. In being our journey, Earth is being its journey. The objective for Earth is not to achieve some grand destination, to complete some cosmic design, or to arrive at some ideal point of existence. The objective for the Earth is to be its journey, to be its becoming. I'd say that the meaning and significance of Earth, like for each human, is in savoring its journey of becoming. Earth, too, is on a never ending journey—the wonder of which is in the journeying.

In our appreciation of life and all its aspects, Earth appreciates itself and all its aspects. And at the same time, Earth's appreciation of itself and all of life is expressed in and through our appreciation. In our savoring of life and all its expressions, Planet Earth is savoring life and all its expressions. For Earth, as for each human, life is for living, appreciating and savoring.

Trying to sort out this relationship of humans and Earth is like trying to sort out the relationship of the mind in the life a person. Who or what is sensing, being aware, deciding, and responding? What and where is self-consciousness? What and where is the *self* that is conscious? Have your go at explaining it.

What I am trying to articulate here is that our role or purpose as humans is not just for ourselves, and in the first instance may not be for ourselves at all. Maybe our role or purpose as humans is to be the means for Earth to create, to engineer, to improvise itself. Maybe our purpose is not to engineer, to create, to improvise ourselves as unique individual humans, as much as it is to engineer, to improvise, to create the Earth's journey. Maybe our role is not to appreciate and savor life for ourselves, but to be the means whereby the Earth appreciates and savors itself and its role in the Kosmos. Really though, it is not an *either/or* situation. Our becoming a human and Earth becoming itself are one and the same reality. Our appreciating and savoring and Earth's appreciating and savoring are one and the same reality.

As someone has said, "a human is a star's way of knowing and appreciating itself." In the same way, humans are Earth's way of knowing, becoming, and savoring itself as the Earth. This could be who we are and why we are here. Oh, what a journey!

g. Relation to the Mystery

When all is said and done, there are major factors in the life of a person about which one knows nothing—the *unknown*. There are also many aspects of life about which it is not possible to know—the *unknowable*. And there are other aspects of life, for which humans have no capacity to comprehend and thus do not even know that we do not know—the *unknown unknown*.

Some of the unknown is because we have not yet discovered all of the details as to how we humans function and interact. Plus, the complexity of life's variables, of their interaction and of the pure creative initiatives of human responses, greatly increases the experience of the unknowable. Whatever clarity, knowledge and increased capacity for knowing that the future may produce, our current experience is that of not knowing.

Whether it is called *luck, fate,* or *serendipity,* whether it is called the *activity of God,* the work of *angels, leprechauns* or *other spirits,* the result of *powers* or *energies,* or the influence of the *stars*—we all experience the operation of some mysterious force in our lives.

What is experienced and known is that our lives are pushed, pulled and limited by unknown and unknowable factors and forces. We constantly show up in situations not of our creation (beginning with our sex, family, race, country and historical time that come with our birth). We experience events and thoughts "out of the blue." We know the validity of *Murphy's Law* as well as its optimistic opposite. Life, with or without or in spite of our self-conscious response, happens.

All of the unknown and unknowable, all of these mysterious forces and factors, I sum up with the phrase *Mysterious Force,* or just the *Mystery* for short. (More about this in chapter 6.)

It might be said that the Mysterious Force is the basic component in the life of a human. Where did each of us come from, how, and why?—finally, the Mystery. Where will each of us go at death? When and why?—finally, the Mystery. Push any event, any item, any aspect of life to its depth and what is found, finally?—the Mystery. It has been said that we live our lives out over nothing, or at least out over a big bowl of Jell-O. This is not a choice—we just show up with nowhere else to live our lives—out over nothing solid, out over pure unknowable Mystery, out over the unknown *Unknown.*

Because the Mysterious Force is such a basic component in a human's life, a person's relationship to the Mystery is critical to the quality of that life. Some believe that the meaning of life is to see the Mystery in everything. I do know that when the mystery and wonder of an event, of an object or of a situation does shine forth, I experience deep joy and satisfaction—a sense of wholeness and goodness that is complete in and of itself. Others have said that fulfillment lies in the awareness of one's self in relation to the Mystery. I do know that when I try to grasp who I am, I become pure mystery and begin to blend in with the Mystery of Life itself—whole and complete as The Mystery itself.

On a more mundane level, if life is about creativity, improvising, jamming and dancing, experience demonstrates that these happen best when a person *turns loose.* When this happens, a person is not focused on playing notes, is not looking at one's feet and gives one's self completely to the event and *lets it flow*. As athletes know, it is when one participates with abandon, when one gives up worrying about the outcome, relaxes, and *lets it flow*, then one does his or her best. Or as the words in the song "Come from the Heart" (by Susanna Clark and Richard Leigh) express it—

"You got to sing like you don't need the money;
Love like you'll never get hurt;
You got to dance like nobody's watchin';
It's got to come form the heart
    if you want it to work."

To take a positive relation to the Mystery—to affirm the reality that one is out over nothing, that one is an essential component of the uncontrollable, unknowable Mystery—is to *turn loose and flow* with the Mystery itself. This is the principle behind the age-old wisdom that in order to live, really and fully, it is necessary to turn loose of one's self—to die to one's self. Or, as expressed in more modern terms, "come on, give it up and get a life!" It is not so much *turning loose* as it is accepting the fact that we have been *turned loose* out over nothing and journey as part of the flow of the Mystery of life itself. When a person accepts and lives the reality that one's journey is actually the journey of the Mystery, then a person is freed from concern over producing, over winning or losing or over success or failure and participates, freely and fully in the journey of being one's life. When a person relaxes and rests in the reality that one is part and parcel with the Mystery, then achieving/failing, winning/loosing, right/wrong fade and he or she fully appreciates and savors living.

To be a human is to be a creative journey. It is a personal journey, the Earth's journey and the Mystery's journey—all one and the same journey.

Oh! What an adventure!

D. IMPLICATIONS OF THE INDIVIDUAL HUMAN

Being human, we have so much more experience and knowledge about this aspect of a Kosmic Story of Life. We also have much more at stake in this aspect of the story. A major shift in this aspect of life's story has many complex implications for us as individuals, as societies, and as the human bio-system. The implications grouped in the subsections below represent only a fraction of the implications of the new image of the human. And each subsection is in no way exhaustive. Each of these sections could be a book or several books. What is done here is but to open a crack in several major *doors*. The reader is invited and encouraged to push the *door* open, go in and explore more extensively.

1. Redefining the *Self*

We are in a period of intensive exploration of the human *self*. People are seeking to discover one's *self* in particular and the human *self* in general. The expanding disciplines and roles of psychology, psychiatry, self-help methods, self-actualization efforts, transpersonal understanding, meditation and various spirit practices are all part of this fascinating effort of exploring the *self*. The results of expanded efforts in brain research, aided by increasingly sophisticated and sensitive technology, are providing increased knowledge of how the brain functions and intriguing insights into the nature and function of the human mind. The billions of cells and connections of a human brain make AT&T's worldwide phone network look small and simple. A related and growing area of research is that of seeking to understand human consciousness/spirit/soul—a major part of which is to define what is meant by these terms.

Along with expanded understanding of the varied, complex, and interrelated aspects that compose a human, we are in the midst of redefining what it is to be a human.

We are just now beginning to learn how a human self functions. For the past three or four hundred years, we have been *meditating* on how the cosmos and the planet function. Our modern scientific knowledge and technological prowess are the results of these efforts. We will likely spend the next two or three hundred years *meditating* on how humans function.

We are discovering that a *self* is a process, not a content; that the self is a continual happening. Being a *self* is an ongoing process of receiving input, processing that input, and responding—all with varying degrees of self-conscious intentionality. The self is a process of participating in numerous relationships and various roles. I am a father, a son, a husband, a brother, an employee, a teacher, a citizen, a homeowner, a group leader, another group member, and the list goes on. How I *play* these roles in any given relationship at any given time varies greatly.

There is no self buried or hidden somewhere to be found and brought out. We are who we are at any given moment—no more, no less. There is no child hidden within, waiting to be discovered and released. There is no wild person crouching within, waiting for an unguarded moment to spring forth. There is no kind and gentle person, no strong and assertive person, no artist, no poet, nor any other type of person, sitting quietly within us, just waiting to be invited to a coming-out party in their honor, or for a chance to "do their thing." There is no potential self to be actualized. There is no encoded self to discover and release to play out its predetermined role. No, we are continually creating, inventing and improvising the multifaceted self that we are. There is no other journey, no other self, than the one a person is at any given moment.

These other types of so called *selves* may be clues or orientations as to how we might decide to respond in any given time as we proceed on the journey; but they are not hidden or lost *selves*. They may be other aspects of our self which, for whatever reason or decision, we have not been aware of, have not cultivated, or have not employed in our *journey equation* and now, because of new stimuli, have become part of our *journey equation*. These types of so-called selves may be "roads not taken" in our journey through life and we may want to explore these "roads" sometime in our journey. We may decide to respond sometimes in a childlike way. At times, we may decide to be a "wild person." We may even decide to radically change our lifestyle. But these are not videotapes of *other selves* which we find stuck away at the back of the shelf and stick in the VCR of life. It is true that we may take a new road, operate out of a different self-image, choose another set of *filters* to see and respond to life, or decide to become a new or different person. But that is a new response, a new creation, a new improvisation; it is not bringing a different *self* off the bench to bat at this time. At any given moment, a person (in all his or her complexity) is the self that he or she has decided to be and created him or herself to be—fully and completely as the only person/self that he or she is.

It is reported that a person, extending his hand, asked Malcom X if he would shake the hand of a white person. Malcom X responded by saying, "I will shake the hand of a human. Are you a human?" The challenge for us in the Ecozoic Age is to be a human. The primary focus is to be an authentic member of the human species. Until one knows how to function as an Earth human, one has limited clues as to how to function as a male or female human, an Asian or African human, an American or Mexican human, or any other sub-grouping of humans. Our first and primary understanding of being a self is that of being a human. Then we can have the opportunity to explore our authentic participation as part of other human categories or groups.

Out of the increased research into human consciousness comes an interesting development. Is the individual self the basic or primary reality of being a human? The witness of John Wren-Lewis and Ann Faraday in articles in the *Noetic Sciences Review*, (Spring of 94, No.29) speak of their individual self becoming transparent and of their experience of a deeper, fuller, more real, more satisfying human existence beyond the self. Mr. Wren-Lewis notes that 'egoic' preoccupations no longer dominate life. We still have the sense of self but it is now experienced as just part of universal aliveness, not as a central anxiety. There is no attachment to personal concerns, because the satisfaction of merely existing far outshines the transitory pleasure that comes from getting my individual preferences met. To my amazement, it even transforms the pains that come when life goes against my personal inclinations." Ms. Faraday writes of losing her sense of self. "I was emerging from a state of consciousness without any "I" or "self" at all. I can't even really say that I experienced it, because there was no experience and no thing to experience. I experience this emptiness as a boundless arena in which life continually manifests and plays, rising and falling, constantly changing, always transient and therefore ever-new. It is the whole obfuscating concept of 'self' which needs to be transcended, for in my experience there has never really been any self to transform, actualize, realize or transcend."

"So, what do you think of those apples!"

I am not advocating a position here. I only want us to note that self-exploration may lead to the questioning of the individual self's primary role and even its reality. Other spiritual leaders throughout human history have noted that the self, or at least the focus on the self, is a hindrance to participating in the fullness and richness of life. Concern for the self and its survival and well-being, which was critical for the survival of the human species in its early development, may now be a hindrance to the further development and evolution of humans. In our next stage of evolution, we may need to move beyond a focus and concern for the self—both for effective individual human functioning as well as for the human bio-system's effective functioning in the dance of Planet Earth. The human self may, as John Wren-Lewis says, be just "a focus of infinite aliveness . . . along the time-line." He goes on to note, "individuality which seemed to mean separateness and struggle to survive, when in truth it is an arbitrary convention, like lines of latitude on a map." Like a relative reference point, the *self* may be only a relative convention. As we look deeper into the *self*, we may just see through and beyond to the deeper and more wondrous reality of being human.

The implication that I want to make here is that we need to be open to the fact that the *self* may not just be the "big cheese" and "end all" that we are wont to think. The *self* and its well-being—which was critical in earlier stages of our development—may now be no more than a false goal, an unhelpful reference point, or a dead end. I find this as frightening as it is intriguing. I did not have this implication in mind when I began—it just intruded during the writing. The more I think about it, though, the more sense it begins to make. Check it out for yourself.

Finally, in dealing with the human self, we are dealing with pure mystery. One cannot finally know one's self, for who is the self that knows the self? The ultimate *knower* is unknowable. Also, a person can never know another human fully. A human is pure mystery.

2. Responsible for Ourselves

The main implication of having to create or improvise our lives at every moment is that we humans are not "mechanical robots." We are not victims. It undercuts the excuse which says, "I had no choice but to . . . " Contrarily, each of us is responsible for each response we make—unless we are seriously mentally impaired. We may not fully understand why we decide to respond in the way that we do, but nonetheless, we do respond. There is no programmed machine inside of us making our responses. There is no "little person" inside of us making our decisions and responses for us. There is no one else moving our feet or lips. There is only the totality of who we are that senses the situation, that is aware of the situation, that weighs the values, that decides and then responds.

It is true that we cannot necessarily control the situations in which we find ourselves, nor control many of the aspects of those situations. We may not be able to control our primary emotional reaction. But we do control how we respond to any given situation in which we are involved, including our relationship to any primary emotional reaction that we have. True, the options may be limited. But within these limits, we decide the response that we make—good, bad, or indifferent.

When a person says, "He made me angry," or "She upset me," they are operating with an image of a human as a robot. They assume that a human is a mechanical object with buttons to be pushed, levers to be pulled and strings to be jerked which induce particular responses. The image of a human as one who creates/improvises life at every moment reveals the inaccuracy of such statements. Humans are not mechanical responders. Humans are creative responders. Yes, I am angry. My response is anger toward another person. But the other person did not *make me angry*. The anger is my response. The accurate statement is, "I got angry." Yes, I am upset and emotionally in distress. But the other person did not make me upset or cause my emotional pain. I, and I alone, chose to respond by being upset. It was my emotional make up, my management of my emotions, and my choice to be hurt.

Each of us is responsible for our responses to a given situation. No one can take this freedom and responsibility away. We might give away that freedom, and many have. But that is our decision. After that, we have no right to blame others for what they do with our freedom. No one takes our interior freedom from us. We and we alone are responsible for ourselves, our decisions and our responses.

3. No Easy Decisions

As expressed in the equation of the human function (sensing, aware, deciding, responding, sensing, aware, deciding, responding . . .), we decide all the time. There are big decisions, little decisions, painful decisions, unthinking decisions. Let's take a brief look at some of the contexts, circumstances, and dynamics within which we decide.

For one thing, life is **radically open**. We are told that "anything is possible." While there are more possibilities than we care or dare to be aware of, we find ourselves thinking thoughts like "I'm trapped; there are no real options for me; I'd like to change but I can't or don't dare." The truth is, as a friend of mine keeps reminding me, that a person has to die before all is really possible. Have you ever noticed how freeing the acceptance of the reality of one's death is for a person—such as a near-death experience or the coming to terms with AIDS? When one turns loose of hanging on to one's self and to one's life, a person is free to do and be about anything. In fact, life keeps cutting us loose from our past, from our very selves. The universe keeps cutting us loose from our stability and security. The ongoing creativity and improvisation of human life constantly presents each of us with new situations and new opportunities to decide. Life is radically open.

On the other hand, we often hear predictions in the format of "if things continue the way they are going, "xyz" will happen." But we can be fairly sure that things will not continue the way they are going. There are built-in ranges and limits that kick in at various times to change the trend. In addition, such predictions usually consider only a narrow set of variables, whereas life is filled with a multitude of complex, highly fluctuating variables. Life is far more open than we like to think.

Increased knowledge and understanding about the universe, the planet, and humans provide ever more choices. Technology, with its expansion and enhancement of human capacity, provides a mind-numbing flood of possibilities for responding. As we turn loose (or are turned loose) of a focus on ourselves and our survival, more and more is possible.

We decide within **tensions**. Life is full of dualities and polar tensions. There is light and dark; up and down; hot and cold. There is positive and negative; male and female; us and them. There is sweet and sour; good and bad; pain and pleasure. And you can extend this list on and on. There is tension between what I need to do and what I want to do; between family and work; between the economy and the environment. There is tension between the various aspects of my self, between the various roles that one plays (parent, spouse, child, citizen, etc.). There is tension between my well-being and the well-being of society. There is tension between all the various groups and players within society—note the special interests lobbying the US Congress. There is tension among all the ecosystems of the planet. And you can extend this list on and on.

We do not like tensions. We seek to escape from them. We seek to reduce them—usually by reducing or denying one of the poles involved in the tension. We seek to balance them. We want authority, rules and standards to resolve them for us. But finally it is not possible to escape or deny tensions. Tensions are an integral part of life. Thus is the universe held together—beginning with the positive and negative electrical charges. Tension is the basis of all creativity. It is the slight imbalance of tensions that causes change and evolution. If life were ever in perfect balance and harmony, all change would cease, everything would remain forever exactly as it was at that moment.

We decide in the midst of the push-and-pull of tensions, of dualities, of opposites. The challenge is to be more aware of the tensions that are at play in our lives and to increase the amount of tension that we can handle so that we can be even more creative. True, a person can be overwhelmed by more tensions than they can handle at a given time, just as they can be overwhelmed by any natural aspect of life, such as water, air, friends, opportunities, and bubble gum. At such times, one may seek to make use of some means to allay some of the tension. This would be part of an intentional way of relating to tensions and of using tensions, rather than an attempt to avoid them.

We also decide in radical **ambiguity**. There are no clean decisions. Often our choices are between good and good—spend time with the spouse or spend time with the kids; help that person or help this person; plant this crop or plant that crop. Sometimes the choices are between evil and evil—blow the whistle and lose my job or let the company keep cheating the customers; both candidates on the ballot are poor choices. But look deep into any decision and we will find a mixture of *good* and *evil* in every decision. Often that which is *good* for someone or some situation is *bad* for someone else or for some other situation.

Finally, one can never know the full results of any decision. Many a great solution has ended up causing more problems than it solved—rabbits in Australia, welfare assistance in the US, World Bank loans to third-world countries, the weed killer that killed all the flowers. The fact that life is interrelated, that there are so many variables involved in any response and subsequent reactions, that the ramifications of any decision are so wide, makes it impossible to ever know the full results of any decision. It is helpful to realize the extreme variety and extent of variables—people, places, energy patterns, perspectives, values, inputs, feedback loops, impacts, responses, events, circumstances, resources, etc.—involved in the implementation of any decision. It is helpful to realize the extreme complexity of the interrelationship of these variables. Then, knowing that it is impossible to know all the facts or all the possible scenarios relative to its implementation, a decision is made in a fog of ambiguity and uncertainty. We are constantly creating and improvising in pure ambiguity.

[We can see here the additional attraction for desiring the old standards and rules that functioned in the past, for seeking some encoded instructions for living, for seeking nature's way, for some authority to just tell me what to do. We want to escape from the ambiguity, from the unknown, from the responsibility of making a decision in the midst of such un-clarity.]

With such radical openness, tensions and ambiguity the natural response is, "It is impossible to make a responsible, intelligent, right, or meaningful decision." If a person thinks much about a decision, they can easily become paralyzed. The reality is that it is not possible to make a so-called "perfect" decision. So how does one decide? Is there any meaning in one decision over another? Why decide?

We decide only when and because it is **necessary** to decide. We decide because life puts us in one situation after another and forces us to decide. (Remember that *not to decide* is a decision, a response to the situation, which has just as many ramifications as any other decision.) In making the necessary decision, we can seek to be as sensitive as we possibly can, to be as aware as we possibly can, to have as much information and knowledge as we possibly can. Then, as ancient wisdom, current studies and my own experience indicate, it is helpful to get as much distance from a decision as one can. Be it meditation, be it conversation with others, be it just waiting or be it taking three deep breaths, it is helpful to step back from a situation to get another perspective. We can weigh the alternatives as best we can. But when life puts the squeeze on us, we have to decide and act—ready or not. All this may be done in the blink of an eye or it may take years.

Once the deed is done, it is **offered up to history**. It is out of our hands. Life, history, the universe, the Kosmos—whatever you call the big drama of which we are part—accepts our deed, honors it and incorporates it into the ongoing process of life. We then move on, in our journey of improvising life, to the next situation and next impossible decision. (From time to time, life may give us feedback on our decision. And over time, history may evaluate our decision, but it is impossible to know the full impact and ramifications of our decisions.)

4. Maturity: Standing and Expanding

Individually and collectively, humans are maturing. Maturing entails increased sensitivity, awareness, decision-making and responses. This increase is in depth, breadth, number, and the quality of our sensitivity, awareness, decisions, and responses. We creatively improvise our lives with greater competence and effectiveness. As our lives are pushed and pulled, repulsed and attracted by the tensions of life, maturity is the ability to embrace more and more tensions. The greater tension and diversity of perspectives that we humans can handle, the more creative we are and the more mature we become.

One of the prerequisites for handling more tension is appropriating the basic tension of life—"to die is to live." The Kosmos creates the new out of the death of the old—constantly reforming, re-patterning energy. The old patterns of responding, the old self, have to die in order for the new patterns of life, the new self, to be formed. It is not an issue of the old or the new, of me or him, of us or them. The issue is that of moving to a larger self that incorporates the previously separate aspects in a new, larger unit—a larger self—whose well-being depends upon all the components functioning well in the new configuration. True, this is happening all the time; it is the way life grows and expands. But as a person self-consciously operates out of this reality, life radically opens and expands for them.

As we move to larger contexts (family, community, bio-socio-economic regions, planetary) and to deeper more complex selves (rational, existential, trans-rational), we will experience an increase in our sensitivity, awareness, decisions, and responsiveness. The jam session gets bigger and wilder. The tension mounts. The creativity expands. The savoring and appreciation becomes more varied, vivid and richer. The wonder, the excitement, the fear and the fascination continually mount. The wonder of the journey expands unbelievably.

[The alternative to this is to sit in the corner, sucking our thumbs, hugging our old worn, tattered self, and complaining about how terribly life is treating us and what a mess the world is. A few may sit in silence, longing for imagined better days in the past or dreaming of how good it is going to be when their luck changes and they get their big chance. If this goes on too long, a person becomes a zombie—just going through the motions of living. We all have had our times sitting in this corner. Enough of this, back to the jam session and the dance!]

As the tension mounts, as the creatively expands, as the sensitivity, awareness, and wonder increase, the challenge is to **STAND**. Do you know what I mean by *stand*? I am referring to the ability to stay in the dance and not to quit. I am referring to the ability to hold this expanded perceptive and not to reduce the tension, not to run from the ambiguity and the fog, not to collapse *in a corner with our security blanket*. I am referring to looking the absurdity, wonder and fear of life in the eye and embracing it. The fear is that the tension will destroy us, that life will overwhelm us and tear us apart. And so it will. And so we live. "To die is to live."

This is not a once-in-a-lifetime decision. It is a daily decision. So, it may be helpful to have a daily ritual to remind us of this decision. A ritual is a symbolic act—words, movement, sounds, objects—which calls attention to our decision and provides the opportunity to make it anew. We need all the help we can get to maintain, expand, and operate out of our self-consciousness, our sensitivity, our awareness. A daily act of standing present to the way life operates and to a decision to participate fully keeps us from reducing our lives under the tensions and wonder of life.

Maturity, with its increased sensitivity to depth and beauty of life, also presents another danger. A person can become fascinated with, and addicted to, one aspect of life to the extent that it becomes the whole of life. We are familiar with those whose world is reduced to money, power, work, sports, cars, clothes, TV, and the like. But there is also the cynic who is fascinated and addicted to the absurdity of life. There is the optimist who is fascinated and addicted to the goodness of life. There is the revolutionary who is focused only on changes that need to be made. There is the visionary who lives in some future world. There are those who focus their expanded awareness on maleness, on femaleness, on peacefulness, on nature, and the list goes on. The danger here is, while being aware of the vastness, complexity and wonder of life a person lives out of only one aspect of that picture. This results in a distorted view and approach to the other aspects of life. This is an ever-present danger to us all.

On the other hand, the challenge of maturity has to do with expanding one's awareness of the depth, breath and complexity of life and with developing all dimensions as an integral whole. It involves a balanced and integral development of various aspects and dimensions of our human potential—physical, mental and trans-rational, internal and external, individual and corporate.[7] (See Chapter 7-C-2-b for a more detailed discussion of this topic.)

Also there is the challenge to develop exercises, techniques and skills to increase our ability to deal with increased tensions and to function in greater ambiguity. A related challenge is to honor the dangers of tension, ambiguity, complexity and one's limited capacity to deal with them.

This is not to lay on us another program for self-development. Rather, it is saying that increased maturity as humans requires increased capabilities. For persons deciding to respond intentionally, a first step is to make a reasonable assessment of their current capabilities. If they do decide to increase them, then a single, integral approach would be the best way to proceed.

Each of our personal discoveries, achievements and areas of growth will contribute to the maturity and growth of the human species. Each individual's development of skills and disciplines for our journey will add to the resources of all humans. Who knows what

---

7. A good introduction to such an integral development is the book *The Life We Are Given* (a long term program for realizing the potential of body, mind, heart, and soul) by George Leonard and Michael Murphy.

we humans will be like after 200-300 years of focused practice!

5. Redefining Lifestyle

What is it to be a human? What is the style of living as a human?

To be a human in this age is to be continually re-engineering one's self. This means that our lifestyle can be recreated at any time. We can change our lifestyle whenever we decide that it is necessary or helpful to do so. In fact, we will probably live several different lifestyles during our lifetime.

A related implication is that we will become more and more open and accepting of the variety of lifestyles. The challenge will be to find ways of permitting differing lifestyles to function together in a creative way rather than a destructive way.

A basic life style implication has to do with saying "Yes" to life.

People who are able to **affirm all of life**, to say "yes" to life, seem to function more fully, satisfyingly and effectively. What is, is, and it is meaningful. What we have is what we have, and it is a waste of time and energy wishing life would have shown up differently. Thus, they are free to engage fully in dealing with the situation at hand. They are free to take any relationship to the situation that they decide to take—all is possible for them. The alternative is to complain that life is not the way that we would like it to be. For those who say "no" to life, options seem to be very limited and such people are either paralyzed, angry or frantic. Affirming life or complaining about life is a decision that a human makes many times a day. As such, a person develops a life style of either affirming or rejecting life.

A friend of mine developed prostate cancer. By saying "yes" to his reality, he came to redefine *healthy* as being more energetic, livelier, intellectually stimulated, rather than just *not being sick*. He changed his self-story from one who had cancer to one who was on an intensive health quest. He shifted his vision from fear of dying to a love of better living. To his surprise, he found his life becoming surprisingly delightful. Before, he was satisfied with his life—can't get much better than this. Now he finds life can get better, and is getting better. New experiments with life produce unimagined pleasures, increased tolerance, dissipating symptoms of sickness, new light in his eyes, new joy in his voice. He still has prostate cancer, but he is one *alive* human being!

Affirming life includes affirming our "dark side." Every person has a "dark side" that we seek to hide from others and even hide from ourselves. Every aspect of our person has two sides—a positive (light) side and a negative (dark) side. One side or the other is usually stronger and is part of our more "public" side. Our tendency is to hide, "put down," deny or otherwise reject the negative (dark) side. At times we seek to get rid of it by correcting, reforming or improving it.

These efforts to reject or get rid of our "dark side" are rejecting half of ourselves. It is not like cutting out the rotten half of an apple; it is more like trying to remove one side of a coin. Without our "dark side" we are not whole—we are not ourselves.

Therefore by affirming our "dark side" we are becoming more integrated and whole as a person. It does not mean letting the negative aspect run wild. But by recognizing the "dark aspects" they are out in the open where we can keep an eye on them, manage them, integrate them into the larger whole and discover the positive aspect of which they are the back side.

Another characteristic that seems beneficial to living the human journey in our era is that of **comprehensiveness**. Life is holistic. For us to be effective parts of the whole, it is helpful for us to be aware of and relate to as much of the whole as we can. Those who have reduced their life to "themselves and their pet" do not seem to have a very rich life.

As we are more and more aware that no one group or approach has all the answers for living, we are also aware that each group or approach has valuable experience and contributions for the human journey. Thus, a stance *above* or *beyond (trans)* any particular approach to life provides a perspective for viewing both the gifts and perversions of a particular approach. This helps move beyond the *either/or, us/them* style of relating to life and moves toward a holistic encompassing of the necessary tensions, the development of the helpful aspects and the guarding against the destructive aspects. I call this life stance a **transic** stance. (This is developed more fully in Chapter 7, Section C)

One other characteristic of a basic human lifestyle has been mentioned several times in this chapter, and that is **intentionality**. I find that people or groups who have made dramatic improvements in their lives by following some method of improvement did so not so much because of the method, but because the method provided a way to be intentional about what they were sensing, deciding and responding to. *Intentionality* has to do with being self-conscious or being aware of one's human equation (sensing, aware, deciding, responding) in any given situation. *Intentionality* has to do with being self-consciously in charge of one's decision as to how to relate and respond to a given situation.

Affirmative, comprehensive, transic, and intentional seem to describe the most appropriate human lifestyle for the Ecozoic Age. These characteristics seem most appropriate for creating and improvising one's life. But these are only my observations. What would be on your list? In your life?

6. Finally

What is finally going to happen to us—as a species and as the individuals that we are? Will we cease to exist? Will there be some final *triumph* or *grand completion*? Will we transit to a new state or form of existence?

The straight, simple answer is we don't know; and right now, it is not even possible to know.

But we are much too curious and seem to have too much at stake to let it go at that. So we are constantly exploring the possibilities, testing theories, and setting forth hypotheses about the conclusion to human life, particularly our own. "Where are we really and finally heading?"

What is going to happen to the human race? Will we finally be destroyed—either by our own hand or by some cosmic force—as some are wont to predict?

To respond to the issue of the human race, it is not so much that we have become more evil, stupid, weak-willed and/or irresponsible, as it is that we have become more aware of the destructive possibilities and aspects of our increased power. This increase of power comes both from the increase in variety and potency of our technological capabilities and from the massive number of humans. Responses to our allurements and the results of our *swirling fireball collision*s have dramatic and far-reaching impact these days. This is the first time humans have had such self-consciousness, such freedom and such control over our own energy and over cosmic energy. For the first time in all of history, we have the capacity to destroy ourselves as a species and to destroy Earth itself. And we are just learning how to use our new and increased creativity and energy. Like a novice at the controls of a bulldozer, he/she can do a large amount of constructive work or he/she can do a large amount of damage. In the same way, we humans, with the knowledge and power at our disposal, can do much creative work or much destructive work.

So what will it be?

Looking at the success of the Kosmos in dealing with swirling and colliding energy patterns over the last 12 billion years and in *managing* the evolution of Planet Earth for the 4.5 billion years of its life, I see no reason not to trust this *management* to continue to manage our situations quite effectively.

True, it is possible that we humans could wreak massive destruction on ourselves and the planet. And if we did, it would not be the first time energy patterns and life forms have done so, or even have come to a *dead end* in the Universe or on Planet Earth. The creative work of life seems to walk the edge between total failure and grand success, with the outcome usually being a nice surprise. We humans walk this edge. And the outcome? Personally, I trust the Kosmos's track record—at least for the next million or so years.

Now, what about us as individuals? We know that each of us will come to an end—we all will die. Birth into Planet Earth is very bad for a person's health—it is 100% fatal. Like a brightly burning light bulb, one day we will just blink out. A human being is a particular energy form. An individual human—however unique, complex and special—is a particular expression of energy, just like a tree, a rock, a butterfly, a fish, a chair, a kangaroo. Like any energy form, an individual human comes into existence and goes out of existence. And if there is some self-conscious force *regulating* this coming-and-going, it certainly gives no consideration to anything like human values or human concerns. Rain and sunshine do not respect human status, wishes, values, or well-being. They nourish or destroy the good, bad and indifferent, the rich and poor, the less and more intelligent, the young and old, with equal disregard. Wind and water will crush, drown and destroy humans just as they do trees, rocks, bridges, crops, cows, bird nests, and frogs. They will destroy nice people as well as evil people; religious people as well as non-believers.

Sure, some people seem to be the objects of fortuitous events. But for each recipient of a fortuitous happening, there are many more who are not recipients. For every time *things have miraculously gone well* for a person, I dare say that there are still more times when *things have not gone well*. So, if there is some self-conscious, regulating force, it hands out ordinary happenings more than it does special happenings. It *hands out* especially bad happenings along with especially good happenings. There is a traditional bell curve for all types of happenings from very bad to very good.

Furthermore, there is another dynamic going on, life will send forth millions of sperm so that one may be successful. How many humans does life send forth so that one may move the race forward another step? Are we just cells in the Global Brain? Are we like cells, which play a special role but wear out, die, and are replaced? Not only are humans just another particular energy form, they seem just as expendable as any other energy form in Planet Earth. In the end, each human will *blink out*, will die.

Yet, this human energy form has the ability to think that there might be more to their existence than this particular expression. Self-consciousness is the ability to stand outside of one's consciousness and reflect on that consciousness. In the same manner, humans can stand outside of their Earthly existence and reflect on existing before and after—particularly after—their physical Earthly existence. So the question, "Is there anything more after death?" Does this self-consciousness, which can stand outside of its physical expression, continue to exist when its physical body ceases to exist? Or are the self and self-consciousness products of the brain which will end with the death of the brain? Or does individual self and self-consciousness exist apart from the brain/body and continue after the death of our particular body/brain?" More particularly, "When an individual human dies, does that individual continue to exist as that individual—somehow, somewhere?" Even more personal, "After my death, will I continue to exist as me in some other place and/or other form? Will I continue to be me after death?"

Trying to discuss this question is somewhat like all humans having been born without eyes and discussing "Is there really light?" and "What would it be like to live with the ability to see light?" Such a discussion would be extremely difficult, if not impossible, even if there were some people with eyes participating in the discussion. How could *have-eyes* persons prove to the *no-eyes* persons that there is light?

There are reports of existence on the other side of death. They are not strange and difficult to understand. And that is exactly what makes it particularly difficult for me to accept these so-called "life after death reports" or "near-death experiences" (NDEs)—the descriptions of the *afterlife* seem to be continuations of normal everyday life, only in a more glorified state. This seems to me to simply be the wish fulfillment of the person(s) having the experience. And this is all quite to be expected, since we are very ego-survival oriented. Furthermore, such experiences can be explained as functions of the brain's neurological processes.

Sure, the experiences are experienced as real—with equal or stronger impact upon a person's life; but, like dreams, the source is from within our physical bodies, not from without. Since there's no possibility of third-party observation or validation of these experiences as having originated from outside of the person who had the experience, I would have to say that it is not currently possible for us to know about human existence after death—one way or the other.

Most discussions on this subject talk of the existence of the ego-self after death and what this ego-self will do and experience. Now the ego-self is a particular invention and phenomenon of human life as part of Planet Earth. In such discussions, *heavenly beings* (humans who are in heaven) seem to be simple projections of Earth beings/selves into a mode of existence where many of the limitations of Earth do not apply. (I say *projections* since all *heavenly beings* reflect the particular traits, customs, values, mores, etc. of the particular people who discuss such *heavenly beings*.)

Another limitation of this discussion is that the ego-self is always associated with the particular physical expression of an individual. But each human will have various *selves* over their lifetime—their baby self, their child self, their teenage self, their *wild oats* self, their family self, their mature self, their weird self, their senile self, their depressed self, their happy self, and the list goes on. Which of these *selves* is to survive after death? In addition, a *self* is a holistic composite of many components, most of which do not survive death. So what kind of *self* will survive?

Some people speak of a *transcendent-self* (or *inner-self*, depending upon the orientation one uses to express the larger levels of consciousness—whether moving into the *deeps* of life or into the *heights* of life) which is somehow differentiated from the physical, planet-Earth-self and which exists apart from the planet-Earth-self. By means of various disciplines, this *transcendent-self* may be experienced directly, intimately and repeatedly. Those who have done the discipline and had the experiences have then come together and validated the common aspects of such experiences. This three step scientific method of validating the true and real thus validates the existence and reality of such a *transcendent-self*. (The written records of such experiences by isolated individuals from various times and locations of history reveal a common experience and thus provide further validation.)

Before one gets too excited about a *transcendent-self*, two related issues should be considered.

First: While my own experience of the *transcendent-self* and *eternal bliss* confirms and is confirmed by reports of others, these experiences could possibly be an electro-chemical experience of the brain—*self-talk* of the brain. We know that electronic and chemical stimulation of the brain, by LSD for example, can significantly alter our perceptions and simulate *transcendent experiences.*

Since we cannot stand outside of our existence on Planet Earth to observe which comes first—the individual self or the brain—then these questions must go unanswered. We stand again in the presence of The Mystery.

Second: The reported and validated experiences of the *transcendent-self* is just that—it is a self that transcends the individual ego-self. The *transcendent-self* is no longer an Earth style individual self. While various levels of development (of inclusiveness) of the *transcendent-self* have been experienced and validated, the point here is that such validated experiences of a *transcendent-self* and eternal bliss are not those of the individual, ego-self. The transcendent-self is a much larger, all-inclusive self. Thus, if we continue to exist after death, it would be as a self that is radically different from any individual or personal self what we know here in Earth.

While near-death experiences (NDEs) may be the result of neurological processes, don't the numerous similar reports constitute validation of the survival of the individual ego-self after death? It would seem so, except there is one critical difference between the NDE and the basic scientific method to which the experience of the *transcendent-self* conforms. The NDE does not have a common injunction (method or discipline) which anyone can learn and follow in order to gather similar experiential data. Thus the NDE cannot be repeated at will, nor can it be sustained, as can the experience of the *transcendent-self.*

In this whole discussion of human existence after life in Planet Earth, for me, the fundamental questions is, "Is the *individual-self* a meaningful concept or function in any form of existence outside of Planet-Earth based existence?" Descriptions of the most wonder-filled, most *real*, most *alive* experiences of existence are expressed in terms of "oneness with all," "oneness with the Light," "oneness with Life," "one with God," and the like. The more profound life experiences are those which are described as being "beyond the individual self" and in union as some larger source of life. This would suggest that, if there is existence after the death of our Earth-based form, such existence would be participation in a wholeness and vastness that is beyond any individualization or ego-self that we know in Planet Earth.

I suspect one reason that the Kosmos does not seem to regard individual humans with any great preference or importance is that consciousness is fundamentally more than individual, human ego-self existence.

Existence beyond life in Planet Earth, if there be such, will most likely be of an entirely different dimension and nature than life as a human here in Planet Earth. It will certainly be a non-brain-based consciousness. The brain does not survive death. Thus we, Planet Earth life forms with brain-based self-consciousness, have no way of grasping or articulating existence beyond life in Planet Earth. The gap is like a baby trying to grasp mature adulthood. Probably it is more like a tadpole trying to grasp a frog—no, more like a tadpole trying to grasp being the music of a symphony!

Since *life after death* is not objectively known or knowable by the human brain, each person will have to develop their own stance in this matter. Such a personal stance will be based on each person's own direct experience and reflection of *beyond-self.*

The value of a person's experience and stance relative to *after-death* existence is not as an escape into dreaming and planning about what such a life is going to be like—it is not the long-desired "super-weekend with no Monday." The value of our experience of, and understanding about, after-death existence is the benefit that it is to our day-to-day living. Several wise ones of our human history speak of the *afterlife* (the eternal, the bliss, the completeness) as something which we can experience NOW in the present planet Earth daily life. We can begin to participate in "timelessness" in the midst of time. We can begin to experience the "non-spatial" in the midst of space. We can begin to experience the "ultimate wholeness" in the midst of many particulars. Such radical discontinuity, such radical detachment, from the present permits us to engage more vitally, more helpfully, more authentically and more effectively in the present.

As we discover more about how the brain functions, we may be able to clear up some of these questions about *consciousness, self-consciousness, soul, self,* and *afterlife.* As we are better able to ascertain the neuro-electric operations of the brain, we may be able to ascertain whether the brain creates consciousness, whether it receives consciousness that exists apart from the brain or whether there is something else happening.

It was mentioned earlier that the next 200-300 years of human history will likely focus on the human. As one can see, looking through the "cracks in the doors" of this section, there is plenty of work to be done—might even take as long as 400 years. But even as such discoveries shed more light on how we humans function, they can never diminish the fact and the wonder of each of each person improvising the journey that is their life!

E. AN IMAGE

We have been playing with a couple of images to hold our fundamental assumptions about the new individual human. One of these is the *jam session*. The other is the *improvisation dance*. The operative dynamic in both of these is the constant, on-going inventiveness and creativity as we respond, moment by moment, to all the life happenings around us and thus produce the life we have. The word *engineer* has also been used to point to the more intentional aspects of building and revising the person that we are.

Another aspect which I feel the image should carry is that of a *happening*—a human life is a constant happening. The fascinating and wonderful thing about a human is not so much the particular content of the happening as it is the happening of a life itself. The content of human lives runs the gamut from the ridiculous to the sublime; but the happening that is a human is always a wonder to behold.

The word *journey* has been used extensively above to talk about a human's life. Though we can take a snapshot picture of a person's life at any given time, such a picture can never capture their whole, full life. A person's life is a continuum over time, which would take something like a videotape to capture. But, as we noted above, this is not a journey in the sense of a trip to a given destination. Nor is it a trip with a given objective in mind—like to discover a lost gold mine or to capture three live wiggle worms. It is more of an exploratory journey to learn about a new land and how to live. It is a never ending journey.

Maybe we could combine a couple of these words to be an operating image for the human—such as *jammin' journey* or improv journey. I hesitate, though, with *jammin' journey* in that this may be too cute or hip. I hesitate also with *improv journey* because the full phrase *improvisation journey* is just too big a mouthful and the shorten word *improv* may not communicate widely. Another possibility is *creative journey*. This would do, if the word *creative* carries for us the flavor of the *jam session*, the flavor of *create on the spot*. This would do if the word *creative* carries for us the flavor of constantly responding in a variety of ways to all that is going on around us. This would do if the word *creative* does not carry the flavor of the long, studied, production of a work of art which takes special talents and skills.

My heart tells me to use *improv journey*. My head tells me to use *creative journey*. I am going with my heart at this time. The proposed fundamental operating image for the new human is *IMPROV JOURNEY*. An individual human life is an on-going happening that is expressed each moment as one journeys through life.

If you wish, try both of the candidate images and see which one works best for you. Please let me know what your choice would be—or some other image entirely.

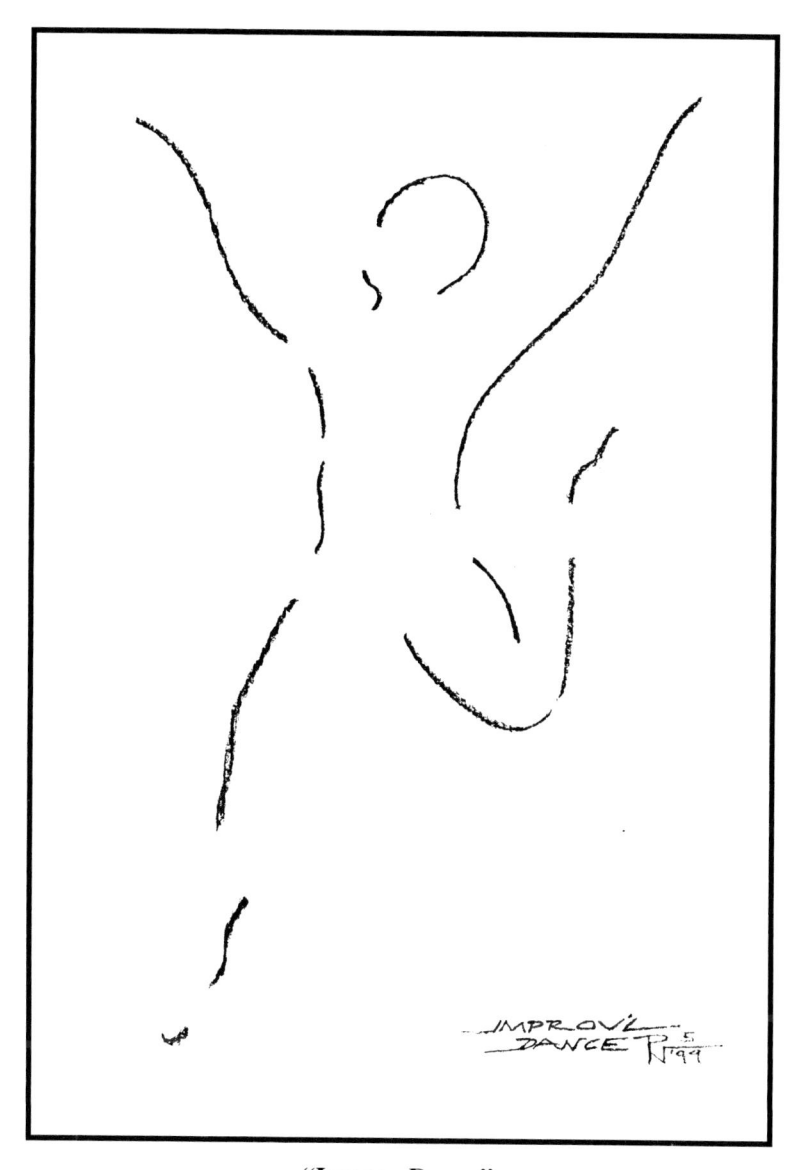

**"Improv Dance"
By Pat Nischan**

Chapter Five

THE HUMAN COMMUNITY

A. THE DIALOGUE—A STORY-POEM
Talk to me!

    What should I say?

I don't know, just talk to me.
I am alone. I am confused.
    I do not know what to think, what to do.
Am I alive? Am I real?
What is life? What is real?
Should I care?
I don't really know who I am.
Talk to me!

    How should I know?

Who does?

    Good question.

What is good? What is right?

How do I evaluate and decide?
What's real and what's fake?

> You're asking me?
> I don't have a clue.

There are so many problems in the world.
Every solution seems to create more problems.
I try to keep to myself, mind my own life—
    so many problems—
        in my life!
What should we do?
Talk to me!

> I'm in the same boat as you.
> You talk to me!

OK. Maybe I'm crazy, but here's the way it comes to me. . . .

> Not bad. What do you think about . . . ?

Interesting. The other day I saw . . . Maybe we could . . .

> I don't know, it seems to me that . . .

You have a point there. I also heard that . . .

> Really! The other day I read that . . .

I think that I'll try . . .

> I think that I'll approach it . . .

Sounds good to me, let's check back next week and see what's new.

> Be talking with you.

This dialogue could have been
    A father and son;
    Mother and daughter;
    Two gals over a beer;
    Two guys over lunch;

> A weekly discussion group;
> A husband and wife;
> Two shut-ins on e-mail;
> A Pakistani and a Kenyan on the Internet;
> Two farmers in Mexico;
> Two corporate executives;
> A group of students . . .

How did it go with you this past week?

> I discovered that . . .
> And you?

It turned out that . . . And did you know that I discovered . . .?

> There's another aspect which I had not thought of . . .

Now that I tried . . . what about . . .?

> This is more complex than we thought.
> This other group said . . .

> "Hey, I've been thinking about that too,"
>   says a person nearby, "May I join you?"

Sure, more minds on this the better.

> Say, Jim, Quang, Rosa, Tamora!
>   you want to get in on this too?

> Sure, why not?

(After more dialogue, it was suggested
        —more likely, it just happened—
    that as a team they could
        come up with a more authentic approach—
            even make some impact on society—
                and they would sure enjoy the whole deal more,
                    whatever the results.)

> You mean that I've got to depend upon you guys
>   and trust you all?

You mean we've got to depend upon you and trust you?

> This would lay some obligation on me.
> I like to do things on my own.
> I don't like to need people and to have people need me.

Hey man, where did you get those chips?

> From the store.

>> How many people does it take
>> for that store to be there for you?

> Well . . .

And where did the store get the chips?

> From a chip factory.

>> And a few trucks and truck drivers.
>> And a few salespersons in between.
>>> Besides, where did the factory get the potatoes?

> From a farmer.

Yeah! In Chile.

>> And a ship and ship operators,
>> a railroad and railroad operators
>> and a few trucks and truck drivers in between.

Where did the trucks and roads,
> trains and railroad,
>> factory and machinery come from?

> Some people or group of people thought them up.
> Other people built them.

>> And where did people learn to do all these things?
>> And how did they keep going when the "going got rough"?

And where did you get the money to buy them?
How is it that your money is good at the store?

> I used a credit card.

>> How many people has it taken and continues to take to enable you to make use of a credit card?

Now, what were you saying about being independent and
>>> not depending on other people??

> OK, count me in. See you next week.
> In the meantime, I'll check out the WEB.

After a few weeks,
> or months,
>> it was noted by one of the team . . . . .

Hey, I could not have thought up all this stuff by myself.

> Neither could I.

>> Neither could any one of us.
>> But together . . . wow!

I didn't know we had so much creativity in us.

> And we sure could not have gotten so much done by ourselves.

Right!
Did you notice how we kept "playing off"
> of each other's contributions?

> Sure did.
>> Building on existing stuff,
>>> Making "leaps" into new arenas,
>>>> Providing a fresh viewpoint . . .

>>>> Yeah. And when we would get "stuck,"
>> someone would always come up with a way to keep us moving,
>>>> provide a "breakthrough."

Awesome!

Come to think of it,
we did not have a leader.

But that logo or symbol sure helped to keep us together.
  Who thought that up?
Sort of made me proud to be one of this group.

And those crazy little things we did and said
to begin each time we got together—
    sure added a bit of class and style.
        How did that happen?

            Now that I think about it,
            they sort of reminded us
            that we were about something more
            than just this task.

What about those times we'd stop and reflect?
Sort of dropped the bottom out of what we were doing;
    connected us with the larger picture of life.

            Maybe the living and
            sharing of living life itself
            is more important
            than the job we were doing.

You think so?

    Could be.
    Anyway, I appreciate just being
            with you guys, and sharing with you.

        What are we going to do next?

Tree? Are you there?

        I'm here. What's up?

These conversations and activities with groups of people are great.
While we are talking and doing,
    I get a feeling that there is something more to living
    than thinking and doing—
        something more satisfying,

            There probably is.

What, pray tell?
What is it for you?
    You just seem to stand there all day,
    soak up water, sunshine and air,
    grow some leaves,
    make some oxygen,
    make some shade,
    wave around in the breeze,
    and shed leaves in the fall.

        True enough.
        But look at it this way—
            I get with the sunshine, air, minerals and water
            that come my way
                (some team, huh?)
            and I transform them . . .
            transform them into leaves and shade,
            transform them into oxygen,
            transform them into branches
                that dance in the breeze,
            transform them into wood that someday may
                build a house, make furniture,
                or warm a body.
        I work with what comes along.
        I transform it into something that contributes
            to the journey of life;
        in so doing,
            I participate in the journey of living.
    Now, that's LIVING!
    I savor every moment of it.

What about other trees, how do you relate to them
    or do you?

        Human child,
            the forest?
            Look at the forest.
            No way could I be a forest by myself.
        It takes a lot of us trees working together
        to make a forest
        and to do all the things that a forest does.
            We protect each other, support each other.

And when I get lonely and discouraged standing here,
    who do you think I talk to?
    Where do you think I
        get all the ideas that I share with you?

Let me see if I am hearing you,
    living is relating as a community,
    working with the ideas and things that come along
        transforming them into a contribution to living,
        being creative in expanding life.
Living is being rooted firmly in the ground while
    reaching for the stars and
    dancing with the wind.
Living is being aware of all this together;
    celebrating all this together.
Is this what you said?

    Yes,
        my fellow journey-person in the adventure of living,
    that's one way of putting it,
    and it will do for now.

Thanks, tree.
    Be talking to you

        And I to you.

Hey, Shanna,
what did you find on the WEB?

    I got some really good stuff
    from the university of Cairo in Egypt.
        This group up in Canada has a great dialogue going
        and I got some stimulating ideas from them.
    An article from Australia will help us a lot.
    A guy in Brazil provided some references that look interesting,
        and I have questions out to them.
    Had a great conversation with a lady in China.

Badri, what did you find out in town?

    I attended three meetings, a conference,

and sat in on two study groups.
I checked out two outfits working on projects similar to ours.
  Their experience will be extremely helpful to us, and
  they were pleased to get an update on our discoveries.
Had coffee with a couple of old friends
  who provided thoughts and references.
While there is a lot of work on aspects of what we are doing,
  no one seems to be putting it together
  like we are
    nor trying to do what we are.
They all can make use of what we come up with.

From the looks of it,
  you'd think we were part of some giant brain—
    variety of sensory experiences,
    observations,
    assimilation at various nodes,
    feedback,
    transmittal to other processing centers,
    creative processing,
    cross processing,
    storage and retrieval,
    updating,
    reflecting,
    analyzing,
    evaluating,
    making decisions,
    initiating action,
    observation, feedback,
    continuous, multi-track processing.

  Do you really think that what we are doing is part of
    some big thinking effort of society?
      Do you think that we are contributing
        to the development of a global mind,
          or at least participating in some global
            minding-like activity?

I don't know;
  but it is conceivable.
    What do you think?
     .

Interesting,
Very interesting.

    Whatever it is,
        I think that we are contributing
        to the evolution,
        to the journey
        of human living and of the world.
Without dialoguing with you guys, I wouldn't have a clue.
    And, besides all this,
           I'm having a *ball*!
           I'm really living—thanks to you all.
    Thank you.

Thanks, and good night, tree.
    Good night, human child.
Thanks and good night, gang.
    Good night, Sharp.

B. CONSCIOUSNESS EXERCISES

- **Your Community:**

The purpose of this exercise is to explore Human Community from your own personal experience with a Human Community. Choose a group to which you belong as the focus of meditation. In a meditative/relaxed state, consider your role in this group, your contributions to it. Now, what do you receive from this group? Next, consider the group's relationship to other groups and to the whole of humanity. What are the benefits and disadvantages of membership in the group?

- **Meditative Council:**

Who would you include in a small group to help you with difficult issues? (This will be your personal advisory council. You may select persons (as well as beings, animals or objects) from any place or time (past, present or future). They may be fictional, family or friends. They may be anyone or anything whose insight or support you would value.) At this time, name the members of your "personal advisory council."

Now, in a meditative state, visualize the location of your council meeting—a round table, an open space in the woods, near a body of water, wherever. Visualize the arrival of each member at this location and greet them. After all are seated, ask their advice, wisdom and input on any subject you wish. Be patient and listen—it sometimes takes a while for our minds to quiet down so that we can hear their responses. Continue the discussion as you would with any close friend.

You can call a close to the gathering at any point. Be sure to thank them for their presence and contributions as all depart.

- **Gifts of Community:**

In a relaxed/meditative state, imagine you are the only human on the Planet. What is life like? How would you live?

Now focus on all the gifts that come from human community—beginning with the language and words you are using to think right now.

- **The City:**

Recall a city with which you are familiar. (Better yet, go to a location on a hill or high up in a tall building where you can look out over a city, especially at night.) In meditation, picture all of the buildings, streets, etc. How did they come to be? Meditate on the water system that provides water at the turn of a handle in every bathroom, or on the communication system that allows one to talk to anyone else in the world. How did this city come to be? What would the region/state/nation be without this city?

• **Talk with a Tree, Rock, Pool of Water, Well or Wise Person:**
This is the same as the last two exercises in Chapter 2, only you ask about the Human Community this time—what is the nature of the Human Community? How does it develop and change? Carry on a lively conversation—speak back, argue, explore wild ideas and above all, **LISTEN!**

C. REFLECTIONS ON THE HUMAN COMMUNITY

1. Fourth Pillar—Community/Corporate Humanness

A human is a community animal. We depend upon interrelationships. Whatever we have, need, or desire for human life is based upon the effort of a group of humans working together. Language, towns, schools, farms, songs, clothes—all take the corporate effort of humans to create. Every individual accomplishment depends upon knowledge and contributions from hundreds of humans of ages past. Even more basic is the deep joy and relief when, in the midst of aloneness, comes the touch, the voice, the face another human. It takes other humans for us to be human. Human identity seems to come from being part of a group of humans. Indeed, before the spread of Western civilization and the rise of the individual as the primary social unit, an individual human had no real identity or importance apart from a human community.

Thus, a major pillar of any cosmic story of life deals with the human community. It seeks to address the basic human questions as: "To what community does one belong?" "Who is *in*?" "Who is *out*?" "What are the roots and destiny of the community?" "What is the role of each individual and how does one fit in?" "How do we live and function as a society?"—that is, "What are the 'rules of the game'?"(In Chapter 4, we looked at these 'rules of the game' from the point of view of the individual. Now we will consider them from the point of view of the human community that is their sociological source.)

The fourth pillar addresses the communal aspect of our lives. After looking at the nature and role of human community in previous eras, we will look at the nature and role of human community in the Ecozoic Age.

2. Previous Human Community

In earlier eras, human communities were relatively stable. Whether tribes, clans, regional groups, ethnic groups, cultural groups or kingdoms, human communities were pretty well isolated from each other. Wherever there was interchange between two communities, there were strong immunities to outside contamination. Changes were few and occurred gradually. It appeared that nothing ever really changed, so people viewed their community as unchanging and secure. Within the larger community, sub-communities and social structures provided extensive means of human participation and interaction. These sub-communities and social structures, as part of the structure of the larger community, shared in the same sense of stability and strength.

Such communities provided identity for their members. The community told each member who they were in the world, and what their personal value was. Communities defined who was a member and who was not, and prescribed the benefits of membership. More importantly, these communities provided nurture and support for their members. The community provided the physical, mental, emotional and spiritual sustenance and support that each human required to live and grow. The community provided and enforced the values, rules, and roles for living as humans.

The community provided a place where people were loved, respected, honored, encouraged, comforted, and cared for. It was a place to grow, to be taught the ways of life, to have give and take in a *safe* environment. A human community was a place where each person had a necessary and significant role to play. One's community provided the sense of *home*—however poor and humble one's position in the community, it was home—a known, comfortable, secure place in life.

The community was also the place where their Story of Life (the religious myth) along with its symbols and "rules for living" were developed, kept alive and practiced. It was around the fires and the tables, at various gatherings and in the many ceremonies that the story was told and retold, the vision shared, the values applied, the rules explained and the journey rehearsed. The community and the myth/story defined each other. In fact, mythic community membership and larger community membership were often synonymous.

Human communities in previous eras operated with mutual trust and commitment. People were committed to their communities and trusted each other to function out of their commitment. People trusted the community to provide support and the community relied upon its people to maintain the community.

Now, all of this is not to say that communities functioned perfectly. They did not. In previous eras communities could be—and were—oppressive, destructive, stifling, unsupportive and ingrown. But, for good or ill, the communities were strong, stable and highly corporate. Survival depended upon it.

With the rise of western civilization, particularly in North America, the individual became the primary social unit rather than the community. Though the power and control of traditional communities were reduced, a multitude of new communities came into being. These were, by and large, volunteer communities—dependent upon the willing participation and support of their members. While providing the basic corporate human functionality, this multitude of communities provided freedom and flexibility for individuals, communities, and society to grow and expand.

Whereas the image of human community in previous eras was stability, its perversion was conformity and control. Whereas the image of the individual in western society was independence and self-reliance, its perversions were "everyone on their own" and isolation—with conformity providing the sense of belonging.

3. New Human Community

a. Global Community

Currently, both the human community and the human individual seem somewhat dysfunctional. Individuals feel frustrated, ineffective, helpless, isolated and ungrounded. Life seems like a big free-for-all marketplace of the survival of the fittest or the luckiest. On the other hand, traditional human communities of all types and sizes are becoming dysfunctional, are disintegrating, or are no longer relevant. With the geographical separation and splintering of extended families, the dissolution of traditional groups and rampant individualism, we live lives of sheer unconnectedness.

As has been noted, we have shown up in a new Kosmos. With the change of basic operating assumptions, previous functional contexts have dissolved, along with the traditional human communities and the social structures that were built on them. As a result, traditional connected relationships among humans are cut. We are left isolated. We can exert our wills, but without connections, the effort goes nowhere.

All of this change seems to be the result of the growth and increased complexity of the human situation rather than the result of degradation and decay. The challenge clearly before us is to give new forms to human community, new expressions to human corporateness that will function well in the new Kosmos in which we have shown up.

Not only have we shown up in a new universe and a new planet as new humans, we have also shown up in a new human community.

The primary human community is now the *global community*. All humans of planet Earth belong first and foremost to the *global tribe*, the *"global neighborhood."* As with all major communities, there are many sub-communities and systems within systems. But the fundamental reality is that the people of Planet Earth are one single community, a single tribe of humans.

This is not surprising. The universe is seen as a single system, an integral wholeness. The planet is seen as a single organism, an integral wholeness. The individual human is seen as a holistic being with all aspects functioning as an integral wholeness. Similarly, humans form a single bio-system, a single holistic community, within the planet.

Though people in previous eras have conceived of such an image and have talked about the "family of humankind," this is the first era for which a global village—a global community—is the functional reality. This reality has been brought about by various recent developments. Instantaneous communication of radio, TV and the Internet not only puts the whole world in my living room, it puts me in everyone else's living room. Rapid and inexpensive global travel creates a steady flow and mingling of peoples. Economically, the world functions as a single marketplace. Science and technology are providing common tools for all peoples. There is a global culture (something more than, and different from, western culture) spreading across the world and engulfing even North America and Europe. The natural resources and environment of the planet are seen as the common inheritance of all peoples. National, political, social, ethnic, ideological and other boundaries are fading. (And people who depend upon such boundaries for their primary identity are ill-at-ease and somewhat threatened.)

Though the global community is our overarching reality, the challenge is to learn how to function in this reality—how to give form and expression to our relations with other humans in our daily living.

Since these questions are yet unanswered, we are in an exploratory mode. It is not an exploration to find what kind of new human community is here. It is rather an exploration to invent, by trial and error, a new human community. We are in an adventure of creating human community. As such, all of our relationships with other humans will now involve a high degree of self-consciousness and intentionality. Let's continue to explore.

b. *Contexts and Dialogue*

It is one thing to realize that we have shown up in a fundamentally different Kosmos in which the previous understandings of the world, humans and life are no longer applicable. It is quite another to develop new functional images and contexts for interpreting and responding to our daily situations. (Contexts include meanings, purposes, values, principals, mores, ethics, social patterns, cultural understandings—the rules of the game, as it were.) Contexts and images are emphasized because once they are established, they are quite naturally given expression in actions and social forms. Without functional images and contexts, there is nothing to express, so actions and forms are random and meaningless. Even more critically, being aware of our own operating contexts and those of others is the basis for cooperation among people.

Traditionally, contexts were fairly stable—usually seen as being provided and enforced by some god or supreme being. They provided a stable frame of reference for daily decisions and actions. Human community was the place where these contexts were passed on, along with the wisdom of how to apply them.

Now, our current universe has added a new wrinkle. Contexts are no longer stable reference points. Contexts are living, shifting and dynamic. As they are put into practice, new experience and new data are generated which update the context. Or our actions expose us to new and different situations that in turn expand our contexts. Thus, contexts are more like *points of departure* for creativity. Rather than firm, fixed frames of reference for social decisions and actions, we have *temporary reference points*, which provide a point of departure and temporary orientation on our journey—both as individuals and as communities.

The challenge for us today is to spin living, dynamic contexts for use as points of departure for creativity. These points of departure will serve as relative reference points until new points are spun into being.

Such spinning, such context developing, such application and creativity, such evaluation of results and re-contexting seem to happen best in community with other humans. Rather than being a place where human culture is passed on, human community now is the place where human culture is invented.

The witness throughout the ages has been and still is that the richer our community life, the richer our individual life. The converse also seems to be true. The richer our individual life, the richer the community life. Being an individual and being part of a group are not contradictory, but complementary. In fact, a person cannot be an authentic human alone. Similarly, there cannot be a strong, vital community without strong, vital individuals as members. There is something about the synergistic effect of individual humans in community that results in power, creativity, and vitality. Each contribution by each individual enhances the whole in a way that releases new and greater responses by others. This synergy is not only among individuals, it is also between the individual and the group. Thus attention needs to be paid not only to how members relate to each other, but also to how individuals and the community relate to each other.

To put it more simply, faced with the challenges and complexity of living in our new Kosmos, it is going to take a extensive dialogue among humans to interpret and to respond to the daily situations life provides. It will take dialogue to develop new operating images, contexts, patterns, decisions, etc. for daily living. It will take dialogue among humans to develop, test, evaluate, and refine new stories, symbols and values. It will take ongoing dialogue to develop, test and refine new models for living—both as individuals and as society. Human community is the place of dialogue about life as well as the place for living that life. We might say, "Where two or three people are talking about life, there is human community, there is life."

Human community is also the place where such life and living are celebrated. It is not easy, and certainly not fun, to celebrate life by one's self. Human community is the place to plan and implement the celebration of the group's effort at meeting the challenges of life.

As the individual human is sensitive, aware, decides and responds to life, so does the human community. It accomplishes this through dialogue among its members. Human community today is a place of give-and-take in exploring the new Kosmos and developing life in the Ecozoic age.

Community is not only a place of corporate dialogue and response, human community is also the place of nurture and support in improvising life—both as individuals and as a group. Relating to life and inventing life, individually and communally, is risky. The process is fraught with doubt, exhaustion and despair, as well as joy, success, and delight—both for us as individuals and as groups. As individuals and groups, we need all the help we can get in the adventure of living. The synergistic dynamic of a human community is particularly powerful and critical in nurture and support. It is in human community that the strength of individuals and of the group intensifies to love, nurture, and heal any manifestation of weakness or pain within the corporate body.

Human community is also the place where things get done. TV programs, sneakers, schools, french-fries, homes and birthday parties all require corporate effort. Social change and social structures also require corporate effort. Again, such effort is the synergistic interaction of human individuals and a human group. The age of the "Lone Ranger" as well as the "tyranny of the group" is past. It is not a case of *either/or*—either the individual or the community. It is the time of synergistic interaction of individuals within a corporate group.

In summary, the synergistic human community is the place where the individual "plugs into life." In the past, community was known as the place of *belonging and source of identity*. Now, community is known as the place for *participation in life*. The main role is spinning contexts of departure and reference points for creating the next step of our life journey—as individuals and as society. Right now *dialogue* seems to be name of the game. Verbal dialogue is not the only form of dialogue. We can also *talk* by means of our drawings, paintings, movement, dances, songs, poetry, movies, and videos. While we all are tired of endless discussions, I am discovering that forced conclusions and premature closure are just as fruitless and just as much a waste of time. Obviously we have work to do on the *how-to* of dialogue.

c. Creating the "Rules of the Game"

My children constantly evaluated my behavior and clothes with comments like, "Dad, you are acting like the '60s; get with it. This is the '90s." Or, "Give it up, Dad, that went out with the '70s." I like to remind them that their children will be saying the same thing to them, "Dad, Mom, you are acting like the '80's, get with it; we are in the 2020s." Or, "give it up, Mom and Dad, that went out with the '90s."

What really "flips" me is to realize that such a conversation is only a fairly recent possibility. People in previous centuries and eras would not, could not, have had such a conversation. Their society changed very little and very slowly from one generation to the next. Cultural values, mores, styles, standards, and codes of all types were thought to be rather permanent. These things were taught to children as the only acceptable way of living. Children taught their children, and so on.

Not to believe and act like one's parents and grandparents was a social disgrace as well as a potential source of disaster for the community. The daily functioning and future well-being of a community depended upon everyone observing the social/religious standards.

The merits and appeal of stability, orderliness and personal identity of such "cookie cutter" societies are strong. But given the new Kosmos in which we live and given what we know about the interchange and evolution of human societies, such eternal *standard rules of the human game* are not feasible or possible in our age. Cultural values, mores, styles, standards, codes, etc. will change constantly as people devise them for their current situation.

This does not mean, though, that there is no need for *rules of the human game*. This has been a false assumption of many people about this freedom from the ways of the past. Society does not function without some rules. Total anarchy in social values, mores, styles, laws, standards, codes, etc. is not a viable or feasible option. (Have you ever noticed the conformity among the non-conformists and rebellious ones? There seems to be acceptable or standard means of not conforming and rebelling.) The Kosmos operates within structured limits and constraints, and summarily dismisses from existence anything and anyone who ignores this reality. Without *rules* there is no *game*. In order to function, to move, to relate as individuals, as families, as communities, as economies, as political entities, as societies, there needs to be common, standard reference points and guidance.

With the old *rules of the game* no longer effective, we are forced to develop new ones—albeit impermanent and relative—to face changing situations. In, and through, us humans, the Earth is creating flexible *rule sets*—more like guidelines—for the *global tribe* just as it created various sets of *rules* for the various tribes and cultures in the past. Through our daily sensitivity, awareness, decisions, and responses to our particular situations, we are creating and improvising the standard values, mores, styles, laws, codes, and the like—as individuals, as communities, as societies, and as a global community. Only today, we know that such standards, such reference points, such guidance, are created by humans and are relative. They are created by humans in response to a given situation and they can be recreated by humans whenever it is deemed appropriate. They are not imposed from *on high*, but grow out of the midst of the people and the situation with which they have to deal. Nonetheless, they are *rules of the game* by which we play.

Creating and deciding such *rules of the game* and doing it fairly frequently, is no easy task. But we do it, for better or worse, all the time. We do it as individuals, as families, as groups, as communities, as societies, as nations, and as a planet. An implication is the need to learn and establish structures for creating, deciding, testing, and implementing helpful *rules of the game* in our families, in our schools, in our businesses and in our society. It could mean significant changes to our current legislative, governmental and judicial structures, which are too slow and unresponsive for rapid, flexible functioning in today's world.

Getting back to the children, while there is no eternal standard set of values, codes, ethics, mores, etc. to teach them and to pass on to them, we do teach them what we parents have found helpful for living. But it is even more helpful to teach them the ability to create their own sets of values, ethics, mores, codes, and rules for living as they journey their lives. Our challenge is to provide them the processes and skills necessary to face new situations and to decide helpful and constructive *reference points* for the journey.

For me, a community is the most effective forum in which to make such decisions about *current, functional rules of operation*. The synergistic operation of two or more persons provides the best chance for a constructive decision about values, mores, ethics, patterns, styles, codes, and the like. The support of fellow humans is needed to persist in the struggle through the *dark night* of such decisions and to validate their result.

In response to the absence of ultimate *rules of the game* and in face of relative, temporary points of departure, many people are seeking to establish new ultimate rules of the game. Many seek to return to cultural the standards of previous eras—to "family and community values of the past," to fundamental Christian values, to the Bible, to Islam, to "native ways," or to "nature" and the like. They all seek to return to some set of values, mores, codes, patterns, rules, etc., which functioned very well at some time in the past—or at least seemed to. (Usually, when examined closely, it is found that these value sets did not work all that well in their day. Memory has a habit of blocking out the unpleasant parts of the *good old ways*.) "If we all could just get back to the basic values of our forebears," they say, "then our lives and society would function properly." Others respond by seeking *rules* in channeled wisdom from the past, in encoded patterns in nature or in our inner being, in cryptic patterns of the stars or of some other objects, or in the words of some guru or of some *guiding spirit*.

Common to these efforts is the attempt to find an external, stable and common standard that will tell us all—individually and collectively—what to do. They think that with a common sheet of music, we will make sweet harmony together. We will then move effortlessly to the desired or planned fulfillment.

This may have been conceivable in earlier ages, in a previous Kosmos. But the reality is we cannot go home to these earlier societies. These earlier *home communities* no longer exist. It is like a person who has been away from the small community where they grew up. They fondly and longingly remember the good, simple life of that community. They long to return to such a good, simple, orderly, predictable, stable, solid life. When they do return to that geographical place, they find the name to be the same, even many of the same buildings and familiar people are still there. But it is not the same community; it has changed. And if they visited around a spell, they would soon discover that they too had changed. The community life in which the person grew up no longer exists. The person who grew up in that community also no longer exists. There is no going home.

Going back to previous *rules* or recapturing the past standards is not possible. The Kosmos, the world and the society of the *good, simple, solid* life with clear eternal standards no longer exists. We have grown up. Our eyes have been opened to the depth, complexity, and constant evolution of life. New people with new ways have moved in. And we ourselves are different people now. We are exploring a new world and creating a new human community in this new world. As part of the process, we are inventing new *rules* for living as humans in this Ecozoic Age.

d. Characteristics of Human Community

The movie *Dances with Wolves* is a story about the intersection of the *gun culture* of the American *white man* of the 1860s and of the *buffalo culture* of the Native Americans of the Plains. In that movie, it became clear that the future lay neither with the *gun culture* nor with the *buffalo culture*; the future lay somewhere else. The future culture awaited creation. At the end of the movie, *Dances with wolves* (the male from the *gun culture*) and *Clenched-fist* (the female from the *buffalo culture*) left their respective cultures, as a committed couple, as a new community, to begin creating the new culture.

The new culture of the Ecozoic age will be created in communities of committed individuals. These individuals will be committed, both to themselves and to one another, to be the journey of life in the new Kosmos—participants in the living planet as improvising humans. While committed communities seems to be the way that any culture has been created, the fast pace and the self-consciousness of the current change makes us more aware of the processes and our involvement in it.

The new thing for us is that the primary community commitment is to the global community not to a particular community. Whenever and wherever they interact with another person (in whatever setting or length of time) they relate as "family." As such they carry on the contextual dialogue, make decisions, engage in actions to give form to the decisions and provide nurture and support to one another.

- *Commitment and trust are primary ingredients for human community.* But commitment and trust will no longer be based on birth, geography, class, organizational membership or any other traditional ways of grouping people. These types of groupings will continue to exist and function, but they are no longer the primary basis of human community. It is the larger commitment to the human journey that makes a person part of the "family," the family of travelers, explorers, and creators of human life. It is this larger commitment that makes for natural and easy groups wherever a person is, for whatever length of time one is involved with others.

The word *commitment* seems to scare people. It is antithetical to the dominant individualism. It cramps one's style. It makes one vulnerable. It allows another to place demands upon one's life. But the growth of an individual, of a group and of society is painful and difficult at times. Developing new contexts and reference points is no simple matter. It is often a knock-down, drag-out affair. Being part of a group is like marriage—it requires a lot of give-and-take among the members. Without commitment a person will not stick with the group through the painful, difficult times. Without commitment, a person will not hang in there through the hard give-and-take of dialogue.

We are not talking *dependency* here. We are talking about the decision to *put one's life on the line* for the group and its members on behalf of the journey. Thus a person is not leaning on others or letting others lean on them. It is not *sucking your life* out of the group or letting the group *suck its life out of you*. Rather it is a joining of your gifts and power with others to enhance and extend the corporate gifts and powers beyond what any one individual could do by one's self.

- Another characteristic of the new human community is that it is a *temporary grouping of people*. The mobility of people, the complexity of current social structures and the inability of any one group to meet all the needs of a person for community, all tend to limit the extent of a person's involvement with any one grouping of people. With the basic commitment being to the journey of life and not to a particular group, a person is able to move with greater ease from grouping to grouping without great disruptions. Thus, a person does not need years and years to become part of a community. One can *plug in* almost immediately, be fully involved for the time one has and then, when necessary, move on to the next situation and a new grouping. In this way, human communities are like temporary *encampments* with people who are *on the journey*. Or they may be like temporary treks or walking together for a phase of the journey.

Previous communities were natural groups of people in which contexts/frames of reference were passed on and a person was *in* until they were put *out*. Now communities are intentional groups of people for developing contexts/frames of reference and a person is *out* until they decide to be *in*.

- While any grouping of people can and does function as a

unit of the new human community, the more that a group is *self-consciously intentional and disciplined* about being a unit of human community, the more enriching and lively it will be. Part of this intentionality has to do with the group's operating vision or mission. The larger a group's operating context or mission, the more helpful it will be to the human and to planetary evolution. Plus, the larger the context or mission, the more significant is one's engagement through that group. (Are we just laying bricks or are we building a local school for global citizens, or expanding the Ecozoic Age educational structures?)

- The new human community is not only reinventing society, it is also reinventing *what it is be a human community*. It is difficult to talk about the form of human community since it is in the process of being created. The main criterion by which the forms will be evaluated is "whether or not they function." The old criterion was "whether or not they fit the pattern." The new forms will be custom-designed rather than standard-designed.
- *Team* is a word that speaks to me about the functioning of community. The word is used too glibly these days, mainly because people have not had not much experience as part of an effective team. For me, a team is a *group of people who are mutually responsible for accomplishing a task*. They take joint responsibility for each other to enable the success of each other as well as the task. They trust and respect each other to make a meaningful contribution, to assume mutual responsibility for the success of the task and to do what is necessary.

The new local human community is a temporary team of individuals committed to the journey. Each team is part of a larger team and finally all are part of the great team, the global team of humans.

e. Human Community and the Human Journey

Humans—individually and corporately—are on a journey. We are constantly creating what it is to live. Human community—dialogue, energy, synergy, power, wisdom, love, affirmation, encouragement, support, nurture, etc.—seems necessary for our journey.

The challenges of participating in a living planet, of living in the Ecozoic age (see Chapter 3) are best met in and by human community. As in early eras of human history, survival in the Ecozoic era will depend upon corporate teamwork. An individual will not, cannot, make it alone. The results are not as immediately obvious as when a hunter-gatherer society confronted wild animals or a devastating winter, but the results will be just as painful—Bosnia (mid 1990s), Israel/Palestine (1960s-90s), and Somalia (1990s) suggest the pain of failure. *Survival Teams* for the Ecozoic age will be bio-socio-economic units of the planet. There are no answers as to the content of the Ecozoic Age—we humans will create them. It will take community dialogue to formulate the new contexts and decisions. It takes community effort to focus the power of individual human efforts to create new forms and structures of society (e.g., social, educational, economic, political, cultural, etc.). It takes a globally contexted human community to sustain and empower the effort to respond constructively to the challenges of the Ecozoic Age. The new planet and the Ecozoic Age are being born and developed. By being alive we participate. The only issue concerns the way in which we will participate.

Not only does a human individual desire all the support, nurture and help of other humans that they can get, somehow a human individual is incomplete without interaction with other humans. As an old song says, "Either love me or hate me but don't ignore me." Remember what happened with the comic-strip character Charlie Brown when he finally met the redheaded girl of his dreams? He did not know what to say or do, so he hit her. Relate we will, one way or another. People are reaching out, unhelpfully as well as helpfully. Note the rise in violence, both domestic and social. Note the phenomena of "12 Step" programs, interest groups on most any topic and Internet chat rooms. We will relate.

The journeys of the corporate human and the individual are not isolated from one another. There is a synergy between the two journeys. There are too many factors, components, and variables to be able to plot the relationship between the journeys. For example, look at the debate as to who or what is responsible for a child's behavior—TV, the school, the family, the individual, poverty, peers, etc. It is clear that today it is not an issue of either one or the other. Both the individual and the community contributes to the journey of each other. To the degree that work on the two journeys could be combined, the more powerful such efforts would be, both for the individual and for the planet.

As we bring self-conscious intentionality to the journey of the planet, the human bio-system and the individual human, intentional human community is a vital component to the journey. Dialogue seems the key ingredient both for the health of the individual as well as the life of the community. Dialogue spins new contexts out of which both the individual and the corporate reflect, decide and act to build the future—both for ourselves as human individuals and as human community.

f. The Evolutionary Edge: Global Minding

In his book *The Global Brain*, Peter Russell developed the image of the human race as evolving to become the brain of the planet (Gaia). According to various brain researchers, the human brain is a living process that is experienced as the human mind and the activity of the brain is called *minding*. Both these concepts were introduced in Chapter 3 where we explored the possible role of the human ecosystem as being the planet's minding process.

I am not a neurological scientist or an expert on the functioning of the brain, nor is this the place to go into any detail on how the brain functions. But as I understand it, the basic operating mode of the brain involves neurological nodes—points of intersection of the brain's messaging system, similar to communication hubs of telephone networks. These nodes are connected to each other in various configurations. These nodes retrieve, receive, send and process various electrical impulses (bits of data) that go into making up a mental result. The nature, content and quality of our brain's activity depends to a large degree upon the number and patterns of connectivity of these nodes, the quality of that connectivity, the functionality of the nodes, the nature and quality of the electronic *message* being transmitted, and other such chemistry between and among these nodes.

The description of the brain's neural electronic network strikes me as very similar to the computer electronic networks being developed today, especially the Internet, linking computers around the globe. But computers are only the means. The content is only as good as what we humans put in.

What really intrigues me is the image that human community units function as the *neurological nodes* of the *global brain*. Human community units receive, retrieve, send, and process various aspects (data, information, knowledge, and wisdom) that go into making up the globe's mental results. Similar to the functioning of an individual's brain, the nature, content and quality of the global brain's activity depends to a large degree upon the number and patterns of connectivity of the human community units, the quality of that connectivity, the functionality of the communities, the nature and quality of the *messages* being transmitted and other such chemistry between these communities.

It would also be interesting to explore the role of individual humans in the image of the *global brain*. They could be seen as individual brain cells and function both as part of a node as well as part of the cortex or other functional areas of a brain. Individuals could also be seen as nerve endings that receive and transmit sensory perceptions of the world and life's situations. Whereas in the brain, cells and nodes are more or less specialized and limited in their functions, humans are versatile and can play various functional roles. Again, this is just a crack in the door to invite more extensive investigation and development—go for it!

While computers are the fastest and most interconnected means of electronic communication, they are not the only means of enhanced communication in our era. Telephones, TV, fax, newspapers, magazines, newsletters, conferences, etc. provide connectivity and the means of sharing *messages* among *nodes* and among individual humans. But with the advancement of the technology of electronic communication, all of these means are being woven together into even faster and more effective means of communication.

But it is important to remember that these technologies are only the MEANS of communication. The important element is the *information* being shared. With the speed and magnitude of developments in all aspects of life these days, potential information is being created in ever-increasing volumes. As a result, it is now recognized that not only is information a basic resource (along with money, property, equipment, personnel and raw material) for productivity. Information is also the primary source of power—beginning with the password. While this is a new development for our era, we are beginning to realize that information has been and is a basic building block of the universe.

With the important role that information plays in the world, I have been disturbed by the imprecise understanding of the meaning of the word information and by the loose way in which the word and concept are often used. *Data* is the basic building block of information. *Data* is a value, plus meaning, e.g., "the 10th month (Oct.)", "10 children", "10 dollars an hour." *Information* is a combination of data in a pattern that resolves a problem—"How many vacation days do I have?" "How much money do I have in my bank account?" "What time is it?" "Who was at the meeting?" *Information is a pattern of data that answers a question.* Everything else is *noise*. When you want to find the telephone number of your friend, the phone number of a good restaurant is distracting *noise*, and the sales price of a new suit is meaningless. When you want to know if there is money in your account for new clothes, the list of all transactions over the last month is distracting *noise*. Thus, all this data which is being communicated and available by the extensive means of communication today is potential information. But, unless it resolves a problem or answers a question for us, it comes as vast, overwhelming *noise*.

The physical universe functions in a similar way. While stars, rocks, plants and animals are full of information (patterns of data), it is meaningful only in specialized situations. The DNA carried by a sperm is a superstructure of patterned data, but this data is information only to the nucleus of an egg cell of its species. To a rock or to a toenail, the sperm DNA data is meaningless and useless.

The developing edge in this era of high-speed communication has to do with patterns of data. The challenge has to do with:
- Making data available for patterning;
- Making data accessible (but not necessarily 'pushing' information);
- Learning how to formulate meaningful questions and problems for the data to resolve;
- Accessing data to create patterns that resolve problems and answer questions;
- And recognizing useful patterns.

Information is not the end of the process. The human mind takes information and develops it into knowledge and then into wisdom. Knowledge and wisdom is information applied within a given context to provide insight and understanding. (Here is that word *context* again.) Not only do humans process information into knowledge and wisdom, the human brain brings self-consciousness to the processing (generating, receiving, applying and sharing) of information.

In fact, one might say that human evolution/history is the result of the flow of information. While individual human minds are extremely good at processing data, information, knowledge and wisdom, several human minds working together do a much better job of processing information, knowledge and wisdom. The high-speed inter-connectivity of modern electronic communication greatly enhances this ability of human minds to develop meaningful patterns of data and to make use of these patterns in generating knowledge and wisdom. Such knowledge and wisdom are also part of the messages communicated between nodes and feed the global minding process. Now expand this self-consciousness and processing power with all human brains functioning as one brain—we can't even begin to imagine the results.

While this analogy of *A Global Brain* cannot be taken too literally or in too much detail, it is useful to grasp the nature of the evolutionary development in which we are participating and of the significant role which human community units play on the cutting edge of evolution. It is also useful to underline the importance of intentional human community units and the dialogue within and among the units to enhance the development of the new human contexts for living in the new universe. This Global Brain image, hopefully, will encourage us in establishing strong community units (nodes) and in developing effective communication between them as our participation on the evolutionary edge of the human race and of the planet. As we are learning how to function in this new universe, I suspect that it will take the power of the corporate human mind to meet the challenge of being the human bio-system in Planet Earth (Gaia).

g. Summary

We have shown up in a new Kosmos. We are exploring and learning how to live in this new world. One discovery is that we are members of a global community—a global tribe. The nature and forms of the sub-community units from families to nations are in the process of being redesigned or created as part of our learning to live and function in the new Kosmos.

With the connectivity and speed of electronic communication, individuals and groups are being webbed together not unlike a giant *global brain*. Such enhanced mode of dialogue, linking the mental capacity of groups and of individuals, begins to function as a *global brain*. This increased synergy of individuals and groups within the global community increases the creativity and power of individuals and groups. This increased creativity and power are needed as we move into the next phase of human and planetary evolution.

D. IMPLICATIONS OF THE NEW COMMUNITY

With the expanded understanding of human community just presented, what are some of the implications for our lives? Since human activity is seldom very logical and often defies even the strongest logic, this section will focus on *challenges* more than *implications*. Below are some particular challenges that have come to mind. Add to the list, share and keep the dialogue going!

1. Commitment

History can and does make use of any community, any grouping of people, from tightly knit traditional local tribes, to nations, to a tailgate party at the football game. History benefits from the sustaining *river* of a strong, ongoing community group as well as the sprinkled *rain* of casual get-togethers.

But the self-consciousness, intentionality and commitment of a group increases its effectiveness as a group and its contribution to life—to say nothing of the increased joy living. The challenge of living today is formidable. To stand present to life as it shows up; to stand within the dualities and tensions and create authentic responses; to push to the edges; to explore all the facets of the new Kosmos and to resist the temptation to escape—all these can best be done in self-conscious community. It takes strong ties among the members of the community to sustain such deep and extensive dialogue, decisions and actions. The tie that binds and holds a community together is self-conscious, intentional commitment and trust. Some basic commitments would include commitments to the human journey, to a basic focus, to each member of the group, to one's self, to the Mystery, and to the process of dialogue and exploration. As a group grows and deepens, other intentional commitments may be added. A related challenge for any group is to find ways (rituals, symbols, practices, etc.) to sustain their commitment.

Two things are being stressed here. First, the effectiveness of a group's dialogue and its impact is relative to the commitment of its members to the journey, the task and the group. Second, being a community is important business. It is a person's means of participating in the evolution of the human bio-system and of the planet.

Some may think that such commitment limits their individuality and their freedom. Quite the contrary. Without structured connectedness individual freedom is meaningless, free-floating energy. Besides, I imagine it is rather lonely and it's not much fun *jamming* by one's self. With structured commitment and connectedness, an individual's creativity is stimulated and has an avenue for effective implementation.

2. Choosing a Community Unit

How does one choose a community unit (group) to which they will commit themselves? Many people look for the *right* group, like people look for "Mr. Right" or "Miss Right." While there is no sure-fire formula to offer for selecting a group, here are some observations.

- There is no *right* group. Even if a person fortunately discovers what seems to be the perfect group, there will soon be the time, if a person is honest, when people or situations in the group are totally disappointing. Participation in a community requires dealing with, putting up with, and working through various weakness and shortcomings of a community and its participants.
- There are likely many groups out there with which a person would be compatible, make a strong contribution, and receive strong support. So, be clear on what you want to contribute to, and receive from, a community. Screen a few, and pick one. Give it a decent try. Then make a decision to stop or to continue. Also, be sensitive to your interior, to your intuitions relative to a group—attraction to a community is most likely not rational or logical.
- We also help to create the group in which we participate. Our participation forms and shapes the group in which we participate. A person can infuse any group with him or herself, with their spirit, their ideas, their energy. Usually in participating, one has more opportunities to participate; in supporting, one is supported; in nurturing, one is nurtured; in adventuring, the group moves. If not, the support, the nurture, the adventuring returns to you and you move on.
- Finally, we participate in several communities at any given time. No one community is likely to provide for all of our requirements/needs for interaction with other humans.

3. Temporary Teams

The major challenge in terms of community over the next several years is to learn how *quickly* to establish self-conscious, intentional, committed communities. These will likely be temporary communities. They may be formed to savor life or to solve a problem. When their purpose or focus is accomplished, they will disband and people will move on.

4. Kosmic Story Community

Within the human community and among the various sub-communities, there is a special community that was referred to above as the *Kosmic Story Community*. This is the community that self-consciously and intentionally maintains the stories, symbols, images, and practices that relate the larger community and its people to the Ultimate aspects of life. Traditionally the religious communities have played this role in the various human communities and cultures of history.

Now that we have shown up in a radically new universe, the previous stories, symbols and images of Life no longer function adequately. As a result, current religious communities no longer function adequately. A new story, new images and new symbols of Life are coming into being.

[But until the new story, the new images and the new symbols are fully in place, the traditional religious communities still have their role to play. The old cannot go away until the new is in place. A "lower level/smaller spiral" of development cannot diminish until the transcending "higher level/larger spiral" becomes stable enough to subsume the functions of the "lower level/smaller spiral."]

Furthermore, traditional religious communities are limited to particular *local* cultures and societies. With the new global community (the global tribe, the global culture) coming into being, traditional religious communities are, by nature and function, parochial. Though each one may claim to be *the global religion*, the other religions stand in witness against such a claim. While it is possible that one of these communities could make the transition to the new story, new images, and new symbols, the *baggage* of its heritage may be too much to overcome for it to be accepted and to function fully as the *Kosmic Story Community* for the global human community. Nonetheless, the new story will likely be told and seen as radically fulfilling the story of each traditional religion.

The new Story of Life will not be "handed down from on high," but will grow up from among the people. An emerging new *Kosmic Story Community* will assist the development of the new Story of Life. As various aspects of the New Story are created, it will gather them, weave them into a coherent Story, and retell the Story. It will gather feedback and enhancements to the story, weave an enhanced story and tell it again. In such a way, this *Kosmic Story Community* will be the midwife of the new Story. At the same time, the new *Kosmic Story Community* will grow with the new Kosmic Story.

This *Kosmic Story Community* will develop the new rituals and practices for rehearsing (the Story of) Life. This Story Community will facilitate the development of new common, global symbols—symbols that relate people to the deep realities of life. This community will also assist people and other communities in applying the new story, images and symbols to the living of life in all its aspects and dimensions. This community will assist in developing the means for support and nurture for our relationship with the Ultimate, with the deep journey of life as well as for the daily journey of living.

As the human community will be creating the new forms and content of community in the Ecozoic Age, so the new *Kosmic Story Community* will be designing and implementing the forms and content of a *Kosmic Story Community* in the Ecozoic Age. It will be self-conscious and intentional about its specialized role in the human community and its responsibility on behalf of the whole Global Community. It will take deep commitment and spiritual skill to fulfill the responsibilities of the New Story Community.

5. Continual Journeying-Learning Units

Every group and organizational unit is a means for community—for context creating dialogue, for building the content of the Ecozoic Age, and for contributing to the evolution of the human race and this planet. Some are very self-conscious and intentional about being a human community unit. Others are not.

As we move further into the Ecozoic Age, I suspect that groups and organizational units will see themselves more and more as journeying communities—*continually* learning, growing, exploring and inventing. No group, no organization, no community unit will ever *have it made, relax and take it easy*. The challenge of living is always present. As members of these groups want to participate authentically in life in all that they do, they will begin asking for continual learning opportunities. Groups/organizations will see continual learning, exploring, journeying is necessary to be effective and viable.

The challenge of the new Human Community—the Global Community—is to expand the self-consciousness and commitment of groups in dialoguing and developing contexts for decision making. A context provides a frame of reference and point of departure for the next steps in the journey of living. Journeying, evaluating, dialoguing and re-contexting are the on-going way of life into the future.

We journey together in a new universe.

E. AN IMAGE

When thinking of an image for the human community, the picture that kept running through my head is that of people sitting around a campfire, talking. They have been on various journeys across the countryside during the day. They have stopped and pitched camp for the night. Others, seeing the fire, join the camp and the campfire. They are talking about the journey and experiences of the day. As they reflect, they learn from each other the nature of the land in which they are traveling and decide how better to journey in it. The next day, they break camp and continue their journeying—some stay together and journey as a core group, others go off on their own or in smaller groups. The next night, as they gather around the campfire, there's a different group of people, dialoguing about life and their journey in it. There are also small groups, each with a common vision and task, who form a team to meet the challenge of seeking a creative solution to the common challenge. They gather around their own fire at night for reflection, support and celebration.

But too many people today do not have much or any experience of hikes through the countryside and nightly campfires.

What I would like to convey in an image for the human community is a temporary dialogue group creating new contexts as points of departure for living our lives, our journey in life.

When no better image came to mind, I stopped and asked *Tree* to suggest an image for human community.

"How about *Global Mind*?" said *Tree*.

"Not bad," said I. "More current, more comprehensive. Have you noticed that the other images have a more dynamic and active feel to them? How about *Global Minding*?"

"That could work."

"*Global Minding* is the activity of a global brain." I suggested.

"Yeah, that would work," replied *Tree*.

So, I offer *Global Minding* as the fundamental operating image for the corporate human, the human community.

The human community, like the mind, is constantly dialoguing with itself about life. The brain processes data and information in and among various nodes and segments of the brain. The brain is not static but very active. Similarly, the human community, in and among its various groups is constantly sharing and processing data and information. Unlike the brain with fixed cells, nodes and sections, humans participate in various groups. Groups form, function, and disband. The participants of one group carry and contribute its wisdom to other groups. The fascinating and powerful aspect of this is the interchange and synergy between various groupings of humans, e.g., political debate, Internet sharing, and break-time conversations at work.

Minding is an ongoing conversation with its environment and with itself. The human community around the world is carrying on a conversation among its components and with itself as a whole. Every conversation, every dialogue that a person participates in is part of the activity of global minding. The deeper and longer a group carries on its dialogue, and the more the group draws from, and contributes to, other groups, the greater the impact that is made upon the *global minding*.

Minding, in and through the brain's nodes, receives input from nerve endings and experiences both pain and pleasure. Similarly, the various human community units receive input from their individual members and others about pain and pleasure as life is experienced. In the group, life is experienced and savored more deeply.

The brain, in its minding activity, processes data, solves problems and creates solutions. The global human community, in and through its various community units, processes data and formulates solutions to life's challenges and problems.

The human community is a global minding effort. Everyone is a participant in it. As a minding activity, the community is experiencing itself and its life—the wonder, the struggle, the joy and the pain of living in the new universe. As global minding, we are dialoging and creating the new contexts and framework for taking the next step in creating life in the Ecozoic age. In every group, we share in the human community, the Global Minding.

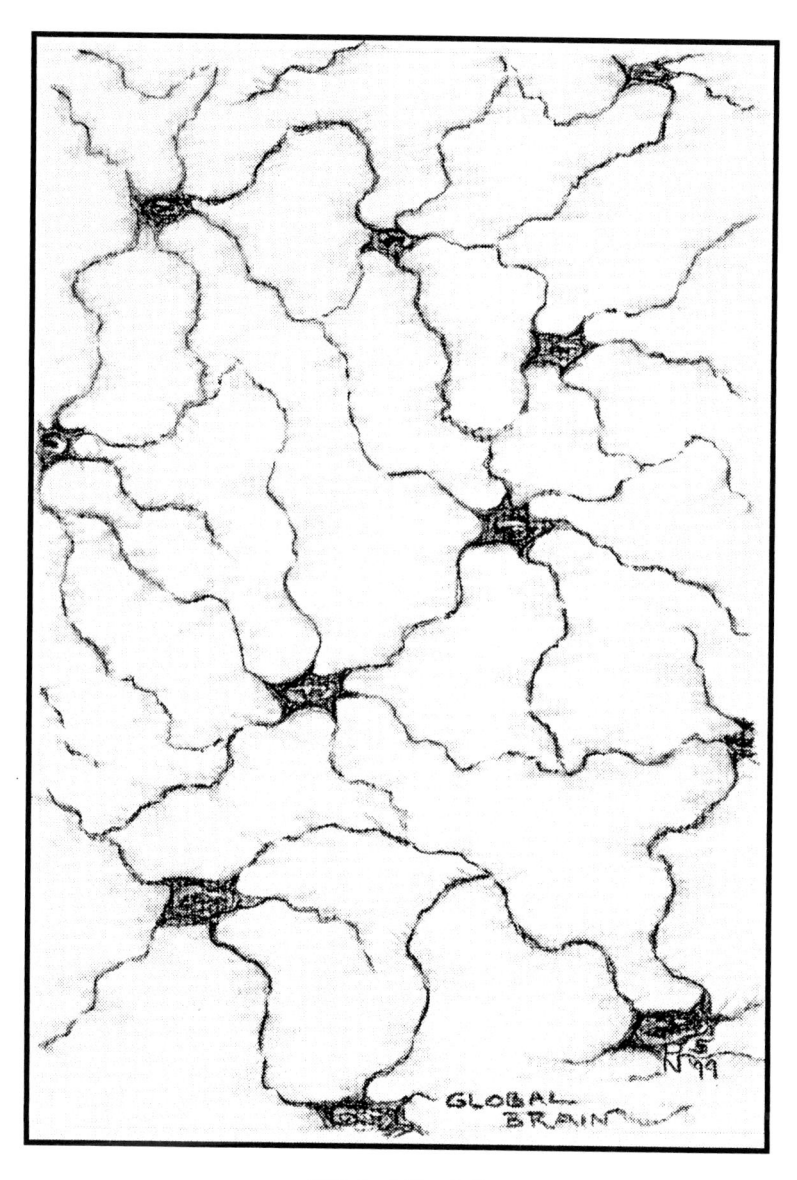

"Global Brain"
By Pat Nischan

Chapter Six

THE ULTIMATE

A. THE WILD WIND—A STORY-POEM

A bare spot of ground;
    a seedling;
        a mighty oak;
            now it is gone;
A great wind snapped it like a twig.

A grandfather's heart rejoices in the birth of a grandson.
    A phone call informs me,
        that after 76 years my grandfather's heart stopped—
            he is no more.

A mother drives her daughter home from school.
    A stray bullet from a gang fight.
        The two paths intersect at a point fatal to the mother.

I am late for the meeting.
    a car turning left jams traffic;
        the traffic lights all turn red as I approach—
            I am late.
I am home alone.

The Adventure of Being Human

My keys are always in my pocket.
    As I return home from a walk to the grocery store,
        I discover I don't have my keys for the locked door.
            Just then my wife drives up
                from a trip to Philadelphia,
                    returning three hours earlier than normal.

The table is set perfectly,
    the pot roast is superb,
        the wine sparkles—
            the evening is flat.

The electricity goes off before the dinner is done,
    and we finish it on the camp stove;
        the wine bottle drops and breaks,
            the beer is warm and there is no coffee.
                Three extra people arrive.
                    Wow, what a glorious evening!

Shall I speak of flowers, birds, mountains, storms, stars—
    from their miraculous birth
        to their eventual destruction?

What is the source of all these things of which I have spoken?
    What is the source of the life,
        the wonder,
            the pain,
                the failure,
                    the fun?
What is the source
    of death,
        inconvenience,
        success,
        joy?
                Chance?
                Fate?
                Unknown pattern of causes?
                God?
                The Devil?
                The Force?
                The Unknown?
                The Unknowable?
                The Unknown Unknown?

Whatever the source,
    Is it my friend?
            or is it my enemy?
    Is it for me?
            or is it out to get me?
    Or does it even care?

A mysterious wind blows,
    and things come into being,
        things happen—
            galaxies and stars,
                a living planet,
                    a flower,
                        dinosaurs,
                            a wedding,
                                me.

A mysterious wind blows,
    and things go out of being,
        things don't happen—
            stars,
                dinosaurs,
                    a flower,
                        a wedding,
                            me.

A wind,
    a wild wind blows,
          sometimes as a gentle breeze,
          sometimes a mighty gale.
A wild wind blows—
    its power pushes and pulls our lives this way and that.
A wild wind blows—
    its power builds Berlin walls and tears them down.
A wild wind blows—
    it enlivens
    a plant, a cup of tea, a mutation of a species,
        the words you speak, the picture you see.
A wild wind blows—
    it deadens
        the taste of food, the glow of stars,
        the advance of a species, the flame of love.
A wild wind blows—

success appears where none seemed possible.
A wild wind blows—
    failure appears where none seemed possible.
A wild wind blows—
    and I am filled with yearning, desire, care.
A wild wind blows—
    and even the fulfilled yearning,
      the fulfilled desire and the fulfilled care
        go flat.
A wild wind blows—
    and happiness and joy depart.
A wild wind blows—
    and happiness and joy appear.

How can people, organizations, nations, societies
    be so brave, so courageous and so brilliant?
      A wild wind blows!
How can people, organizations, nations be
    so stupid, so cowardly and so fearful?
      A wild wind blows.

Mysterious Power blows life this way and that,
    Ultimate, Uncontrollable Power gives and takes away—
      pure fear and fascination is generated.
In fire,
    in mountains,
      in the stars,
        in the lotus flower,
          in the trees,
            in the sun and Moon,
    that Power has been sensed and experienced
      by people of old.

Today,
    that power,
    that Mysterious Force,
    that Wild Wind
        is most strongly experienced in
people,
    especially in large masses of
people.

People—
what power!
    to destroy,
    to tear down,
    to pollute,
    to contaminate,
    to mess up,
        lives and eco-systems!
what power!
    to hurt,
    to hate,
    to cause suffering and pain!
People,
    seen as the source
        of most of life's problems!

People—
what power!
    to create,
    to build up,
    to clean up,
    to heal,
        lives and eco-systems.
People—
what power!
    to love,
    to ease pain and suffering.
People,
    to them we look
        to solve most of life's problems.

People . . . what power!

People—
    how fearful and threatening to my being!
Look into their eyes—
    the eyes of the beggar, the CEO,
        the student, the grandmother!
Look into their eyes—
    the eyes of the African, the Mexican,
        the Chinese, the French,

the Indian, the Arab, the American...
They present so many different ways
    of approaching and organizing life,
  each different way
      challenges my own neat little world.

People—
  how fascinating and enlivening to my being!
Look into their eyes,
  feel their touch,
  hear their affirmation,
  sense their support—
    a smiling child,
    a loving spouse,
    a trusted team member,
    a twinkle in their eye,
    a hug, and
    the whole cheering mob.

People!
  Such fear and fascination.
  Such uncontrollable power.
People!
  They are not the Mysterious Force.
    They are just where we experience it.
We flee the cities where it is so focused.
We are attracted to the cities where it is so focused.

Ah! the Mysterious Force!
  The Wild Wind blows!
    My life crumbles;
      My life rises from the rubble,
        greater, more wondrous than before.

The issue is not the particular situation
  in which we find ourselves—
    that was blown to us by the Wild Wind.
Little Johnny's baseball broke the window.
  That cannot be changed.
  We have just been given a broken window.
We have been given a "C" on the test,
  a dog mess in the kitchen,

> a word of praise from the boss,
>> a traffic jam,
>>> a cold beer.

The essence of our life is not the givenness of a situation.
The essence is how we decide to relate to that situation.
> Our anger
> or our joy
>> is part
>>> of the givenness to which we relate.
> I can decide to yell at Johnny.
> I can decide to beat Johnny.
> I can decide to ask him to sweep up the glass
>> and help repair the window.
> I can tell his parents and ask them to pay.
> I can say nothing to Johnny and fix it myself.
> I can let it ruin my day.
> I can reflect on my neighborhood ball games as a child—
>> and the windows we broke.
> I can use it as a chance to get to know Johnny better.

I can decide to respond in various ways.
> And that response determines the quality of my life.

Most fundamental of all
> is the relation
>> that we take
>>> to the giver of the situation—
>>>> the Mystery,
>>>> the Wild Wind.

The choice is simple.
> I can reject the situation—
>> I can complain and blame;
> Or I can say "thanks"—
>> accept the situation,
>>> use it,
>>> respond creatively.

Yes,
> the choice of relating to the given situation
>> is simple—
>>> bitch or dance.

The quality of your life
> turns on that simple choice.

The laundry is there to be done.

You can leave it.
You can do it
    and complain the whole time.
You can do it
    and explore
        the wonder of how each piece was dirtied,
        the wonder of the ingredients in the soap,
        the wonder of the marvels of a washing machine.
in that decision is
    damnation
        or salvation,
    a bitchy hell
        or a heaven of adventure and wonder—
the choice is yours.

The Wild Wind blows—
    situations come and go—
We relate
    and relate—
the quality of our life rides
    on how we relate
        to the Giver and Taker
            of life situations.
The Wild Wind blows!

B. CONSCIOUSNESS EXERCISES

The following exercises are provided as a means of experiencing The Mysterious Force more directly and personally. They are opportunities to visit and reflect with the Wild Wind.

- **The Wind:**

In a relaxed, meditative state, visualize a wind blowing. It may be a gentle breeze or a strong, powerful wind. Stand in the wind. Feel it on your skin, in your hair, through your clothes. As you stand there, it may change—stronger or gentler. Sense it. Where does it come from? Where does it go? Let it speak to you.

- **A Cloud:**

In a relaxed, meditative state, visualize a cloud or a fog surrounding a mountain or over water. Focus on it; contemplate it. What is inside? Behind? How do you "grasp" it—literally and figuratively? Continue to contemplate it.

- **A Storm:**

In your relaxed, meditative state, visualize a storm, a mighty storm—a snow blizzard, a hurricane, a tornado, a rainstorm. Stand in the midst of it as best you can. Feel its power and force. From whence does it come? Why? What does it mean to be human in the midst of this? What is happening here? Let the storm speak to you.

- **Positive Moments:**

In a relaxed/meditative state, recall a moment in your life when you experienced vibrant aliveness or exquisite joy. Visualize that moment—what is the setting? Who is involved? Savor it. What forces are operating there—physical, emotional, mental, cultural? Follow one of these forces to its source. What is the source of life/liveliness in you?

- **Negative Moments:**

In a relaxed/meditative state, recall a moment in your life when you experienced deep pain, deep "darkness," intense hatred or fear or anxiety, sickening evil—a really bad time in your life. Visualize that moment, return to it—what is the setting? Who is involved? Hold it close as you would a small hurting child. What forces are operating there—physical, emotional, mental, social? Follow one of these forces to its source. What is the source of pain or misery in you?

- **The Other:**

With your index finger, touch the index finger of another person—either physically or in a visualization. Sense the Mystery (The Other) in this other person.

- **The Masses:**

In a relaxed, meditative state, visualize masses of people—like a city full of people or thousands of people at some gathering or however you can imagine huge numbers of people. Contemplate a mass of people. Sense their power. Sense your fear and fascination of these people. What attracts you to them? What repulses you from them? Continue to sit in contemplation of masses of people.

• **Talk with a Tree, Rock, Pool of Water, Well or Wise Person:**

This is the same as the last two exercises in Chapter 2, only you ask about The Ultimate/The Mystery this time. Ultimately, what is real? Ultimately, what is going on? Ask any questions that you have about Ultimate Reality. Carry on a lively discussion—speak back, explore wild ideas and above all, LISTEN!

C. REFLECTIONS ON THE ULTIMATE

1. The Fifth Pillar

Wandi, a ten-year-old girl in a Central American jungle of 1038 A.D., screams. A snake has bitten her. She dies before reaching her home. Is that all there is for Wandi? Is this just another young living thing that happened to die early, just like a young plant trampled by a grazing cow or a young rabbit killed by a fox? Or is there something more—something beyond dying—for Wandi?

Life seems to mock us humans. For all our evolution, our greatness, our achievements, our uniqueness, we die just like a cow or a fish. A person's life is a nanosecond blip in the life of the universe. Our efforts seem futile. Is there more to life than eating, sleeping, working and dying?

There is an emptiness within us which cannot be filled with anything known. There is an incompleteness about our lives. There is an indefinite longing for something more. Is there more?

Who I am, ultimately?

What should I do, finally?

How be I, really?

We look into the clear night sky, at the stars, at the darkness beyond. What is the source of the universe? Of the planet? Of us humans? Where did it all come from—originally? Ultimately? Why these energy forms, at this time and in this place? What sustains the universe, the planet, us humans, and all the other forms and patterns of energy—ultimately?

So much of what happens is inexplicable—describable, but inexplicable. So much is unpredictable. There are forces and powers operating in the universe over which we have no control—that we do not even understand.

We fear the unknown and the uncontrollable forces of life, both creative and destructive. We want greater power over these forces. We want the controlling power on our side, or at least not against us. We are also fascinated with the unknown. The overwhelming wonder and enchantment of life attracts us. We want to be associated with the controlling force of this dimension of life.

Is there something controlling or guiding this whole show of existence? Are there "higher beings" or "guiding powers?" Whether there are or not, it seems that there should be. What is beyond the here and now? What is deep within it? Ultimately? When all is said and done, what do we finally have to deal with? Ultimately?

These questions arise in the midst of our daily lives and come to us in the stillness of the night. Eventually, everyone asks these questions about the ultimate—
  the ultimate power,
    ultimate reality,
      just **THE ULTIMATE.**
The effort to answer the Ultimate Question forms the fifth aspect of traditional Kosmic Stories.

Previous Kosmic myths provided answers to the question of The Ultimate. These stories began with a "face of God." This "face of the Ultimate" was the source of the Universe, of the Earth and of Humans; the Ultimate sustained them all. It was also their ultimate conclusion.

In this new Kosmic Story of Life, I thought best to begin with what we know and experience. It is in the midst of the mundane that we experience the supra-mundane. It is in the midst of the ordinary that we experience the extra ordinary. It is in the midst of the known that we experience the unknown. It is in the midst of the particular that we experience the Ultimate. For us, it is in the midst of the known Universe, Earth, Human Individual and Human Community that we experience whatever we decide is their Source, their Enlivener, their Sustainer, and their Conclusion. The other pillars have set the stage to be able to explore The Ultimate.

2. Previous Faces of the Ultimate

From the earliest of times, humans sought to answer the Ultimate Question, to identify the Ultimate Power, to explain the Ultimate Reality, to give a human face to The Ultimate.

Humans were awed by the wonders and forces of life—birth, death, and the precariousness of life itself. What was the source of life? What took life away? They were threatened by wind, storms, floods, cold, heat, drought, fire, and wild animals. They were inspired by the sun, rains, flowers, stillness, gentle breeze and a loving touch. What was the source of these forces and what controlled them?

In dancing flames, awesome mountains, searing deserts, luscious rain forests, rolling seas, starry heavens, fertility and death humans experienced fear and fascination. What was the source of such power? It had great impact upon their lives, both positively and negatively. This power was very strong and capricious. How could humans relate to this power so that it would help and not destroy them?

The answers to these questions, which provided the content for this pillar of their Kosmic Myth-Story, took the form of some supreme being or beings—Allah, Yahweh, Krishna, Shiva, Zeus, The Great Spirit, Goddess of Mercy, Iris, Ra, Earth Goddess, etc. These gods and goddesses were set forth in terms of a supreme leader or an ideal human within the culture or society in which the story grew. Mid-Eastern gods resembled desert clan sheiks. Tribal gods resembled tribal chiefs. Greek gods and goddess resembled ideal Greek humans. Chinese gods resembled Chinese warlords and emperors. Fertility goddesses resembled ideal mothers and matriarchal leaders. Each culture modeled its gods and goddesses according to its own social structures and character traits. The realm in which these beings lived and functioned was described in terms of the society's idyllic vision. Furthermore, the characteristics, values, and responses of supreme beings were described in terms of human characteristics, values, and responses similar to the culture of the people telling the story. These supreme beings were associated with places the storytellers deemed awesome. For some it was fire, for others it was mountains, for yet others it was the stars and the heavens. Later, by association, it was temples.

The more enlightened tellers of these stories were aware of the inadequacy of human words, images, expressions and forms to describe a being and a realm which were radically other than the human realm. Yet, they were aware of the necessity to point to the force that was beyond human comprehension but acted upon human lives with such profound impact.

Some societies moved beyond ultimate beings and beyond a human "face of god," talking instead of ultimate concepts. Some developed stories of an ultimate spirit that functioned in and through all things. Others developed stories of an ultimate way-of-being. But, because they were so esoteric, these ultimate spirits and way-of-being were surrounded with gods and goddesses who were go-betweens for humans as well as managers of Earthly affairs. Also, because of the common desire of people for the tangible, the spirit worlds were filled with very particular structures and standards that mirrored Earth's. While these general principles of *Ultimate Spirit* or *Way-of-Being* may contribute to the understanding of the Ultimate in any age or place, their particular context and content are subject to the limitations of all previous stories of the Ultimate.

The lives, functions, and mode of operation of these gods and supreme beings were described in terms of the Universe, the Earth, the Human Individual and Human Community as these were understood by the era in which the stories were developed and told. In fact, the stories about these supreme beings were the vehicles for explaining and communicating a society's understanding of the Kosmos, as well as their answers to the ultimate questions. These myths were a society's way of communicating its collective world view and wisdom about the most effective way to function in that world.

With the disappearance of their initial Kosmic contexts, these gods have lost their vitality. The previous understandings and stories of the Universe, Earth, Human Individual and Human Community are no longer adequate. Therefore, the gods and the stories associated with them no longer provide suitable answers or assistance to people who now live in a very different Kosmos.

Efforts made to modernize these gods by translating them and their story into the present age are just that—translations or explanations. The process can be likened to explaining a joke whose punch line was missed; a person may appreciate its humor but they cannot experience the spontaneous laugh. The same goes for the gods and the images or poetry associated with them. An explanation cannot provide the authentic experience. The power of these gods in previous times was that people EXPERIENCED them! The language used to describe the role and functioning of these gods was the language of everyday life. These terms spoke directly to the lives of people and evoked a direct response. Today's translations produce a secondhand understanding, but not a direct experience—which is about as exciting as secondhand love.

More recently gods or supreme beings have been replaced in some societies by physical cause and effect (the natural laws) or by a combination of randomness and natural laws. But such stories are inadequate to explain all the aspects of the Universe, Planet Earth, Human Individuals or Human Community as we currently experience them. There is just too much serendipity, too many gaps in the equation where a *miracle happened*, too many "one in a trillion chances" which cannot be explained by these methods. Humans sense that their lives are more than just the outcome of an equation or the "roll of the dice." We sense that our future (individually and collectively) is more than the result of mathematical probabilities or set of instructions whether embedded, encoded or activated by some other operative mode. Modern science now concedes that ultimate reality is outside of its domain. In fact, modern science is becoming aware that its methodology is based upon unarticulated assumptions about the Ultimate. Modern science is also becoming aware that it uses poetry (symbolic words) and myth-like expressions to articulate its discoveries. One of the results of science and rationality is to bring us to the edge of a great, dark abyss—The Ultimate!

3. The New "Face" of The Ultimate

What is The Ultimate? What is that which we ultimately must face?

The task of naming and describing this pillar is uniquely different and more difficult than naming and describing the other pillars. For the other four pillars there was something to name and describe (e.g., stars, water, plants, nations and human relationships). In each of these previous four pillars there is something that impacts our sensors, something to be measured and objectively verified. We can send forth stimuli to them and receive feedback stimuli from them.

But for this fifth pillar, there is nothing there. There are no sensations. We send forth various stimuli and we get no feedback. We ask questions; we seek signs; we cry into the darkness. There is no feedback. There is no answer. (Oh yes, we, and others, sense some kind of "answer" at times, but it is not independently, "objectively" verifiable and it is not repeatable by others.)

So how do we describe that which is "not here" and "not there?" How do we talk about that which by definition is the source of all things, but cannot be a thing itself? We begin where people have always begun in identifying the Ultimate—with our experience of it.

a. At the Edge

One thing we do experience is the edge of our experience. We experience an area of life where there should be something but we experience nothing. We experience a place where something seems to be operative, but we have no direct experience of it—only an indirect experience by inference.

Since the Ultimate is not "some-thing," we might say that the Ultimate is "no-thing"—the great NOTHING. The flip side is that the Ultimate encompasses everything—both known and unknown. This has led some to say that the Ultimate is the ALL, or the TOTALITY, or the UNITY, or the ONE. As a combination of the NO-THING and the ALL, some have spoken of the Ultimate as the NAMELESS ONE. Others use the term VOID—the total emptiness that contains the total fullness.

Some come to the edge and experience the absence of everything—the DARKNESS. Others come to the edge and experience the presence of everything—blinding LIGHT.

Another approach is that the Ultimate is radically different—is radically other than us humans and existence as we know it. It is not just past the edge of experience, it is a totally different realm of existence. Thus, the Ultimate has been described as The OTHER or even the Radically Other—the TOTALLY AWESOME ONE that blows away any and everything a person has considered real.

We also experience the Ultimate at the beginning and the end of existence as we know it. Words like the SOURCE, the GIVER OF LIFE and the CULMINATION have been used to describe the Ultimate. Similarly, the Ultimate is experienced as the SUSTAINER of life. But that which gives life also takes it away. And so people have spoken of the TAKER OF LIFE or the DESTROYER. Together, as the source, sustainer and end of all existence, the term GROUND OF BEING has been used to point to the Ultimate. As some people examine the workings of the Universe, the Planet Earth and Human lives, they notice a NUMINOUS quality at work. This is an unexplained agent, ethereal or spirit in nature that is beyond what is observable, but present in all things. A common word used to describe these various experiences at the edge is "MYSTERY." Such "MYSTERY" is more than something that is presently unknown. It has to do with that which is not knowable by our senses and that which we do not know that we do not know.

What launched the Cosmos?
    Some MYSTERIOUS FORCE!
What brings into being the particular energy patterns from stars to snowflakes to unique humans?
    Some MYSTERIOUS FORCE!
What brings an end to stars, to eco-systems, and to unique individual humans?
    Some MYSTERIOUS FORCE!
Where does it all come from ultimately? Where does it all end ultimately?
    At both edges: The MYSTERY.

b. *In The Midst*

Whereas the experiences of the Ultimate at the edge may be somewhat abstract and infrequent, the experiences of the Ultimate in the midst of our daily living are direct and frequent. In the midst of life we experience the impact of a force.

Daily we are pushed and pulled to live; we are driven to provide for ourselves and others, to achieve, to grow, to know and to improve. Some force drives us to care about life. At the same time, we are confronted by limits and constraints on our living. For all our providing and preparing, our lives are never secure. There are limits to our caring. We all know the truth of the sayings such as "The best laid plans of mice and men often go astray," and "If something can go wrong, it will."

Daily, we are driven and limited by some force. There are so many things which we are driven or attracted to accomplish and which we are not able to do or to complete. We want to jump higher, to run faster, to read more, only to hit the limits of what we can do. We are driven to know, only to experience knowledge's limits. We are driven to relate to others, to love and be loved. Yet, in spite of close relationships, for which there never seems to be enough time, we often experience being alone. We are pushed to avoid the painful and are pulled to seek pleasure. Pleasure does not last long enough, the painful lasts too long, and there is no "control knob." In such situations we experience a power, a force—a MYSTERIOUS FORCE.

In the midst of our lives, we experience many things happening coincidentally. We experience times of serendipity—things just happen, come together, in a wonderful, inexplicable way. People, things, answers, resources, help, etc. just show up unexpectedly at the right moment. MYSTERIOUS FORCE is experienced. Conversely, we experience things going wrong in a frightful, inexplicable series of mishaps. People, things, answers, resources, etc. don't show up as needed or desired. A MYSTERIOUS FORCE is experienced.

Lives are lifted high or dashed low without any consideration of human values or concerns, without so much as an "excuse me!" A bumper crop here, a killer drought there. A tornado levels one house and leaves the next untouched. A young, healthy, brilliant life is struck down. A mean, cranky, sloppy life lives to be 95. A MYSTERIOUS POWER is experienced.

There are times when we are permitted to experience great beauty. Other times there is only dreariness and drabness. There are times of great insight and clarity. Other times only dullness and fog (ask any writer or poet). A MYSTERIOUS FORCE.

Whenever we push and explore any aspect of life to its depths, we drop into a vast hole of overwhelming complexity—MYSTERY.

People of old often identified a primary location or situation where they experienced the mysterious in an overwhelming way. For some it was fire. For others it was the night sky or a scared mountain. For yet others it was a lotus flower or a tree. Today, we experience the mysterious force most deeply in other humans.

Whom do we blame for the world's ills and society's problems? Humans. To whom do we look for solutions to these ills and problems? Humans. What is our greatest enigma? Humans—some we can't live with, some we can't live without and none that we can fully understand. Notice how people are attracted to cities—great masses of humans? Notice how people flee in fear from cities? The magnitude of human power—to create and to destroy, to love and to hate, for brilliance and for stupidity, for complexity and for simplicity—is a source of profound fear and fascination. The *otherness* of people threatens and attracts. Just spend some time in another culture and you will notice your irritation with the ways they think and act. Their other-than-our-ways threatens our own, customary ways. And yet it is the *otherness* of people which holds a deep attraction for us.

The vast cosmos as a whole and Planet Earth in particular are places for experiencing great fear and fascination. But human beings—with their love and kindness, hate and stupidity, extreme complexity and unpredictability—are a means of experiencing supreme fear and fascination. Humans constantly break open our comfortable, complacent lives and provide opportunities to expand our lives and to mature.

c. The Quest Goes On

At the edges of life and in the midst of life, we experience the effects of a Mysterious Force. I would suggest that the reply to the ultimate question is *The MYSTERIOUS FORCE*.

This is not an answer. The Ultimate Question cannot be answered, cannot be wrapped up. My experience of life is that whenever I think that I have the answers and have life all wrapped up, something pulls a string and it all comes unraveled. I am left with more questions, and the quest goes on. For now, I am recommending *The MYSTERIOUS FORCE* as a temporary "face of the Ultimate."

In the previous eras, learning was in the format of *question and answer*. There was first a question for which a person sought and learned the correct answer; then there was another question, the answer to which was learned; and so it continued. Tests determined how well a person had learned the proper answers—

    question, answer;
        question, answer;
            and so on.

The answers were then evaluated as correct or not.

In the Ecozoic era, the response to a question is another question. Now, learning will be in seeking the next question. Tests will be composed of questions followed by questions—

    question, question;
        question, question;
            and so on.

The MYSTERIOUS FORCE, as a response to the ultimate question, is basically another question. It is an invitation

to explore,
> to go questing,
>> to seek the unseekable,
>>> to find the unfindable,
>>>> to struggle and wrestle with life
>>>>> and with its questions,

to go beyond,
> to expand,
>> to push the limits,
>>> to risk,

to create,
> to dance,
>> to journey.

d. Quality of Life Depends on Relation to the Ultimate

The search for a more adequate "face of God" is not an academic question or an esoteric concern of philosophers or religious professionals. It confronts us every time we wish that we were somebody else or that some things about our life were different. It is raised every time we complain about life. Underneath it all we are asking, "Why couldn't it have been different—better—than what I have?" Half facetiously and half seriously, we are wont to ask "Where do I go to exchange my life for one that works better or at least get a refund? Who's in charge here to whom I can give my complaints and/or suggestions for improvements—or at least get a satisfactory explanation for the way my life is?"

The question of the "face of the Ultimate" comes every time we are overwhelmed by success, by beauty, by affection from another human, or by the pure wonder of existence. It is raised every time we are having fun or we are happy. "Where did all of this come from? Whom do I thank? Why can't life have more of these pleasant and wonderful times?"

Sooner or later we grasp what we have always suspected—we cannot provide or ensure either protection from the undesirable happenings of life or the presence of the very desirable happenings of life. These things just happen. Why? The givens of life are just that, given—given to us by the Mysterious Giver of Life. The Mysterious Force—in and through the workings of the Universe, the Planet Earth and Humans—provides the life situations that we have. You see, it is not possible, at any single moment, to have any other life or situation than the one that we have at that moment.

Deeper reflection, by many people, on the non-satisfying as well as on the satisfying experiences of life reveals that the satisfaction or dis-satisfaction have more to do with the person's relationship to the given situation, rather than with the content or nature of the situation. It is not so much an issue of the situation being pleasant or unpleasant that makes for a satisfying or non-satisfying experience. It is more an issue of how a person relates—affirming or rejecting—to the given situation that makes for a satisfying or non-satisfying experience. This is more than an emotional or instinctive reaction of like or dislike. This has to do with a person's basic stance about life—affirming or rejecting. Even more fundamentally, it has something to do with a person's basic relationship to the Ultimate, to the Mysterious Force. Is our relationship a positive one or a negative one?

The response to the Ultimate Question has not only to do with the "face of the Ultimate" but also whether that "face" is a "friendly face" or not. Is the Mysterious Force for me or against me? People find that with a positive answer to this question they have a satisfying life, no matter the situation in which they show up. People with a negative answer to this question find life to be non-satisfying, no matter what the situation in which they show up.

Our lives and their current situation as they are at any given moment are the result of the Mysterious Force. This said, we have two basic choices:

- We can blame and complain about our situation; or
  we can be pleased about it.
- We can reject it, wishing life would be different; or
  we can accept it and appreciate it as it is.
- We can try to run, hide, and escape from our life and our
  situation; or we can deal with it.
- We can live our life; or
  throw it away.

When the MYSTERY has given us lemons, we can complain and throw them away; or we can make lemonade. Which would be more satisfying? It's our choice.

The dishes need to be washed. I can try to run and escape. I can wash them grudgingly, or I can wash them as a gift that may reveal something interesting about life. Which would be most satisfying? My choice.

My hair is gray, my face is wrinkled, my body is growing weaker. I can sit around and wish I were younger and stronger, or I can be a fantastic elderly person. Which would be more productive and exciting? The choice is mine.

And those other people—so different, so disturbing, so uncomfortable to be around—their way of life calls into question my "world" and my way of life. Do I reject them and try to hang on to my way of life or do I seek to relate to them and to expand my life? Which would be more lively and interesting? The choice is mine.

The quality of our life –
>being a complainer or being one who is pleased with life,
>being a nay-sayer or being an affirmer of life,
>wishing life were different or dealing with it—

depends upon our choice as to how we relate to the Ultimate. If you do not believe that there is a real difference in your life based on how you make this choice each morning, just ask a member of your family, a co-worker, or a friend. They can tell if you are living that day as one who is embracing life or as one who is rejecting life.

This is a choice that we make constantly. We make it over and over, day in and day out. Every time life gives us a new situation, we make the choice anew. But the choice that we make is enabled by a basic commitment about the Mysterious Force. Do we decide that the Mysterious Force is "friend" or "foe?" Do we accept that which the Mysterious Force has provided as a gift or not? On this basic choice rides the reality of a satisfying, lively life or an empty life. The choice is ours—to dance with life or to sit on the side. This is not a moral or religious choice. This is a life choice that we make, consciously or not, every day. It is the ultimate choice.

How can we say that the "pusher and puller of life," the "giver and taker of life," is our "friend?" What happens to enable a shift our response from "No" to "Yes," from complaining and wishing life would be different to affirming life and living it?

Some have been hit extremely hard by reality, like being "slapped upside the head by a baseball bat." Some have had all their props knocked out from under them and have "hit bottom." Others have been fascinated "off the sidelines into the dance." No matter the means, the basic experience was that it happened like other aspects of life—it was given by the Mystery.

The dynamic goes something like this. These people were just going about their lives—floating or struggling as usual—when a message of affirmation was communicated to them. Somehow they "got the message":

>that they were affirmed and accepted just as they were,
>that life was significant and wonderful,
>that they were a significant being,
>that their life was approved and loved just as it was,
>that life was open to all kinds of wonderful possibilities.

They experienced themselves as part of a greater whole. There was deep satisfaction and fulfillment in being part of this greater existence.

Some speak of it as a "light dawning." Others speak of it as having their "eyes opened." Whatever, the only response "asked" of them was
>to say "Yes" to the message,
>to accept their acceptance.
They found themselves saying, "Yes."

Everything remained the same, yet everything was radically different—transformed. Life was the same, yet they saw it differently, they related to it differently. The quality of their life changed. Some have described the transformation as "being alive" whereas before they had been "dead."

>[*Suffering, Death, and the Dark Side:*
>
>*One of the main aspects of life that remains the same but is related to differently is that of the brokenness of life. Pain, suffering, destruction, death, imperfections and the dark side of our selves are part of the givenness of life. They are part of the growing, changing, evolving, expanding, experimenting, learning and developing dynamics of the Universe, Planet Earth and Humans. They are part of the economy of life itself. Out of pain, destruction, and death comes new life. Life seems to permit and tolerate, to some degree, perversions, imperfections and mistakes in normal operations. In fact many aspects of our life come with two sides—a positive side and a negative side.*
>
>*A positive relationship with the Mysterious Force does not mean that the Mysterious Force is going to "fix things" for us. It does not mean that the Mysterious Force will save us from pain, suffering, mistakes, "goofs," destruction and death. These are part of the givenness of life. The broken things are part of the wholeness of life.*
>
>*But trusting the Mysterious Force as friend and saying "Yes" to the givenness of life transforms the brokenness of life. The brokenness is still there, the dark side is still there, but the way in which we relate to it is transformed. We are released from our fear of pain, suffering, and death. We are free from our efforts to deny it, to escape it. We are free from the control under which fear and denial of brokenness had put us. When we reject and deny the broken and dark aspects of life, we cut out large portions of life. When we affirm all aspects of life as accepted and significant, then all of life is given back to us and we are made whole. Pain is still pain. Suffering is still suffering. Death is still the end of life. But in accepting them, we participate in and assist the newness of life—not only for ourselves, but for others, for society, for the planet.*

Be it facing terminal illness or experiencing near-death, those who have been able to accept their final death, who have been able to say "Yes" to the end of their human existence, have experienced a calmness, a joy, and a freedom to live more fully than they ever had before. Those who have been able to embrace The Mystery and their death have experienced a freedom to embrace life, to risk, to explore, to journey, to create, to love, to relate as never before.]

The "face of the Ultimate" brings with it a decision—is the Mysterious Force friend or foe? For us or against us? Do we run from it or embrace it? The quality of our lives depends upon this decision. It opens life to a whole new dimension of authenticity, of wonder, of power, of joy, of peace and of vitality. The arm is still broken. The dishes still need to be washed. The gray hair and wrinkles are still there. Society's problems still exist. The people at the office are still the same and so are the kids at home. The neighbors still see life differently from me. Yet there is wonder in it all. There is a mysterious ability to do what needs to be done. All of it participates in a mysterious harmony. All of it is a source of mysterious joy.

But whether we decide "Yes" or "No," the Mysterious Force is still there—giving us another situation . . .

e. Finally

Finally, where do we come from? Only Mystery.
Finally, where do we go? Only Mystery.
Finally, what and who are we? Only Mystery.
Finally, how do we live? Only Mystery.
    Life—existence—is pure Mystery.
Finally, we are pure Mystery.
  I am Mystery
  You are Mystery
After all is said and done,
  we will cease to exist as individual human beings and . . .
Silence.
Finally, Silence.
  No questions.
  No responses.
Finally,
  beyond talking and thinking…
Finally,
  only Silence…
  emptiness of all;
    fullness of all.

D. IMPLICATIONS OF THE ULTIMATE

Given the fact that we have a very different set of experiences to be covered by a new "face of the Ultimate" than humans who have gone before us, what are the implications for us and for our lives? With the new basic assumption that the Mysterious Force—which blows like a wild wind through the Universe, Planet Earth and Human lives—is a proper response to the Ultimate Question, what are the implications for us and the way we live our daily lives?

In keeping with the nature of the Mysterious Force and with the nature of the new learning mode of "question: question," these implications are explorations and observations which reveal more questions to be explored.

1. Is the Mysterious Force a Self-Conscious Being?

Is the Mysterious Force conscious? Is it self-conscious? Is it intelligent? Is it even a being? Is it one or is it many?

As the Mysterious Force is beyond the physical and rational realms of existence, it is not possible to use physical or mental scientific methods to discover and to validate knowledge of it and thus to resolve these questions. The realm of existence beyond the material and mental realms is that of Spirit. Therefore *Spirit scientific methods* must be used to experience, discover and validate direct knowledge of Ultimate Being.

The Mystics of all ages and cultures have systematically learned and applied methods of direct experience/awareness of the Ultimate. Those who have applied and continue to apply such methods are the only valid source for confirmation (or rejection) of data about the Ultimate.[8]

All of these mystics (scientists of the Spirit) attest to the difficulty of trying to express direct awareness of the Ultimate in the language of our mental and physical realms. They use terms such as *Oneness with all creation, Oneness with the Divinity, Oneness with Oneness Itself—for which there is no second, Oneness as Pure Being Itself, Pure Light, Joy and Clarity, Formless Fullness* and the like. You are encouraged to read documentation of or about any of the classical Mystics. Their

---

8. For a thorough discussion of the levels of existence and the ways of knowing appropriate to each —particularly the "higher" levels of Spirit, I refer you again to books by Ken Wilber—*Spectrum of Consciousness*; *Sex, Ecology, Spirituality*; *Eye of the Spirit* (Chp. 9-12); and *Marriage of Sense and Soul*.

witness is dramatically similar, no matter the tradition or culture that they practice. Better still, you are encouraged to learn the spirit scientific methods for investigating the Spirit realm (classic traditions of contemplation and meditation) and explore this realm yourself.

On one hand, the Mysterious Force is present in and through every aspect of existence and thus we experience it constantly—no way to avoid it. On the other hand, the realm of Spirit is so different from and transcends the normal physical and rational realms that it is not possible for the physical and rational realms (our normal level of consciousness today) to comprehend the Mysterious Force at all directly. Though we use terms like *Self-conscious*, a *being, intelligence* in discussing the Ultimate, these are rational level terms and concepts. And while there may be some correspondence between them and aspects of the Mysterious Force, the Mysterious Force transcends these concepts.

This radical otherness is part of our relationship with The Mystery. As such, it is a vital aspect of our liveliness and growth as humans.

2. Is there a Non-Flesh-Based Aspect of Human Life?

The question itself represents a dualistic understanding of life in which either a soul is outfitted with a body for its visit to Earth or the body has a soul strapped on it like a fanny pack. It is raised precisely because modern scientific thinking, by and large, rejects the reality of anything non-physical based.

True, there are emotional, mental, psychological and personality aspects of our lives that are more than pure body functions. But are these anything more than complex expressions of body organs—primarily the nervous system? Alterations of brain cells and/or their functioning cause major alterations of the emotions, of the mental functions, of the body functions, of the psychology and/or of the personality of a human.

There is research that indicates humans are capable of other and more direct means of sensing and communicating—such as ESP. But still these aspects seem to be functions, albeit very specialized, of the brain. I am overwhelmed by the change to a person that Alzheimer's disease (of the brain) causes—the person I once knew is no longer there. Alterations of brain chemistry and brain cells dramatically alter a person's humanness. Dreams and other mental visions/images, for example, are experienced by the body and/or personality as though physically real.

On the other hand, we all experience that there is something about ourselves that is independent of our physical body. We sense that we have an ability to reflect, decide and initiate activity that is other than the physical aspect of our existence.[9] But the vast number of interrelated variables and expressions involved in the human brain, psyche, emotions, thought patterns, and personality (along with the varied social and cultural influences) make it almost impossible to isolate and identify a "non-physical-based" human aspect.

A more helpful approach would be to see existence as evolving from the **material level** to the **mental level** (which integrates material as part of a greater whole). Then the mental level matures to the **Spirit level** (which integrates material and mental in a greater whole). Each of these levels has its particular way of looking at life—the eye of flesh, the eye of mind, and the eye of Spirit. Each of these levels has an **exterior**, objective and physically measurable dimension—both as **individual** units (an atom, a tree, a brain, etc.) and as common **groups** (a forest, a bowling league, a government). Each of these levels also has an **interior**, subjective and experientially measurable dimension—both as **individual** (personal) units and as common **groups** (cultures). Each level is a whole that is comprised of four dimensions—exterior individual, interior individual, exterior corporate and interior corporate.[10] In this approach all elements and all experiences of our existence have a legitimate place, along with the corresponding methods for validation. That is to say, all elements and experiences are all real, are part of the whole of existence and are a source of truth.

No matter what approach one takes, no matter the results of research in this arena, the basic dynamics of our journey and of our relationship with The Mystery will not be changed, only enhanced. However we understand the relationship of the so-called "physical and non-physical," however we understand our existence as humans, we journey, we quest, we seek to expand the experience of living.

3. Is There Life After Death?

In chapter 4 the issue of life after death was viewed from the perspective of the human individual looking beyond his or her death. In this chapter the issue of life after death is viewed from the other side.

---

9. This arena is under increasing research and discussion, particularly the subjects of consciousness and valid ways of knowing. It is an extensive and complex effort. Those who are interested to pursue it are referred to various publications and writings on the subject.
10. Wilber, *Sex, Ecology, Spirituality*. The "four quadrant" structure is presented here in detail.

In traditional Kosmic Stories, life after death was to be spent in the realm of the Ultimate. From the perspective of the Mysterious Force, what happens to a human when they die? As we asked before, when the human Earth organism dies, does a person continue to exist as an individual? Is there a *me* that continues after *I* die? If so, what is such existence like?

The simple answer is that we don't know and may never know. But humans usually don't take "not know" for an answer.

The traditional religions, in their Kosmic Stories, have provided elaborate descriptions of existence after death. Each of them described the afterlife in the most idyllic conditions and experiences of the culture from which the stories come. The life after death was often seen in terms of a continuation of life on this Earth, only in the most desirable of conditions and of eternal duration. The early American Indian looked forward to an ideal and happy hunting area. In the Middle East heaven was seen as a rich, bejeweled palace in a lush oasis. Some traditions in China sent (by burning symbolic representations of money, houses, food, clothes, transportation, etc.) to the departed who were seen as needing these things in the afterlife just as they did in this life. For many present-day Americans, heaven is imaged as a place of perfect and happy relationships with family and friends, of peace and harmony or of the perfect weekend that lasts forever. The more heady descriptions see the afterlife as a time of peace, light and understanding. In all the stories, the afterlife included some form of direct communion with the deity of their culture.

In addition, there are reports by individuals of "Near Death Experiences," "visits to heaven," "communion with dead people" and other *after-death* experiences that also provide descriptions of life after death in the realm of the Divine. These reported descriptions are, as the others, in terms and images of the particular religious and/or cultural background of the reporter.

[Communication from or about after life:

Before we continue, I would like to make a couple of observations. Since in life after death we are dealing with non-physical existence, the whole discussion of non-fleshed based aspects of life, from sub-section 2 above, applies here.

Furthermore, any reports or descriptions of the afterlife are dealing, by definition, with a level of reality beyond our human physical and mental realities. Humans do not normally, at this time, have the capacity to communicate directly with such advanced existence. Therefore, some people contend that any communication from or about the afterlife, if it exists, would require some form of communication which humans can currently comprehend. If this is the case, and in principle it is true, then all such communication from or about life after death cannot be taken literally at "face value," but rather it must be seen as representing something that is beyond, greater and radically different than our current existence. As such, these reports cannot be considered as physical data or physical realities and thus require other appropriate means of validation.]

As noted previously, the fact that the afterlife is seen in terms of continued individual, personal existence strongly suggests that we are dealing with projections and other brain functions.

More importantly, from the point of view of the Ultimate, individual, personal existence is an Earth-human phenomena—and then, maybe only for certain levels of Earth-human existence. While concern of an individual for its particular well-being may have been necessary for the survival of the human race in previous times, it may not be the most helpful mode of existence now and into the future. Many great spiritual leaders have spoken of the hindrance to full life that comes from concern for the self and individual well-being. These leaders speak of moving beyond the ego-self and individual concerns in order to function as a larger network of beings and/or in unity as a larger Being.

The individual self, in fact, may be only a temporary convention for functioning in Planet Earth, or just for the early levels of human development in Planet Earth. Already we are seeing our knowledge and our minds being linked by computer networks. No one person's mind can contain all of human knowledge and experience. But now we have greater and greater access to more and more human knowledge as a single *mind*. Individual human learning and wisdom is now common learning and wisdom for all. As I push to the edges of my personality, of my being, it is difficult to discern where I end and other persons begin—we are so inter-dependent and involved with each other's lives. For example, I cannot think (and you cannot read this page) without words and meaning provided by the common life (i.e., culture) of many humans over the ages. Who can tell what we humans will evolve to be!

So, to lock the convention of the *individual self* into all eternity does not seem very authentic. If life after death is supposed to be an improvement, the continuation of individual personalities is not likely to be the best way to go.

At worst, the concern for the continuation of individual personal existence after death is an escape from the reality of physical death.

All Earth organisms die. Death is part of the natural process and the economy of Planet Earth. All energy forms and life organisms are born from, and live off of, the death of other energy forms and life organisms. We are an Earth organism. Any denial or escape from death is a denial of, and failure to experience, our full humanness.

Is death, then, the end of our humanness? At death, our unique combination of body organs, our particular emotional patterns, the unique functions, memories and mind activities of our brains, all that makes us the individual we are, cease to function. Death is the end of our particular individual body, mind, emotional and psychological unit. The wholeness that is *me* is no longer whole. What happens to us at that point when we are no longer physical humans is mystery, pure mystery.

I think that I am safe in saying that what the Mysterious Force has in store after death is beyond anything that we can think or even imagine. To use the analogy of a seed, the seed dies and a plant grows. The plant is a radically new form of existence as compared to the seed. A seed cannot imagine a plant mode of existence. At death, we are likely to *explode* into a whole new dimension of being.

My personal response to the question of life after death would go something like this. Just as we exist now as an expression of the Mystery, as part of Being Itself, after death we will continue to be an expression of the Mystery, a part of Being Itself. We cannot get outside of Being. As our lives are a continuous transition from one state of existence to another, physical death is just another transition. Be it living or dying, we dance and journey with the same Mysterious Force.

4. What About Angels and Demons?

There seems to be much interest in angels these days. Demons? No. But angels seem to be "in."

In religions of previous eras, angels and demons made sense. Gods, like all great rulers, needed a court full of people to take care of all the work that needed to be done—armies, messengers, servants, musicians, artists, entertainers, keepers of this and keepers of that. Heaven was populated with all kinds of beings. Then, there was the work in managing the Earth and looking after all the people for which the gods needed extra help. Also, I imagine that people did not feel too comfortable dealing directly with a god, so there were intermediaries with whom people could relate. This population of the heavenly realm was called, in general, *angels*. Particularly, angels were seen as the source of personal messages from one's god and the source of many, small acts of helpful intervention and fortuitous events in people's lives. (Remember that there was no e-mail, phones or fax machines in the era when the concept of angels came into being. In those times, communication was delivered by messenger, especially from persons of importance—often verbally. Angels were the messengers—the means of communication—of the gods.)

Conversely, the gods of the underworld (of evil) needed the same kind of personnel to take care of their courts, of the work associated with running their kingdom and of their business on Earth. These personnel were *demons*. Demons were seen as the source of lies and all unhelpful messages from the evil gods as well as the source of many small harmful and bad events in the lives of people.

Granted, today, with the lessening power of science to explain everything and with increasing sensitivity to the interior deeps, we are becoming more aware of direct inspiration and so called *spirit messages*. We are also becoming more aware of serendipitous events and fortuitous coincidences in our lives. But why do we need to revert to a bi-level universe and a population of angels as a source of wonderful insights, positive changes in our lives and fortuitous events? Why do we need to explain such happenings as, or reduce them to, personalized intervention by some "higher source?"

But given this current mode of thinking about angels, I am particularly puzzled by the lack of any attention paid to demons, who are the negative counterpart to angels. For every direct, inspired, constructive *message* there are numerous direct, inspired, destructive *messages*. If angels are seen as the source of the *good* stuff, why are not demons seen as the source of the *bad* stuff? For every serendipitous creative happening, for every significant coincidence, for every fortuitous intervention, there were numerous other occasions when the serendipity was destructive, when things did not come together, when the "sparks did not fly," when there was no helpful intervention. Should not these be credited to demons? Or were the angels just busy elsewhere or asleep on the job?

Things do happen which we want to label *miraculous*—for good *and* for ill. Things can go inexplicably wrong as well as inexplicably right—both are equal experiences of our Friend, the Mysterious Force; no need for any intermediary forces, such as angels or demons.

5. The Ultimate Has No Regard for Human Values.

The Mysterious Force is no respecter of persons. The sun shines on good people as well as on bad people and the rain falls on the good guys as well as on the bad guys.

In the same vein it can be said that the Mysterious Force does not seem to take human concerns or values into consideration. A flood will wipe out the homes and businesses of both good and evil people with the same devastating force that it tears up trees and rocks. A drought will destroy the crops of those who pray to their god as well as the crops of those who have no use for god, of the rich as well as of the family trying to get back on their feet financially. Car accidents kill loving mothers as well as irresponsible drunks. Atheists have their cancer miraculously go into remission as well as devout believers. And I can personally attest that absolutely no consideration to human effort, worthiness, talent, passion, desire, deserving, prayer, faith or any standards of fairness and good will is given in regard to my efforts to catch fish!

Life is not fair. Life is not equal. The Mysterious Force gives and takes as it will, without any regard for the human condition of those involved.

6. The Ultimate is Not Tame.

The Ultimate is not tame. The Mysterious Force is not predictable. It comes and goes, does or does not, when, where, and as it, and it alone, decides. (I know, *decides* is a human characteristic—but the sentence required a verb of some kind. Nor do we have the slightest clue as to how the Mysterious Force involves itself with what happens or what does not happen.)

The Mysterious Force is not tame. It is not domesticated. It is not safe, sterile, hygienic, pure, moralistic, or nice. It is wild. It does not go by the rules. It does not necessarily play fair. It makes the rules and it breaks them. It is not consistent.

I find it difficult to understand people who counsel (or seek) the use of spirit exercises and disciplines as a means to tap into the spirit forces of the universe so that a person can use this power for self-development, healing, and dozens of other personal and social ends. It is like advising a person to tap into a tornado for a personal source of power. Once you touch a tornado, it grabs you and takes you for one helluva ride, turning you every which way but loose! One does not use the Mysterious Force. It uses us. If a person is not prepared to be grabbed and used, to have their life turned inside out in ways they least expect, they should not attempt to tap into the Ultimate Force of the Kosmos.

I am amused by some teachings about various transcendent worlds—worlds of the Spirit or some kind of "other world." These teachings seek to make such worlds function like this world with scientific, technological and mechanistic "cause and effect." They seek to spell out the laws or rules or operating principles of these "other worlds." A person is then to employ such laws and rules to manipulate these Spirit worlds and the Transcendent Power for his/her own purposes and desires. It seems that such Transcendent/Spirit power is just another tool for achieving desired "this world" control and results. And in terms of functioning in such "Spirit or Transcendent realms," people seek to get ahead or prosper in these realms, just like they do in this world.

But for me, any such Spirit worlds, like the Ultimate Force, would function in ways that we humans cannot fathom, much less control and use. The Mysterious Force does not bargain or negotiate, and is not subject to laws or rules. The realm of the Mysterious Force, like the Mysterious Force itself, is radically other than our ordinary, everyday world.

7. We are Not in Control

The other side of the Mystery not being tame is the fact that we humans are not in control. After 300 years of concentrated efforts by science and technology to gain some control of our lives and our destiny, it is rather difficult for us to entertain the thought that we are not finally in control. Our whole mindset is that we are in control and it is just an issue of finding and applying the proper formula, technique, tool, or approach to manipulate ourselves and our situation to provide the results that we desire. What we find is that life does not always fit neatly into our prescribed patterns. There are too many variables at work that we do not know and/or cannot fully take into account. Life is often inconsistent and arbitrary. To state it more colloquially, "life happens."

The struggle to accept the reality that we cannot finally control life is difficult—particularly for managers, leaders, and other people who have been given responsibility for keeping things organized and for producing prescribed results. (Parents can fall into this category.) The challenge is to sit loose, be aware, use common sense, develop corporate and delimited goals, provide structures which encourage and facilitate constructive interaction and communication, set wide parameters which are firmly held, focus on open and flexible processes, and trust the Mystery. (Now I am sure you are going to be able to remember all these "8 Fantastic Steps to Whatever" the next time life begins to come apart at the seams! But just in case you don't, the short form is "sit loose and trust the Mystery.")

The key ingredient is trust. Trust people; trust yourself; trust the Mysterious Force. It also helps to appreciate all the people and their participation as well as all the happenings and all the results, in which total disaster as well as glorious successes are equally valid.

[*Failure is valid:*

Currently there are many methods that encourage one to follow and trust the "flow," "deep intuition," "the underlying dynamics of life," or "transcendent wisdom" of various kinds. Did you ever notice that they only speak of the positive, successful outcomes? They never seem to consider that the "message" from any such source may be that one should not continue with a particular endeavor, or that a particular personal trait is not changeable and you will need to learn to use it constructively. The "flow" may be "downward" as well as "upward." The fact is that these "deep dynamics" and "transcendent insights" may lead to disaster as well as to success. While the underlying principles of this approach may be true, it needs to be recognized that failure *is as valid an outcome as* success.]

It seems that life is lived in the tension between (1) being responsible with the knowledge, tools, power, and opportunities that we have and (2) not being in control of all of the factors and results. If you take it too seriously, it will drive you crazy. It is best to play at this. The journey into the uncharted world of the new Kosmos continues.

8. Development of "Spirit" Sensitivity

The word *spirit* can have various meanings, connotations and uses—often within a single paragraph. Its imprecise and inconsistent use these days can be confusing and unhelpful, resulting in both unrealistic claims and out-of-hand rejection.

In relating to the Ultimate, to the Mysterious Force, we are dealing with at least two distinct and meaningful uses of the word *spirit*.

First, *spirit* (lower case "s") is used to denote one component of our make-up as individuals. It is one component along with other components such as our cognitive abilities, our psychological components, our physical abilities, our ethical capacities, our inter-personal abilities, etc. This *spirit* component is described differently by different people—such as our relationship with the Divine or as our "Ultimate Care." We grow and develop in our *spirit* abilities just like we grow and develop in our physical, mental, emotional, psychological and other aspects of our makeup as a human. The challenge here is to clarify what comprises the *spirit* component and then keep the distinction clean in dealing with the other components of a person. *spirit* is not a catchall term for a person's inner life. Nor is *spirit* to be confused with the moral, emotional and psychological aspects of a person's life. *spirit* is only one aspect of a person's inner life. It is only one aspect alongside moral, emotional, mental, social and other components of a person's life.

Secondly, *Spirit* (capital "S") is used to denote a level in the developmental continuum of existence—as we have discussed earlier. This development is more like expanding concentric spheres than a straight line. Each succeeding sphere encompasses and integrates the preceding sphere into a larger whole. Beginning with the physical sphere, organic life emerges. From organic life the complex nervous system emerges. From the nervous system consciousness emerges, followed by the emergence of self-consciousness with its various levels of human mental development. From self-conscious, rational thinking there emerges a trans-rational or *Spirit* mode of existence. The *Spirit* sphere of pure awareness may itself involve various developmental spheres or degrees of direct awareness of the Ultimate. This understanding would be in line with the experiences of the great mystics of all traditions as they give witness to the growth of a person's relationship with the Ultimate beyond our normal physical and mental levels.

Notice the distinction of *Spirit* ("S") and *spirit* ("s"). *Spirit* (upper case "S") is a level or sphere of development—the trans-rational, pure consciousness level. *spirit* (lower case "s") is one component among the many components of a human being at any and all levels of development. *Spirit* is a level of maturity. *spirit* is one of several human components or "lines" of development that run through all levels of an individual's development. It might he helpful to refer to these two realities as *Spirit level* and *spirit line* Both are very important, but very different, subject areas. It is important not to confuse or mix these two arenas.

Often times the word *spirit* is used to refer to the personal inner life of humans. This is a carryover from times when knowledge of the inner workings of the human was very limited. There was basically mental activity, emotions and then spirit to cover all the rest—especially the more ethereal aspects of life. But now that we have more extensive understanding of the interior workings of the human personality such as the various dimensions of the emotional, psychological, interpersonal, social, sexual, psycho-somatic, consciousness and unconsciousness aspects, to name a few, as well as the *spiritual* as defined above. While *Spirit-level* and *spirit-line* interact with and impact on all these other interior components, these two lines should not be confused with the other lines of personal development. Furthermore, personal interior development is the cutting edge of our development as the human bio-system. To group all these various lines of development as *spirit* is unhelpful in terms of accurate analysis, development and/or correction of any of these lines of development—especially *spirit*.

When a person seeks to deal with or mature in their emotional, interpersonal, psychological, spiritual or other interior components (lines), it is important to use methods and exercises appropriate to the development of the emotional, interpersonal, psychological, spiritual or other particular interior component of their concern. Now *Spirit/spirit* methods and exercises may be adapted for use in the development of various interior components, but it needs to be clear that such methods are being used for the development of some other line than *spirit*. It also needs to be clear that *Spirit/spirit* development is not a substitute for other aspects of personal interior development and that personal interior development is not *Spirit/spirit* development.

There are still many human interior phenomena that have not yet been clearly distinguished or identified. People are still wont to use spirit to talk about such phenomena. While these phenomena currently seem ethereal, they have not been clearly categorized. Until they are, it might be helpful to coin a new term to cover such not-yet-distinguished and identified, ethereal phenomena—a term like *Xological*.

However one approaches Spirit-level and spirit-line, it would be beneficial to expand our sensitivity and awareness in both these arenas. It would seem helpful to expand our capacity and participation in both of these aspects. There are various exercises that we can do to increase both our Spirit-level and spirit-line sensitivity. The first thing is to accept the reality of Spirit-level and spirit-line dimensions as legitimate parts of our life as a human. Get familiar with both Spirit-level and spirit-line. They exist. They are real and not weird. Basic exercises that can be done would involve some type of meditation or contemplation. These exercises can be used for both Spirit-level and spirit-line development as well as for the development of other components that comprise a human being. So one needs to be clear as to what they wish to develop and accomplish in their use of any Spirit/spirit exercises. Pick a discipline, determine what you are trying to accomplish with it and stick to it as long as necessary; then do another. Writing—stories, poems, songs, etc.—is another helpful exercise. Sing, dance, paint, draw, sculpt, garden—any kind of creativity is a means for developing both Spirit level and spirit line sensitivity. And above all, follow the lead of The Mystery; give expression to the experiences of the Spirit/spirit—let both Spirit/spirit flow in and through you. Don't try to hang on. The Mystery is like the wind, you cannot hold it—only let it blow and enjoy its presence.

9. Enchantment

The Mysterious Force opens up the Spirit-level dimension of existence in an enticing way. Every situation, everything is an opportunity for experiencing the Mystery. As such, we are permitted to enter the world of enchantment in an authentic way. (*Enchantment* means to be under a magic spell, to be delighted or charmed greatly. It is to be pleasingly transported out of the ordinary into another realm that operates with its own set of rules.)

Human societies of all ages and cultures are filled with stories of enchanted worlds, places, and people. For many people of those times, these were real worlds, places, and people—or at least such were within their realm of the possible. For modern, educated folks, these are just make-believe stories. We have science fiction instead.

Many of us desire to experience enchantment and enchanted situations; but we doubt the reality of their existence. We would like to share the pleasing experience of the extra-ordinary, but we fear escapism. For us there seems to be a conflict between the cold, hard facts of physical reality and enchantment. But our scientific exploration is revealing that cold, hard facts may not be so cold, so hard, or even facts. When someone pushes reality to be real, they often end up in enchantment—in a wholly different realm or dimension of existence. The Mystery awaits just below the surface. How often do we ask, "what is really real?" Explore that question thoroughly and honestly and see where you end up.

Other times, enchantment just erupts in the midst of every-day events. We turn on a water faucet and the enchantment of the world of water overcomes us. A smile from a stranger sends us into the enchantment of people and relationships. We look at a flower, see a star, listen to music or read a book and life shines with a strange *light*—The Mystery, enchantment.

What is real, really? The experience of enchantment—of the transworld, of this other dimension—seems far more real than reality.

Jesus, Buddha and other Spirit leaders have given witness that, to live more completely, it is necessary to operate beyond simply the physical and mental realm. They point to a realm of existence beyond the physical and mental—a trans-rational realm or *Spirit* realm. The Spirit realm builds on and incorporates the physical and rational realms into a more inclusive (deeper, higher, wider) and more complex state of existence.

Experiences of enchantment may differ from person to person and time to time. But each experience may just be a different window into the same *trans-rational* dimension of life. The point is not to debate them but to explore them—and share what we find. At least, when you find yourself in a world of enchantment, wander around in it and enjoy. With the Mystery blowing loose in the land, it is OK to do so.

The presence of the Mysterious Force in the midst of life frees us from the ordinary and opens the world of enchantment. Or to state it another way, the ordinary world is a place of enchantment, a place of experiencing the Mysterious Force. Wonder and mystery are everywhere. Nothing is as it seems, only more so.

10. Prayer

How does one pray to "The Mysterious Force?" In the new Kosmos, with its new "face of the Ultimate," what is the role of prayer?

Recognizing that an adequate response to this question would involve a book of its own, I will risk a few general comments.

Prayer is communication with the Ultimate. Prayer is a dynamic, not a form. But this dynamic is expressed via form. The form of prayer is based upon a person's perception and understanding of the Ultimate. Whether it be "dark spirits," "nature spirits," "the Supreme Ruler," "a Loving Father," "The Way," or some other god or goddess, each one is approached with a different form of prayer (communication).

The content of prayer expresses one's relationship to The Ultimate, to life and to one's self. Since most prayer is "one way talking" to some supreme being, how a person talks and what a person talks about are extremely revealing of that person and his/her basic assumptions about life. Basically prayer falls into two general types: 1) expression of thankfulness, and 2) requests for help—either for one's self or for others. While there are many occasions of formal prayers, most prayers are spontaneous "Thanks!" or "I need help!" or "Please help them!"

So in a new Kosmos of constant creation, complex networks, personal inventiveness and an unpredictable Mysterious Force, what is the role, form and content of prayer?

Obviously, in communicating with the Mysterious Force, a person is not out to impress, to influence or to ask favors. Rather, prayer is more of a statement of the way persons understand and relate to the Ultimate, themselves and life. Spontaneous expressions of thankfulness and calls for help to something beyond ourselves are still appropriate. But in these expressions we now recognize our affirmations of being pleased or of being vulnerable.

From my experience, a more appropriate form of communication with the Mystery is some form of quiet communication with the interior deeps of life. Most any mediation, contemplation or centering prayer practice is a way to do this. The Consciousness Exercises of each chapter are examples of this form and content. The emphasis in all practices is on being aware of or listening to what is being communicated to us from within or beyond ourselves. Personally, the Mystery is a wise friend with whom I have many long conversations. We meet in any and every situation, person or object. From a dirty dish to a mountain, from a child's smile to a body in a casket, from a tree to a computer, we meet and explore life.

[*An invitation to try something new:*

For persons of various religious traditions who are at more elementary spheres (levels) of development, their traditional prayer forms and content are still adequate and useful for them. These traditional forms and content express their current understanding of and relation to the Ultimate. And this is fine.

At the same time, they are encouraged to be sensitive to the pushes and pulls of life to expand and grow. I would invite them to test their current understandings and assumptions about the Ultimate in light of their experiences of life and to expand these understandings and assumptions as they are able. I would also invite them to try some forms of more direct communication with and experience of the Ultimate—either from their own tradition or some other.

There will be no gold stars, "smiley faces" or other rewards. It surely will be uncomfortable for a while. But I can almost guarantee that their lives will become more exciting and satisfying.]

Quiet communication with the Ultimate, whatever form a person uses, enhances a person's self-consciousness of all aspects of life. It is a means to struggle with all of life's relationships. Such quiet communication is a means to integrate the various aspects of life into a longer whole. And it is a primary way of beginning to move to the Spirit-level of direct awareness of and oneness with Ultimate existence.

More and more research is revealing the influence of directed thought—both by individuals and by groups. Thus, prayer (directed thought) for assistance on behalf of others is appropriate—at least it does no harm while enhancing our relationship toward them.

It goes without saying, prayer, along with all other aspects of living in the New Kosmos, is being reinvented. You are encouraged to try out various forms, modes, styles and content of praying.

11. Keep the Relationship Strong

As noted in the reflections above, the quality of our lives depends upon our relationship with the Mystery. A natural implication is to keep this relationship strong and functioning well.

The Mysterious Force is a "being" of action. It is not much for words—at least not directly. And when there is communication of words—either through actual talk of other humans or in our personal thoughts—a person has to decipher and decide what the Mystery is communicating. One's "state of being" may be the best clue as to the health of our relationship with the Mysterious Force, with Life itself. But unfortunately we humans are not very advanced in this arena.

The bottom line is we also have to do some actions to keep our relationship with The Mystery strong. In addition to the exercises for expanding our sensitivity to the *Spirit/spirit* dimensions of life our lives, there are some activities that will help us keep our relationship with the Mystery strong and affirmative. Here are a few categories that have proven helpful:

- Create and/or chose symbols of your relationship. Display them where they will be noticed regularly.
- Life and its relationships are a drama. Rituals rehearse one's relationship with life and with other beings. They get you ready to do well in the real thing. Select or create meaningful rituals and practice them regularly. They may be personal or communal.
- Songs are a powerful means for expressing and keeping alive the relationship. Write and/or select songs that express and motivate the relationship with the Mystery that you want cultivate. Then sing them regularly, most helpfully in a group setting.
- Write and read poetry—a creative means for expressing and enriching relationships, particularly with the Mystery and with Life.
- Decor. Your surroundings impact your whole being. It is helpful to surround yourself with decorative items that remind you of The Mysterious Force.
- Participation in a community of like-journeying people is critical for sharing and nurturing one's relationship with the profound dimension—the Mystery—of Life. It is an opportunity to express, to get feedback, to learn, to test, and to develop a corporate mind, spirit and synergy of human beings.

- Conversations. Talking with other humans about one's relationship with the Mystery provides stimulation, support, clarification, self-correction and inspiration—among other things.

These are only generalized suggestions. We are in a new land, a new world, a new era. On your own and/or with others, explore, test, evaluate and share the results.

E. AN IMAGE

For this pillar, since there is no object to name; images are about all that we have been using. Conceptually, we are dealing with the Ultimate dimension. We actually experience the results of some unknown force. That force we have called the *Mysterious Force*, which is as much an image as a name.

But as an operating image—a picture of how this force operates in our lives—"*Wild Wind*" seems very appropriate.

The Mysterious Force is like the unseen wind, known only for its effects—a caress on the check, flapping flags, ripples on the lake. Like the wind, the Mysterious Force is unseen but forceful—turning windmills, toppling trees, etching rocks.

The wind, like the Mysterious Force, is capricious and wild! One never knows when or how the wind will blow. Sometimes it blows gentle and caressing. Sometimes it blows savagely and destructively.

In many ancient cultures, the wind is seen as the source of life, as the breath of life. The wind enlivens people and situations with vitality. The wind is the creative and enlivening force. The same can be said of the Mysterious Force.

The Mysterious Force, like the wind, blows in and through all of life—creating life here, destroying life there, calming a situation here, stirring up a situation there. The Mysterious Force, like the wind, blows in and through all of life—refreshing a heart here, turning a life inside-out there, clouding an issue one moment, clearing the air the next.

From gentle spring breeze to raging hurricane force, the Mysterious Force blows like a *Wild Wind* through the Universe, the Planet Earth, and Human life.

Thus, as the fundamental operating image for the Mysterious Force, I propose the image of the *Wild Wind*.

"Wild Wind"
By Pat Nischan

Chapter Seven

DANCING

A. THE GREAT DANCE—A STORY-POEM

The Wild Wind blows.
    Dance Kosmos, dance!
        Dance the Great Dance.
The Wild Wind blows.
    Energy swirls
Physical Energy expands, swirls and dances.
        Quarks, quantums, neutrinos join and dance.
        Protons, electrons, and neutrons dance as atoms.
        Atoms dance with atoms as molecules.
        Clouds of dust swirl and pulse with swirling energy.
        Stars dance with stars in galaxies.
        Planets dance with stars, moons dance with planets.
        Dances within dances.
    Physical Energy swirling through space and time,
        —an ongoing creation—
    creating space and time,
    creating the edge of the physical universe.
    (And beyond?
            beyond all space, all time, all matter?

Ask the Wild Wind.)
Racing away,
    racing together,
        attracting and repulsing,
  spinning, colliding, exploding, regrouping…
Swirling energy—
    patterns and configurations,
        within and upon,
            patterns and configurations,
    continually creating
        patterns and configurations,
            dances within dances.
A star explodes, dust swirls.
A planet spins and cools.
The Wild Wind blows.
    Energy swirls in a new form—living cells.
Biological Energy swirls,
    life bursts forth—
    erotic patterns of living energy
        dancing,
            spiraling, entwining, dividing,
              joining, multiplying, evolving,
        dancing within dancing;
    exotic patterns of living energy
        dancing,
            squiggling, squirming, bursting,
            blossoming, waving, swimming,
            flying, running, walking, crawling, burrowing,
            fur, shells, skin, scales, cloths, feathers, leaves,
        dances within dances;
    the coloring of a planet,
        the life-ing of a planet.
A Blue Marble
    dances in the spotlight of the sun—
        a living, breathing, nurturing, swirling, planetary dance—
The Wild Wind blows.
    Energy swirls through the network of nerve cells in a brain.
    A new kind of swirling, a new dance emerges—
        mental patterns form and reform,
            patterns within patterns,
                configurations within configurations,
                    thoughts within thoughts—

Mental Energy swirls.
    The human mind,
        the human self,
           comes alive and dances.
Another round of erotic and exotic creativity bursts forth;
    new patterns, new configurations, new swirls of energy—
        words, sentences, stories,
           chairs, wheels, philosophies, spears,
        houses, TV, dresses, guns,
        money, paintings, medicine,
        planes, computers, songs.
Mental Energy as the human self emerges and dances,
    dances with other humans—
        relationships within relationships,
    savoring itself
        and the dance of life.
The human self is not a solitary dance but
    an integral part of the human community dance.
The Kosmic dance becomes even more complex,
    more dances within dances—
        values, morals, laws,
        families, towns, cities, kingdoms, nations,
        schools, stores, factories, offices,
        discussion groups, committees.
The human community emerges from
    and is an integral part of
    the communal dance of planet Earth.
The Wild Wind blows—
    Physical Energy swirls.
    Biological Energy swirls.
    Mental Energy swirls.
    Is there more?
The Wild Wind blows—
    Spirit Energy swirls
        deeper,
           within,
               beyond,
                   deeper,
                       within,
                           beyond,
    beyond all knowing and
    beyond all doing

The Adventure of Being Human

                    at the center
                    one—
a oneness
        a wholeness
            a peaceful at home-ness
                with
                    and
                        as
                        all physical expressions,
                        all life expressions,
                        all mental expressions,
                    in timeless thereness
                as Spirit Itself.
Spirit Energy swirls
    an aliveness beyond alive.
Spirit Energy swirls
    in and through
        every physical, biological, mental energy swirl.
Spirit Energy swirls
    as one great dance,
        as the dance itself.
The Kosmos dances—
    dances within dances—
        one great dance
The Wild Wind blows in and through all—
    the very swirl and dance itself.

The Wild Wind blows.
    Dance, oh Planet Earth, dance!
The Wild Wind blows.
Planet Earth dances,
    a living, growing communal dance,
        dances within dances.
Land, air, water, biological life and mind
    dance a wild and passionate dance,
        alone and together.
Land—structural patterns and configurations—
    Lava flows, rocky layers form,
        mountains rise and fall,
            continents dance with continents
                sand and dirt sway back and forth.
Air—the blanket of gases—

      blows hot and cold,
          fierce and gentle,
              streams, swirls, and hovers,
                  lifting, mixing, putting down,
                      enlivening.
Water—Ah, the Water dance—
    clouds, rain,
    splashing, flowing, crashing;
        streams, rivers and seas;
            washing, dissolving, carrying,
                refreshing.
The Wild Wind Blows and
    out of the dance of land, air and water
        life dances forth.
    Bacteria, algae, fungi,
        bugs, fish, trees, flowers,
            reptiles, animals, grass, birds.
    Big ones, little ones,
        Simple ones, complex ones.
    Hard things, soft things.
    They wiggle, flap, swim, crawl, run,
        bite, suck, scream, sing.
    They eat,
        they reproduce
            they die.
    Each kind of living thing is a complex life system,
        a living community
            complex set of dances in itself.
    And they learn to dance the dance of life together,
        with land, air, and water,
            ecological systems within ecological systems;
    each contributes to the living dance
        that is Planet Earth—
            dances within dances—
    each is enlivened by the dances of the others
        and by the communal dance
            that is Planet Earth.
 The Wild Wind blows . . .
    the brain of the one of the life systems
        develops self conscious thoughts—
    the human mind begins to dance.
        This is ice cream.

The Adventure of Being Human

    I like ice cream.
      "Jim, I like ice cream! Do you want some?"
      "Sure. Where's my dish?"
    "This is the best ice cream I've had in a long time!"
    "And eating it together is something extra special."
The Earth knows the wonder of itself—
  the mountain is magnificent,
    the river is refreshing,
      the flowers are lovely,
        the beaver is clever.
The human mind
  self-reflective,
    plotting its destiny.
What shall I wear today?
  Whom shall I marry?
    Where shall we put this road?
      What will be produced by splicing these genes?
    Let's try this and see what happens.
      Why? How? Can we . . . ?
        Should we . . . ?
In the human brain, Planet Earth
  reflects on itself,
    learns of itself,
      manages itself—
        haltingly, stumbling,
          the dances take on a new dimension,
            learning new steps.
As humans communicate with humans,
  a global neural network is being built,
    a global brain is forming,
      global minding is happening.
In the human mind,
  the Earth steps back and looks at itself,
    takes in larger and larger vistas,
      even steps off and sees itself.
A single dance,
  swirling through space,
    living systems within living systems,
      living communities within living communities,
        one great communal dance—
  dances within dances within dances,
    constantly learning new dances.

The Wild Wind blows.
Dance, oh Human Being, dance!
    I see so much,
        hear so much,
            smell so much,
                touch so much,
                    taste so much,
    think so much,
        speak so much,
            do so much,
                feel so much . . .
And I am aware that I do.
So many variables,
    so many options—
    What shall I say?
        What shall I think?
            What shall I touch?
                What move shall I make?
    What is my decision?
        How shall I respond?
There is no answer,
    except my answer.
        The only response
            is my response.
Each sensation,
    each awareness,
        each decision,
        each response . . .
    a part of my dance,
        a part of the dance.
I make it up as I go—
    pure improvisation!
        pure creativity!
Other dancers,
    other dances,
        swirl around me,
            within me—
    Evoking a response,
        providing new patterns,
            new moves.
My self,

  my dance,
    pure improvisation.
Am I going anywhere?
  Maybe,
    maybe not,
      sometimes "yes,"
        sometimes "no,"
  I just enjoying dancing.
I dance with my body-world,
  with my self-world
    with my family-world,
      with my neighborhood-world,
      with my area-world,
        with my nation-world,
          with my planet-world
            with the universe.
And in me,
  the body, the self, the family,
  the neighborhood, the nation,
  the planet, the universe
    dances.
I pick up on all the dances that have danced,
  and are dancing
    to dance them with my flavor.
I push the edge,
  deeper, wider, higher, beyond—
    the inside is larger than the outside.
  My dance,
    the dance,
      becomes larger, more complex,
        dances within dances within dances.
I dance,
  I am part of the Great Dance,
    The Great Dance
      dances in me, through me, as me,
  I and the Great Dance are one dance—
    there is only one dance—
      it swirls ever larger, ever more complex.
I enjoy it all,
  appreciate it all.
    I let it roll around in my mouth
      and savor it fully.

Life,
    an adventure,
        a wonder,
           a dance.
I dance.
Who is the I that dances?
    what matter?
  I, the dance,
    swirl and flow,
        the Great Kosmic Dance.

The Wild Wind blows.
Dance, oh Human Community, dance!
    A human-individual
        does not dance alone.
Humans dance in community.
    The words, the language,
        in which we think our thoughts
           come from a community of humans—
        relationships within relationships
Human communities—
    family, friends, neighborhood,
        the folks at work,
           groups,
    local village,
        local tribe,
           race, religion, culture,
  and now
    the global village,
        the planetary tribe,
           the world community,
              a global culture.
    The development, the project, the suburb,
        the town, the city, the country—
           all now part of
              the living planet.
Communities within communities,
    dances within dances within dances
        participants in the planetary communal dance.
In communities,
as teams committed
            to the journey,

The Adventure of Being Human

            to the dance,
we decide and learn
    what is good, beautiful, real;
we decide and learn
    ethics, values, morals, rules, justice, mercy—
        how to live and dance together;
we learn who we are
    what life is all about—
        the contexts within contexts—
            how to live;
we build and create
    the structures and forms of human society;
we sing and play;
we learn to dance
    a larger dance
        to include more people and more kinds of people
        to include more space
        to include more dimensions of life
            interior
            exterior
                individual
                corporate
        dances within dances,
            deeper, wider, beyond
                more complex,
                    more singular.
In communities—
    as teams—
    we are nurtured, supported, and affirmed
        in body,
            heart,
                mind,
                    Spirit;
In communities—
    as teams—
    we provide nurture, support and affirmation
        in body,
            heart,
                mind,
                    Spirit.
In groups/teams here,
    in groups/teams there,

the DIALOGUE goes on,
    the contexts, the values, the guidance—
        contexts within contexts—
            for launching new creativity
            for expanding the journey, the dance,
are raised, discussed, designed, tested, evaluated
        —constant dialogue—
    as we build the common music, the global song
    as we learn how to live,
            how to dance,
                authentically
        with other humans
        with other life systems
            as individuals,
            as community.
Human individuals linked with individuals,
    human groups linked with groups
        the global communication network
            like a global brain
        links the sensitivities,
            the awareness
                the reflections
                    the decisions
                        the actions
    of the planet
        as a single, living being
        a single dance
The global brain pulses with
    global minding activity—
        the human community learns to dance
            more gracefully
            as one of the life systems
                in the planetary communal dance.
A global mind,
    a planetary self-consciousness,
        a global vitality
            emerges—
    Planet Earth matures,
        expands its self-consciousness,
            matures in its dancing—
                gliding, stumbling,
                    swirling, tromping,

                        leaping, tripping,
            having it together,
                    falling into disarray and chaos,
                            coming together yet more gloriously
        ever maturing,
            ever expanding the dance,
                    more complex, wider, deeper,
                            moving within and beyond,
                                ever one dance.

The Wild Wind blows,
    The Mysterious Force blows
            in, through, and as all things,
                        all happenings.
The Wild Wind blows,
    things,
            events,
    feelings, thoughts, insights, experiences
            come into existence
The Mysterious Force blows;
    things,
            events,
    feelings, thoughts, insights, experiences
            go out of existence.
Look closely at every
    thing,
            event,
                experience—
    the Mystery shines forth
        in glorious beauty and wonder—
                the awe of eternal Being
                    dissolves us,
                            expands us,
                                    transforms us,
                                        fulfills us
            with Life,
                with Being
                    Itself.
Life is beholding the Mystery in all things,
    is beholding all things as the Mystery,
        as The Dance,
The fullness of life is awareness

of ourselves as The Self,
....as The Mystery,
........as The Dance
............as Fullness Itself.
The Wild Wind blows,
....The Mysterious Force dances
........the Great Kosmic Dance.
There is only one dance,
....the Great Dance,
........dances within dances within dances.
There is only the Great Dance,
....constantly creating itself as it dances.
The Wild Wind blows
....and daily life dances—
........the child smiles, the flood rages,
............the gun cracks, the lips touch,
................the bread is made and bought,
....................music washes through, the engine roars,
........................the dog barks, the bird sings,
............................the report is written, the ball thrown,
....the galaxy spins, the star burns,
........the leaf falls, the virus infects,
............the apple is eaten, the egg is fertilized,
................the water is drunk, the cloud drifts—
The Wild Wind blows,
....The Mystery dances.
All forms and experiences of existence
....are expressions of the one Dance.
There is only the dance—
....the dance of dances within dances.
There is only the dance,
....The Great Dance.
There is only the Wild Wind blowing and dancing.

The Wild Wind blows and
....I, the Self, dance the Great Dance,
........I am the Great Dance,
............there is only the Dance.
The Wild Wind blows and
....the Great Dance dances me, you, us
........i, you, we dance the Great Dance—

                    there is only the dance.
The Wild Wind blows and
    i, you, we
        dance the Great Dance—
            the swirling energy,
                the planetary communal dance,
                    the individual improvisation dance,
                        the global minding.
There is only the dance—
    i,
        you,
            we
                dance it
                daily,
There is only the dance,
    i, you, we
        have always danced it.
There is only the dance,
    i, you, we
        will always dance it.
The Wild Wind blows,
    i,
        you,
            we
                dance with the Wild Wind:
    we are swirling energy;
        we are part of the communal dance;
            we are an improvising journey,
                we are global minding.
By waking up,
    by breathing,
    by thinking,
    by going to the bathroom,
i, you, we
    dance with the Wild Wind,
        the one Dance.
Dare
    i, you, we
                dance it
            with full awareness?
Dare

    i, you, we
        savor each step of the dance?
Dare
    i, you, we
        appreciate and enjoy
            each swirl, each move
                of the one dance—
                      dances within dances?
Dare
    i, you, we
        know ourselves as one with the dance,
        as the dance itself?
The Wild Wind blows,
    The Great Dance dances.
Dance, oh Dance, Dance!

B. CONSCIOUSNESS EXERCISES

Every moment of your life, of all life, is participation in and experience of the Kosmic Dance. Be aware of and savor that participation. As a means to enhance awareness and experience of the Kosmic Dance, the following exercises are offered.

- **Dance:**

Play music that moves you or calms you. Standing in the middle of the room, close your eyes and feel the music. Let it flow through you and begin to move you—your head, your arm, your feet—slowly, involving more and more of your body.

Open your eyes and let your body move with the music. Sense yourself moving with the universe of swirling energy, with the planet as a communal dance, with yourself, improvising each move, in dialogue with all humans as a global minding pattern. Sense yourself as the dance.

- **End of Day:**

Sit quietly and reflect on your day: (1) as part of the ongoing physio-mystery creation; (2) as participant in the planet as a living organism; (3) as constantly creating/improvising your life; (4) as a participant in the integral maturing of the global community; (5) as enlivened by the Mysterious Force.

- **Create your own Kosmic Story.**

Possible starters are:

-Write a paragraph about each of the five images.

-Write a poem or story based on five phrases: "I am swirling energy;" "I am planetary communal dance;" "I am a creative journey;" "I am global minding;" "I am the wild wind."

- **The Contributors and the Contribution:**

In a relaxed state, meditate on all that has contributed to the life you now live—all the physical aspects of the Universe, all the biosystems, all the social structures, all the culture, all the people. Where do "you" stop and begin?

Continue to meditate on all aspects of life to which you contribute; then meditate on all that will come after you and will be influenced by your life and your decisions (and non-decisions).

- **Walking Meditation:**

Do a walking meditation using the following phrase: "I DANCE THE KOSMIC DANCE HERE, NOW."

C. REFLECTIONS ON LIVING

"You are at a watershed where the given world diverges sharply from everything you have known and have been, into the unknown." So begins an article by Paul H. Ray in *Noetic Sciences Review* (Spring 1996, p6ff). It continues, "in the next two decades our world will either be dramatically better or dramatically worse. The one thing that cannot happen is just 'more of the same'.... The quality of our 'image of the future,' and the quality of our creative efforts based on it, will determine which way our future develops over the next generation or two."

The article is a report on the results of his survey, profiling a group he calls the "Cultural Creatives"—44 million US adults who are the standard bearers of Integral Culture. This new subculture includes, among other things, a "new set of concepts for viewing the world" (In this book I have used terms like "new basic assumptions" and "new fundamental images" to express a similar thing). This Integral Culture "will succeed precisely to the extent that it solves the problems of a whole planet that is starting to be 'one world' for the first time." This new subculture and the Cultural Creatives "means being FOR something" as it centers on integration, at a higher level, of that which has now been differentiated or has collapsed from increased complexity. It also has to do with "self integration and authenticity, integration with community and connections with others, nature, etc.—a synthesis of diverse views and traditions." (page 13)

Mr. Ray describes the Integral Culture as a "creative time, a cultural revitalization movement which says 'the old story does not work and we will invent a new story.' Such movements create new images of 'who we are,' play with new symbolism and archetypal imagery, ... try to invent new ways of life to replace others that don't work, and are hopeful about the future."

This book seeks to contribute to the effort of inventing the new story. It is also an invitation to live our lives as an adventure of creating one's own life and the new world that is emerging. It is an invitation to be an explorer of this new world as we are learning to live in it.

This last chapter is not a "wrap up"—life cannot be "wrapped up;" life is radically open. This chapter, for sure, is not a conclusion—we have just opened lots of doors for exploration—we are just beginning. This section continues the exploration with a conversation on living in the new Kosmos. Now that we have shown up in a new Kosmos, now that we have some new images of life in this new Kosmos, how do we go about living our lives? As I have said before, I am leery of prescriptions for improving one's life and/or the human situation. There are just too many variables and unknown factors for any prescription to address. In addition, there is always that "wild card in the deck"—the "human factor." Furthermore, there are no answers—we create the answers with our living. So this section is not a prescription or an answer. Personally, I would rather open a door and begin to explore together what it might be like to live out of the new story, the new assumptions and images about life.

1. The Dance

Atoms and galaxies swirl as precision dances of energy—swirls within swirls, dances within dances. Biological life forms are complex organisms comprising even more complex life systems—dances within dances. The Planet Earth is a communal dance of life system dances. My life, your life, each human life is an ongoing dance, improvised at every step and movement. Mental activity is an intricate interplay—a dance involving millions of inputs—that is constantly growing and expanding in its complexity. The human community, groups within groups—again, dances within dances within dances. Within and beyond all this—the Spirit realm—these dances begin coming together into larger, deeper, and more complex dances of dances within dances. The Kosmos, as the totality of all existence, is one great dance, composed of all the dances—dances within dances within dances. . . . Finally, there is only The Dance.

Another way of talking about this reality is that there is only The Dance of which all particular dances are expressions and in which all particular dances participate. The Kosmos is one great dance. Stars, rocks, trees, bugs and cows are all expressions of and participants in the one great Kosmic dance. Your life and mine are expressions of and participants in the Great Dance.

The Dance is constantly creating itself, as it dances, in and through each particular set of dances—dances within dances within dances. This is a living dance, constantly creating itself, constantly creating new stars, new toothbrushes, new personal relationships. In and through our particular creative journeys, in and through our many sensitivities and responses, the Kosmos is creating itself. I get up in the morning and take shower—the Kosmos is dancing. You work at your desk, the Kosmos is dancing its dance.

The Ultimate Reality, the Mysterious Force, the Wild Wind expresses itself as the Kosmos, as The Dance. The Kosmos is not a product of the Mysterious Force, it is the Mysterious Force. The Kosmos—all of existence, in its many shapes and forms—is not a product of The Dance, it is The Dance.

There is only the Wild Wind. There is only The Great Dance. There is only Being, only Self, only Dancing. Each of our particular lives is an expression of and participant in The Great Dance. Or to say it another way, the Great Dance creates itself in and through our dancing. There is only the Dance.

This is difficult for our brains to grasp. It is even more difficult to put into words. Those humans who have developed and experienced trans-rational or Spirit means of "seeing" speak of such oneness. They experience life as only Self, which is expressed in each of our particular selves and in all things.

From this perspective, we and the Mysterious Force are one reality—one in the beginning, one now, and one in the future—three ways of talking about one reality. The Kosmos is a never ending story told many ways—from fullness to fullness, a living circle, a living dance, always complete, always becoming.

The Universe, the Planet Earth, Individual Humans, the Human Community and the Ultimate are all one living process, one reality, one happening—dances within dances as The Dance.

It is difficult to talk rationally about something that is beyond reason. And yet, this is part of the enchantment and wonder of our lives. We have had tastes of another dimension or level of life. There have been witnesses by a few people who have experienced deeper or greater aspects of life.

This is by no means an attempt to provide a thorough discussion of this aspect of life. It is only calling our attention to a larger context that is necessary to experience the full richness and wonder of our day-to-day lives. It is only trying to provide some beginning expression of a larger, unifying context. As we move into an era of integrating the vast particulars of life into more complex, greater and deeper wholes, such a larger context is important. As we create new images and a new story to hold all of life and to open us to the deeps and wonder of being human, such a larger picture provides the framework.

2. Life Style

Life is in the living, not in the talking about it. The joy of dancing is in dancing, not talking about it. The validity of the new story is not in talking about it, but in our daily living.

Life style is about the way we relate to and participate in life. Life style is about putting it all together in living our lives. We talk about the various life styles of people—flamboyant, extravagant, simple. We even talk about some people as really living life with *style*—meaning that they have a very distinctive, sophisticated, self-confident way of relating to life. We all have style. We all relate to life and express our lives; the only question is what kind of style? And how self-conscious are we about that style? As mentioned earlier, there is a desire to live authentically, to be real, to be **ALIVE**. This has to do not only with the story/images out of which we live but also with the way we participate in life out of those story/images—**STYLE**.

This section introduces some facets or characteristics of a new Kosmos life style. It seeks to increase our consciousness of the life style of a person who lives out of the new Kosmic Story of Life. It is about being self-conscious of the practice of living.

a. Aware, Enchanted, Savor

Be aware! Life is extremely complex and involved. Each moment is filled with a variety of objects, happenings, relationships, sensations, and thoughts. Each of these is a *door* into hundreds more. The first aspect of living is to be aware of as much of a given moment, of a given situation as possible. Awareness is to some degree the given state of all humans. To increase awareness is to increase one's experience of life. There are many ways to do this, but it mainly involves slowing down, relaxing and being open to what is happening.

Related to awareness is affirming or accepting the existence of all that we are aware of. It is being enchanted or fascinated with all of life as we become aware of it. In the first instance, this involves not evaluating or judging anything, but rather just recognizing that something is and letting it reveal itself more fully. Awareness, like each of ourselves, is cautious. At the first sign of an unfavorable reaction, awareness withdraws and closes down. Making evaluations and judgments have the effect of being "show stoppers."

Sure, we make judgments and evaluations. But be slow to make them until the full *picture* has come into view. Then, in kindly dialogue with the situation, assessment can be made. In the process, we can also seek to be aware of the assumptions that are in use at the time. If life comes to you as a problem, then check your assumptions, your images about life.

Life is enriched by seeing each aspect as enchanted. It is seeing the wonder and excitement of a night sky, an older person's wrinkles, a committee meeting, a cool drink. It is experiencing the awesome wonder of a car, a flower, a touch and even a hateful remark.

The other dimension of this is appreciating all our awareness—savoring it, enjoying it deeply, appreciating it for its being. Be it positive or negative, pain or pleasure. We often say how we should "stop and smell the flowers," But we do not necessarily have to stop. It is more like living in a perpetual state of appreciating and savoring all of which we are aware. Style has to do with being aware of, being enchanted with, appreciating and enjoying our dancing the Dance.

b. Transic and Integral

Transic is a word that I have invented to refer to the style of transcending or moving beyond one stage of development to the next stage. The new stage does not reject the earlier stage but rather incorporates it into a larger whole. This is the mode of evolution in which simpler forms are integrated to form larger, more complex wholes—atoms to molecules to cells. . . . It is also the mode of mental development. It is the style of synthesizing two or more aspects of life (such as values, viewpoints, cultures, world views) into a new whole that is greater than each of the components while incorporating the useful aspects of each.

[Transcending:

Ken Wilber has developed a very comprehensive structure and extensive discussion of this transcending dynamic in his various books, particularly Sex, Ecology and Spirituality *and* The Eye of Spirit. *I enthusiastically refer you to his books for a thorough discussion of this life dynamic. I present here only his summary of the process.*

"Thus, at each point in growth or development, we find: (1) a higher-order structure emerges in consciousness; (2) the self identifies its being with that higher structure; (3) the next higher-order structure eventually emerges; (4) the self dis-identifies with the lower structure and shifts its essential identity (proximate identity) to the higher structure; (5) consciousness thereby transcends the lower structure; (6) and becomes capable of operating on that lower structure from the higher-order level; (7) such that all preceding levels can then be integrated in consciousness, and ultimately as Consciousness. We noted that each successively higher-order structure is more complex, more organized, and more unified—and evolution continues until there is only Unity, ultimate in all directions . . . "[11]]

I use the word *transic* in referring to a life style of transcending or moving beyond any current stages of development to more comprehensive and complex stages that incorporate the various aspects of the former stages.

---

11. Wilber, *The Eye of Spirit*, pg. 238.

The *transic* life style is of particular importance in dealing with more inclusive world views, cultural values and relationships as we learn to live in the new Kosmos. While it makes sense rationally to transcend one stage of life to a more comprehensive and fuller stage of life, the actual experience can be painful and strongly resisted. To transcend, a person must give up, let go of or "die to" the current stage of development at which they are living. For example, one must give up childhood to move into youth and then one must "die to" youth in order to move into adulthood. Whereas such social/mental transitions of an individual (though painful) are well established and supported as normal, other transitions that push the edge of evolution (e.g. trans-cultural, trans-established-social-patterns, trans-rational) are strongly resisted. We see evidence of this in the painful struggle from tribal and ethnic life to nationhood, from traditional religion to progressive to trans-religion or, more mundanely, in many meetings of your local school board. We have become very good at differentiating and evaluating various components of life. The challenge now is to integrate these components into a more comprehensive whole. The *transic* style is critical for both personal growth and assisting others to make the transitions.

Besides the various stages (levels or spheres) of development, each stage has four dimensions or quadrants that were considered in the previous chapter. As a reminder, these quadrants are (1) the interior individual, (2) the interior social (cultural), (3) the exterior individual and (4) the exterior social. The interior is the subjective dimension. The exterior is the objective dimension. We live in a time in which people tend to focus almost exclusively on one quadrant or another. Some focus only on the external individual—if you can't touch it or isolate it or measure it, it isn't real. Others, in reaction to this, focus only on the interior personal subjective—only that which a person feels, experiences and/or is in their mind is real. Still others stress only the social interior (cultural)—if you do not believe and value what my group does, you are not fully human. And still others focus only on how things are organized structurally (external social)—if it does not work functionally, it is of no use. But healthy existence and growth depends upon a balanced integration among all four quadrants. Seeking to reduce life to one quadrant not only reduces one's experience of life, it also hinders the progress of evolutionary development of life.

In addition, there are various streams or lines of development, such as cognitive, moral, emotional, spiritual, psychological, physical, sexual, interpersonal—to name only a few. Each line matures through all the basic stages of development, in all four quadrants and with impact on each other.[12] What I want to stress is that living as a human involves all levels, all quadrants and all streams. A strong, healthy development of one's human potential would seem to involve all these aspects in a conscious, integrated fashion. This approach to life is spoken of as an *integral* approach or style. Besides Paul Ray and Ken Wilber, Michael Murphy and George Leonard address this very issue of an integral life as well as provide exercises called the *Integral Transformative Practice*.[13]

In summary, living in the new Kosmos involves *transcending* current levels of evolutionary development and self-consciously *integrating* all previous levels, all quads and all streams at a level/sphere which, for lack of a better word, I would call the *Integral Level*.[14]

On into the future, once life has evolved to a fairly stable (normal) *Integral life*, it will once again transcend to a larger, more comprehensive, more complex whole of a new level of evolution. Though this major transition beyond the *Integral* Level will be far beyond our lifetimes into the future, I find it exciting to contemplate the future development of Planet Earth and humankind. So let's take a break and enjoy a short side trip. (If you do not wish to join, just skip this side road.)

[Side Trip: Future Levels of Human Development

The four basic levels (or spheres) of evolutionary development are matter, biological life, mind and Spirit. Each level develops all four quadrants and various streams to a point where it transcends to the next level. For billions of years the Dance spun itself out in just the physical sphere. Then the Dance transcended to biological life which, though resting on the physical, moved into more complex, comprehensive levels of development. For several more millions of years the Dance spun itself out in the development of the biological sphere.

Then the Dance transcended to mind and mental activity which, though resting on the physical and biological, moved into the even more complex, comprehensive (both in depth and breath) sphere of mental development in all four quads and various streams/lines. This development at the mental level has been under way only a few 100,000 years and fairly intensely

---

12. Wilber, *The Eye of Spirit*. This book provides an excellent treatment of human development in all quads, all levels, all lines.
13. Leonard, George and Murphy, Michael. *The Life We Are Given*.
14. Ken Wilber uses the terms vision logic and centaur to refer this next normative level for human society.

only for the last 10,000 years. As a normal operating level across the planet, we are only now beginning to reach the upper levels of mental development. (Though a few individuals during the last four or five thousand years have developed to the highest levels of mental development, the human race as a whole is just now approaching the upper levels.) In succeeding years, more and more individuals will reach the highest levels of mental (rational) development. Gradually, all quads and all lines and all preceding levels will be integrated into a new whole (Integral Life) *at this upper rational level. Though this may take another 2,000 or so years, it is exciting to think about the highest level of rational development being expressed in a balanced, integrated way in individual personalities, in individual things (like technology), in worldwide cultural forms and in worldwide social and political structures. As the Human Potential development effort reminds us, we have only begun to realize the potential of the human mind. (Remember that* living life fully, authentically and vibrantly *is not equated to* realizing one's full potential. *Human life is lived completely, fully and authentically at any point in a person's development.)*

Following this, there will be a sphere/level in which the Dance transcends the rational and the personal into direct consciousness of the Dance itself. At this point, the Dance will spin itself out in the development of the Spirit sphere as normative for human society. (While many individuals have experienced one or more of the several identified levels of the transrational, very few have transcended to an operating stability at any stage within Spirit sphere.)

Can you begin to imagine what it might be like for all the people of the planet to experience some level of unity with or as the Divine, the Mysterious Force, the Dance or whatever your name for Ultimate Being? Mental development would be accomplished rather quickly. Then students would advance through various degrees of direct, consciousness of the Ultimate. Everyone would be living beyond the personal in various degrees of unity with all of existence. What would it be like for this experience of unity to be expressed in cultural forms and social structures? What kind of things would be produced? What would travel be like? Medicine? How would individual entities communicate in a level of Unity consciousness? How would humans go about their daily lives—what would life be like—at a trans-rational, trans-personal or Spirit sphere as the normal operating level of existence? What kinds of struggles, pain, mistakes, brokenness would be experienced? What would provide pleasure, joy and happiness for them? It is beyond imagination! And how many more years of evolutionary development are we talking about—50,000? 100,000? 200,000? Or will the development possibilities be limitless at the Spirit levels?]

Back to the "main road." The gift of this is to be aware of the role that the *transic* and *integral* style play in the maturing of our personal lives as well as the maturing of the Kosmos. In this we can self-consciously mature to our next level of development in an integral—all quad, all level, all stream—fashion.

c. Being our Becoming

As we consider the development of the planet, both its past and its projected future, it is rather obvious that we humans have a lot of development ahead of us. Though we are at the leading edge of evolution, we are nowhere near the end of the evolutionary process—for humans or for Earth. Our lifetime will only be one small step in this long journey. Thus, waiting for the full development of human life to appear is not a winning model. It is also obvious that we have not even reached our own personal potential as a particular integral being of matter, body, mind and various streams of our personality—which will take our full lifetime, if not more. So how can we talk about experiencing and enjoying the fullness of being human now?

On the other hand, there are "schools of thinking" that stress the fullness of life is in being who we are, right now. So be yourself! Don't try to be someone else. Be the person you are—warts and all. You are a great, wonderful person, just as you are. Or as many of the world's religions and many of the spirit leaders today stress, life is one and we are part of life's oneness. Life is whole—one great harmony. Or if it is a redemption religion like Christianity, God has already forgiven us and made us whole. Either way, we are whole, wonderful, totally significant beings just as we are. Therefore, BE the whole, wonderful person that you are!

Using these over simplified pictures of two views of human life, I would remind us of two types of experience that we all have: (1) "I am very incomplete and nowhere close to my potential in any and all of the aspects of my life, but I am working to improve;" and (2) "I am accepted, loved and wonderfully whole as I am." Becoming or Being? Is the fullness of life *becoming* the person that I potentially can be? or is fullness of life *being* the person I am? How often do you catch yourself alternating between the two—struggling to become the person you desire to be and just being who you are?

When someone says to me "you are accepted and OK just as you are" or "Just be the person that you are," I find myself asking, "Who is the 'me' that I am?" "Who is the 'me' that is OK?" "Who is the person that I am just to be?"

My answer goes something like this:

"I am the sum of all my living up to this point. I am the sum of all the things I have experienced, consciously or unconsciously, all the responses that I have made—said, thought and done—good, bad or indifferent. I am all my relationships—constructive and destructive—now and throughout my life. My life has been a journey from the time of my conception, through birth, through childhood, through teenage years, through young adulthood, through marriage and raising a family. I am constantly growing. My personality, my emotions, my psyche, my understanding, my body—all have been on a journey—exploring and changing. I am a process. There is not some real me hidden deep inside. The real me is the sum total of all my life as I express it at the present moment. Tomorrow, I will be a different person since I will have added another 24 hours of experiences to my present me. Each time I think something, say something, or do something, each time I evaluate and respond to a situation, I am creating who I am. Therefore, to be me is to be my process.

"To be me is to be my becoming. As such, I am whole, complete and fulfilled. At any and every moment my life is an expression of the Great Dance which is always whole and which is constantly being created. My life-in-process (filled with pain as well as joy, failure as well as success) is the Kosmos which itself is Life-in-process and which is whole and complete at every moment."

Wholeness is not a goal to be achieved. Completeness is not a place to arrive and set up housekeeping. Harmony is not a level of development to be achieved, at which point you can stop, retire, and live happily ever after. Wholeness is a way of being; it is a state of consciousness; it is an experience of awareness. It is similar to how light affects the mood of a situation. Change the light in a room and the whole mood is changed or an outdoor scene looks different at sunset than at sunrise. The light does not change the situation, it just changes how one sees and relates to the situation. A state of being is something like that—how we see and relate to a situation.

Wholeness is like a line of color on a canvas, seen just by itself, it may seem meaningless or ugly. But seen as part of the whole picture the line has meaning and beauty. As part of the whole picture, the line is complete, just as it is. Each of our lives is like an ongoing line of color in the great painting of the Kosmos. Each day we add twists and turns and color to that line. These twists and turns contribute to the whole picture which The Great Mysterious Force is creating. As a work of the Ultimate, the picture is good, whole, complete at any and every point. This is true whether you and I realize it or not.

In summary, I show up in the midst of an ongoing Dance. How I am to participate is not clear. I am constantly becoming, constantly inventing my life. I am an improvisation dance. This dancing-which-is-me exists in an eternal state of being whole, complete, and wonderful because it is an expression of The Great Dance—Being Itself.

As a life style, this can also be described a "flowing" or "shapeshifting." It is responding to the creative edge of life wherever the edge shows up for you. It is the style of being aware of and adapting readily to the changing situation that life is constantly providing of us. Robert Jay Lifton in *The Protean Self* (Proteus was a Greek god who could take various forms) offers a helpful discussion of this human tendency not only to survive traumatic changes, but to grow stronger from them. As the world is constantly changing, the ability to shapeshift is critical to functioning well in the world today. This is not an issue of "will we finally get it all together, perfectly." Rather, it is participating in the evolving process of life—dancing at the edge of life and creating the emerging Kosmos.

d. Technique and Skill

"How do we be our becoming?" "How do we improve our *dancing*?" are legitimate concerns of implementation. What are the techniques and skills which help us be more sensitive and aware, and to help us in our decisions and responses? How do we improve those techniques and skills?

Although this book is not a "how-to" book for change and improvement, life style does have to do with the use of techniques and skills for enhancing our lives.

Today there are an abundance of techniques and skills to help us *dance* our lives. There are literally thousands of books, methods, programs, seminars, classes and exercises offering direct help or guidance in answering questions of becoming. These resources provide techniques and skills in all four quadrants, especially for the individual interior and exterior quadrants. The majority focus on the various lines of personal development such as emotional, psychological, spiritual, physical, health, mental and the like. A few provide skills and techniques for the cultural and social quadrants. More and more the integral approach across all quadrants and/or several lines is being promoted.

So how do we relate to these many and varied resources for techniques and skills? Cautiously and with heightened "sensitivity, awareness, decision and response." One has to pick and choose according to one's need—like the selection and use of any tool.

My personal reason for caution is that these resources too often build on and encourage our desire to have a different, more perfect life as well as our dissatisfaction with the life we have. These resources and their use are often based on a life understanding that "if I can only change and improve my current life situation, then I will have a real, happy, satisfying life." Or they are based on our desire to gain life by being successful in some area or achieving some goal. I have attempted throughout this book to show how this is not an appropriate way to relate to our lives. Another concern that I have is that many of them seek to offer a quick, easy "fix" to deep, complex, ingrained problems and life styles which have been years and years in the making.

But the depth issue is this. *If real, satisfying life is in living our lives—dancing and journeying as part of the dance of life—why should we be concerned to change or improve our lives?*

In the first instance, we shouldn't.

We really change only when life forces us to change and improve.

Life forces us to change in one of two basic ways. The first is through pain or collapse of our current way of living. Some experience of physical, mental or spiritual pain and/or collapse makes it clear to us that it is not possible to continue to live as we do. The second is through the fascination or attraction of some potential newness. Some passion, some yearning, some joy, some unknown "out there" fascinates and attracts us to new ways of living. Either way, something about life calls into question our current images or mode of living and *invites* us to change, to create a new or improved understanding and mode of living. Such *profound invitations* may be dramatic, such as (negatively) the breakup of a marriage or a serious illness or (positively) a deep insatiable yearning to create something or an opportunity to explore a new dimension of life or the chance to live in another part of the world. Such *profound invitations* may be triggered by ordinary, everyday experiences, such as being criticized, a friendly smile, or reading a book. As a result of such experiences *we decide* to make a change—the emphasis is on *we decide*.

Sometimes a *profound invitation* may not seem like an *invitation* at all. These are the times when we are *dancing* just fine, but we would like to enhance the pleasure and joy of it. These are times when we want to expand our understanding, our skills, our abilities just for the pure joy of it or to be more effective in our *dance*. These are times when we realize that we have more potential as a human than we are exercising and *we decide* to grow and expand.

These invitations, I would contend, are just the self-conscious experience of the underlying evolutionary process of the Kosmos. They are part of the ongoing maturing of life to ever higher, more complex wholes. Therefore, if you respond to a *profound invitation* to change or enhance your life, I would encourage the use of techniques which promote integral development of "all quads, all levels, and all lines." Also note where you are in your development along the various *lines*, then use exercises that are appropriate to the *line* and to your current level of development in that line. (For example, you may be at an expert level intellectually, a beginner level physically and intermediate level emotionally.) We could call it *integral development* or *integral becoming*.

Whenever any one undertakes an effort to change or enhance their life style, there is an important fact of life to be aware of. The current structures of one's life that have been developed over many years and, like all structures, they are resistant to change. This resistance to change is a self-regulating characteristic in all forms of life (known as *homeostasis*) and it is critical for maintaining life within acceptable tolerance levels. It resists all major change—good or bad. Therefore, any real change in our lives is going to be met with serious resistance from all fronts—including friends and family who are used to relating to us in our current life style.

This does not mean that real change is impossible. It means that real change—in response to a *profound invitation*—most often takes long, hard work. We have not only to develop the new or improved aspects of our lives, we also have to be prepared to deal with the resistance that will naturally confront us from those around us as well as from within ourselves. Style-wise, self-improvement takes serious commitment, intentionality and support. More importantly, change or improvement is most successful when it is undertaken for the pure joy of it. That is, the process must be satisfying, not just the end result.

In the process, remember that life is in the *dancing*—whether that *dancing* be daily activities or efforts of improvement. *Improving our dance skills does not get us any closer to dancing.* We are *dancing* fully, we are living fully, all the time—whatever the level of our skills.

e. *Responsibility*

Another major aspect of the life style of a person in the New

Kosmos is that of responsibility. In the New Kosmos we are aware that we are constantly exercising our ability to respond.

Responsibility is not an obligation that has been laid upon a person, either by themselves or others. Responsibility is not "you should do . . . ; you ought to do . . . ; or you need to . . ." Responsibility is responding to the various situations or occasions that the ordinary process of living present to us. Usually when people talk about "being more responsible" or "the responsible thing to do," they are talking about being more self-conscious in responding and about increasing the context of concern that is used in making a decision.

Responsibility is a combination of three dynamics. It is the tension between *freedom* and *obedience* in *surrender*. Every response is in obedience to some factor—laws of physics, personal principles, people to whom one reports, a sense of concern for the well-being of others, etc. Every response involves a free choice among alternative options—even as to what we will be obedient. Thus, it is not an issue of obedience or freedom. We are always obedient and we are always free. In fact, the larger our area of obedience the larger our area of options and freedom. Total obedience to the most comprehensive context and to all the particulars of life provides total options and freedom. Obedience to 1000 people gives you more options than obedience to only five. As one's awareness and integration expand, does one's obedience and freedom expand.

So in the tension of obedience and freedom, we make our decisions and our responses. Are they right or are they wrong? It depends upon who is evaluating. Most likely it is some mixture. As the results of our response ripple throughout the Planet, the Universe and all of history, who knows for sure whether our response was helpful or not? Our actions are like children—who knows what will they be when they grow up—*demons* or *angels?* More likely they will be a nice mixture of both. Thus, we make our response and then we surrender our actions to the Kosmos, to the Mysterious Force, to history for the final decision. Our responses come from and contribute to The Dance.

Responsibility means increasing the awareness of the situation, expanding our awareness of all to which we are obedient, expanding our awareness of all of our alternatives, then deciding and acting, and finally, surrendering the deed to The Dance—which put us in the situation that required the response.

More and more these days I hear the response, "We can't deal with those kinds of issues, nor make decisions about them—that would be 'playing God'!" The fallacy of this statement is the words "playing God." We humans do not "*play* God." In the New Kosmos we are aware that we humans "*function* as God" all the time. We make "God" decisions all the time. A dramatic example, for instance, would be "Who gets the kidneys that are available for transplant?" If I ask you, "Will you make your kidney available?" then your answer, either "Yes" or "No," is a "God" decision.

On a more mundane level, an example would be something like who gets access to available medical resources? Only those with insurance or money? And who gets the available government money? Shall we keep a few people alive at all costs or keep many people generally healthy for the same costs or less? Or shall we do both and reduce spending for other things? The fact that we know how babies come into being makes even the decision not to have sex a "God" choice of denying the possibility of a life being created. And given the very fact that we know that it is possible to abort a fetus, then every thought and decision to continue a pregnancy is a "God" choice about the life or death of a new human. In fact, all decisions that we make affect the life and death of others—not only physically, but mentally, emotionally and otherwise. So again, we offer up our decisions to The Dance and keep dancing.

Actually, in the New Kosmos there is no distinction between "God" choices and "human" choices. There are just choices. Each choice/response is part of the Great Dance. Take for example the choice to go to a school of higher learning or not. If so, then there is the choice of where to send an application; then the choice of which one, if any, to attend. One's future occupation is impacted by these choices. Sometimes people meet a person at such a school, whom they later marry. With that spouse a child may be created. That child's existence is a result, among other choices, of a decision about attending a school of higher learning. And the world is a different place because of the life of that child.

We are responsible. We are constantly exercising our ability to respond. The issue is, how aware, how intentional are we about our responses and about the assumptions/images out of which we are responding? And then, how aware are we in appreciating and savoring our responses?

f. Mutuality

Life in the New Kosmos is not so much about how you should respond to me (my rights) or how I should respond to you (your rights), but more about how we interact with each other (mutuality). Another term for this is *teamwork*. The style of life in the New Kosmos is that of mutuality or teamwork.

As part of the Great Dance, as the creative edge of evolution, we explore and create together—not just with other people of all kinds, but also with other life systems. Since all that one does has an impact upon everything else, it is more helpful to consider the mutual benefit of our actions than a narrow focus on benefits for one's self or one's group. With the great complexity of life, it is more effective to combine all our thinking and acting.

Teamwork and mutuality are somewhat new for most of us. Yes, there has been corporate effort and teamwork in our history as humans. But because human individuality had not yet strongly emerged, such corporateness was more an undifferentiated mass—like a school of fish. With the emergence and strong emphasis on the individual in current *western culture*, particularly in the United States, mutuality and teamwork by strong, self-conscious individuals are not too familiar for us. Though we may be familiar with the importance of strong individuals working together to have effective orchestras and sports teams, this mode of operation is less common in businesses, families, education or politics. Though studies upon studies document the effectiveness of teamwork and mutuality, it has yet to become our normal operating style.

In the New Kosmos, as we become aware of ourselves as part of the life flow of the Kosmos, we will respond more and more as part of the synergy that is life. We will be moving from current *homocentric* (focusing on humans as the center of life) to *planet-centric* (focusing on the planetary communal dance as the center of life) and, later, to *Kosmocentric* (focusing on the One Dance as the center of life).

But let's take one step at a time. The next step is to *planet-centric* living. (This is not to be confused with *nature-centric* which focuses only on the so called *natural world*.) *Planet-centric* as a style of life is focused on all the life systems dancing together for the mutual well-being of the whole planet and thus the enhanced well-being of us all. Our way of life is teamwork with all life systems for the continued evolution and enhancement of life.

Since life is composed also of physical, cultural and social *quads*, life style is not purely an individual affair. We give cultural expression and create social structures to reflect lifestyle. We express it in our common images, language, and values. We give it form in our educational, economic and community structures. Life style also relates to how we (individually and corporately) relate to the physical aspects of life. In fact, all four quads work together in mutuality and teamwork to make up our style of life. (How's that for opening doors to further discussion and dialogue!)

3. An Adventure

And so we end where we began—the alarm is ringing; we awake to the adventure of living.

Many of us desire a more authentic, satisfying life, a more complete, vibrant life. We may talk about it in a variety of other terms, such as the desire for happiness, stability, success, "the good life," the Kingdom of God, Nirvana, Enlightenment and you can add other terms to the list.

The reality is that we wake up each morning in the Great Dance. You and I wake up in the midst of the fullness of life. There is no seeking it. We are in its midst. Living is an adventure. In the movie "Flashdance," a girl is dancing for her life. As she sails through the air, will she succeed? It does not matter! Her life is dancing. In dancing she has succeeded, she is living fully.

What is life all about? What is your life all about? How shall you appropriate your full life, really? In his novel *Skinny Legs and All*, Tom Robbins expresses it so well, "Everyone has to figure it out for themselves . . . Even though the great emotions, the great truths, were universal; even though the mind of humanity was ultimately one mind, still, each and every single individual had to establish his or her own special relationship with reality, with the universe, with the Divine. . . . Everybody had to take control of their own life. . . . and when you finished, you didn't call the Messiah. He'd call you." And the interior voice continued, "We're making it up. Us. All of us. It. All of it. The world, the universe, life, reality. Especially reality. We make it up. We made it up. We shall make it up. We have been making it up. I make it up. You make it up. He, she, it makes it up."[15]

You have to figure it out for yourself—each day, each moment. As a wise friend of mine was fond of saying, "The life you have right now is the only life there is. . . . There isn't another life somewhere else." The fullness of life is living the life you have—right now—the one that you "have figured out and made up." Being a human is pure adventure. Easy to do, impossible to avoid.

Energy patterns swirl all about, a planet of life systems dances all around, billions of humans improvise their journey on all sides, the global neural network awakens, the Wild Wind blows and in the midst of this we emerge as we dance our lives—what a dance! What an

---

15. Robbins, Tom. *Skinny Legs and All*, pg. 467-469.

adventure! Successes, failures, pain and pleasure, suffering and joy, calm and excitement—all part of the dance, the adventure of living as a human.

The alarm goes off. You have awakened in a new Kosmos. You invent, you "shapeshift," you dance life another day. You continue the adventure—the adventure that is your life, which is the Great Dance. Easy to do, impossible to avoid.

D. IMPLICATIONS FOR OUR LIVES

Considering thoughts presented in this book as a whole, what are some implications for our lives? I will first discuss some possible responses that one could make, followed by an invitation that is implicit in these pages. And finally . . .

1. Response to This Book

Each of you is going to have your own, very particular responses to this book. I would like to suggest a couple more for your consideration.

One premise of this book has been that our lives are full, complete and whole at each moment. To experience and enjoy them as full, satisfying and exciting has to do with how we relate to the situation of the moment. This in turn is based on how we see the situation—the assumptions and story we have about life.

Another premise, relating to how we see life, has been that the dramatic increase in our sensitivity to the universe, the planet and human life reveals that we are living in a Kosmos very different from the ones inhabited by previous generations of humans. We are now in the process of creating new fundamental operating images or mental models for the new Kosmos and human life in it. A new Kosmic Story is coming into being. Based upon the images in this new story, we can increase the wonder and excitement of living our lives while, at the same time, creating a new era in human civilization as we live .

One response might be to review your own basic operating assumptions or images. Write them down and test them. Are they adequate? Do they help you appreciate your experiences of life? Do they help you function adequately? Just check them out.

A second response might be to test the five basic images introduced in this book against your experiences. Are they helpful? Meaningful? If not, create ones that hold life for you. Create or adopt images that help you appropriate, experience and savor life more fully. If you find yourself saying, "That's not so!" then ask yourself "Why? Who said so? and Where do my values or assumptions come from?"

Human civilization is currently in a "story creating" mode. We are exploring our new Kosmos and learning how to live in it. We are observing, reflecting, interpreting and deciding. We are discussing and recording our observations, reflections, interpretations and decisions. We are reflecting on our basic assumptions and stories of life. We are updating our images and stories. We cannot live and function without some assumptions and images, without some story. The new thing today is that we know we are creating our Kosmic Story. We are participating more and more self-consciously in the process. A key component is providing and getting feedback on all of our language—our symbols—to help us learn to speak that same language and function in the same world.

Thus, a third way to participate more self-consciously in the birth of the new Kosmic Story might be to use the new images in this book or your own to create your own version of the Kosmic Story. Or you could begin with the Kosmic Story that this book introduces as a starter story and modify it. The new Kosmic Story will be created by ordinary people telling and retelling it.

2. Dare We

A new Kosmic Story is being created. A new era in the evolution of the planet and human life—a global community—is dawning. A new life style—an integral culture—is emerging. We are participants in it.

We are the forward edge of explosive, continually creative, swirling energy.

We are a participant in the huge bio-system known as planet Earth and of the human life system which is one of the life communities of the planet.

We are a focal point of self-conscious response to all of which we are sensitive—a life journey that is constantly creating itself.

We are participants in the global minding—a corporate integral maturing of the human community.

We are blown this way and that by the enlivening Wild Wind.
In all of this, we are an expression of and participant in the Great Dance.

We are. That is not an option.

The choice is self-consciously to appropriate and live out of this new story. Dare we appropriate and live out of this emerging story?

What are the new decisions that you need to make relative to:
    the Universe?
    the Planet Earth?
    yourself as an Individual Human?
    the Human Community?
    the Ultimate?

The Wild Wind blows, we dance the Great Dance
—swirling, dancing, journeying, minding.
    In waking up each morning,
    in breathing,

in speaking,
in moving
we participate in the Great Dance.
Dare we dance it self-consciously?
Intentionally?
The Kosmos dances the Great Dance.
The fullness of life is present at every moment.
Participate we do. Easy to do, impossible to avoid.
We are People of the Kosmic Dance.

It seems, though, the more self-consciously we participate, the more intentionally we live, then the more meaningful, satisfying and exciting a human life is. Thus, the choice is ours—how self-consciously and intentionally dare we participate? How fully dare we experience our experiences, our lives—LIFE!

Dare we be the People of the Kosmic Dance?

The wonder, excitement, joy and satisfaction of being a human seems to be enhanced by increased awareness. As awareness expands, our experience of life expands. And, in practical terms, our life expands.

The issue is, who can stand to look,
who can dare to look,
at life
with fully open eyes?
Who can bear the pain and agony,
the wonder and ecstasy,
the deep darkness and the brilliant light
of life?

The invitation is to stand, to look and to be aware as much as one can be, for as long as one can.

3. Finally

Finally?
Ultimately?
SILENCE.
Beyond talking.
Beyond thinking.
SILENCE.

When we come to the final edge of development in any phase, when we come to the time of transcending to the next phase, we face an end—death of all that is known. There is only emptiness and silence.

When we push anything to the deeps, the bottom drops out—

> Silence!
>> And the Wild Wind blows
>>> a grand, wonderful, ultimately pleasing
>> Silence!

Finally—as it was in the beginning and is now.
Finally—there is no beginning or end; there is only Is-ness—
> there is The One,
>> The Emptiness, The Fullness,
>> The No-Thing, The All.
>> The Awareness.
>> The Dance.

Whatever the name, it is beyond time and space and things, yet all time, all space, and all things exist in it and are expressions of it. It is beyond our ability to articulate. Yet we are expressions of it—our life, our awareness, our dance. We stand, we rest, we be, in silence—enchanted!

> Daily we participate in the fullness of life.
> In silence, be aware, savor it.
> Then respond in creativity to the drives and attractions of life,
> in silent wonder and joy.

Finally, ultimately,
> our Earth-lives arise from silence;
> our Earth-lives return to silence—
>> the silence of enchantment,
>>> of a grand symphony,
>>> of a grand dance.

The grand silence.
> Don't ask.
> Don't talk.
> Don't move.
> Don't think.
>> Be still;
>>> Be quiet.
>>>> Turn loose of everything.
>>>>> Be open—Be receiving.

Rest in the Silence,
Rest in the Symphony,
Rest in the Dance.
> Be still,
>> Be silent.

E. AN IMAGE

I do not need to retell the overarching image for the Kosmic Story. Nor do I need to explain it further. This whole chapter has been about the Great Dance, the **KOSMIC DANCE**.

The Kosmos is the Dance.
Our lives are the Dance.
To be fully human is
    to participate in the Great Dance.
        This we do each day—easy to do, impossible to avoid.
To experience the fullness of life
    is to experience our dancing.
        This we do each day—easy to do, impossible to avoid.
May we know the joy and wonder of so living, of so dancing!

As they say in dance classes, "don't look at your feet; look into your partner's eyes, feel the music, move, and enjoy."

So, look into the eyes of life, feel the **KOSMIC DANCE**, live and enjoy.

"Dance, my friend, Dance!"

"Kosmic Dance"
By Pat Nischan

Addresses

Send your comments or responses to the author at one or more of the following addresses:

Physical mail:
Basil P. Sharp
1354 K St. SE
Washington, DC 20003

E-mail:
mbsharp@igc.org

Fax:
202-544-0529

Internet (Web Site):
http://www.wel.net/integratedlife

Bibliography

Berry, Thomas. The Dream of the Earth, San Francisco, Sierra Club Books, 1988.
Houston, Jean. The Possible Human, Los Angeles, J.P.Tarcher, Inc, 1982.
____. The Search for the Beloved, Los Angeles, J.P.Tarcher, Inc, 1987
Leonard, George and Murphy, Michael. The Life We Are Given. New York, NY, G.P.Putnam's Sons, 1995.
Lithon, Robert Jay. The Protean Self. New York, NY, Basic Books, 1993.
Kazantzakis, Nikos. The Saviors of God: Spiritual Exercises, New York, Simon and Schuster, 1960.
Kornfield, Jack. A Path With Heart, New York, Bantam Books, 1993.
Moore, Thomas. Care of the Soul, New York, HarperPerennial, 1992.
Owen, Harrison. Spirit-Transformation and Development in Organizations, Potomac, MD, Abbott Publishing, 1987.
Robbins, Tom. Skinny Legs and All. New York, NY, Bantam Books, 1990.
Russel, Peter. The Global Brain. New York, NY, Putman Publishing Group, 1983.
Satir, Virginia. "I Am Me," from Self Esteem. Berkeley, CA, Celestial Arts, 1975
Swimme, Brian and Thomas Berry (contributor). The Universe Story: From the Primordial Flaring Forth to the Ecozoic Era-A Celebration of the Unfolding of the Cosmos, San Francisco, Harper, 1994.
Wheatley, Margaret J. Leadership and the New Science, San Francisco, Berrett-Koehler Pubishers, Inc., 1992.
Wilber, Ken. The Spectrum of Consciousness, Wheaton, IL, Quest, 1977
____. Sex, Ecology, Spirituality. Boston, MA, Shambhala Publications, 1995.
____. The Eye of Spirit, Boston, MA, Shambhala Publications, 1997.
____. The Marriage of Sense and Soul, New York, NY, Random House, 1998.

About the Author

Basil Sharp—ordained minister, college professor, organizational developer and computer system designer—has been a writer all his life.

He graduated from Davidson College with a BA in Psychology and went on to attend Union Theological Seminary where he received his MDiv and STM. After becoming an ordained Presbyterian minister and serving in Oklahoma, Kentucky and Tennessee, Sharp left the United States for Taiwan to become a Professor of Religion and Society at the Tainan and Taipei Theological Colleges. Both in Taiwan and back in the States, he was a regional director for the Institute of Cultural Affairs, a global effort of church, community and organizational renewal. He has since moved on as a consultant in the field of Information Systems Engineering.

He and his wife Marie Blessing, live in Washington, DC. They have three children—Heidi, Jane and Otto.